# BROOKINGS&WHARTON

# papers on URBAN AFFAIRS

## 2000

*William G. Gale and*
*Janet Rothenberg Pack*
*Editors*

BROOKINGS INSTITUTION PRESS
*Washington, D.C.*

BROOKINGS-WHARTON

papers
on
URBAN
AFFAIRS
2000

**Purpose**    The *Brookings-Wharton Papers on Urban Affairs* is an annual publication containing the articles and formal discussant remarks from a conference held at the Brookings Institution and arranged by the editors.

The annual forum and journal are the products of a collaboration between the Brookings Institution Center on Urban and Metropolitan Policy and the Zell Lurie Real Estate Center at the Wharton School of the University of Pennsylvania. All of the papers and discussant remarks represent the views of the authors and not necessarily the views of the staff members, officers, or trustees of the Brookings Institution or the Wharton School of the University of Pennsylvania.

**2000**    Individuals and institutions  $24.95
**Subscription**
**Rates**    Standing order plans are available by calling 1-800/275-1447 or 202/797-6258. For international orders add $8.00 surface mail and $16.00 airmail.

Send subscription orders to the Brookings Institution, Department 037, Washington, DC 20042-0037. Or call 202/797-6258 or toll free 1-800/275-1447. Or e-mail bibooks@brook.edu.

Visit Brookings online at www.brookings.edu.

Brookings periodicals are available online through Online Computer Library Center. For details contact the OCLC subscriptions department at 1-800/848-5878, ext. 6351.

# Preface

The *Brookings-Wharton Papers on Urban Affairs* is devoted to bringing cutting-edge research to bear on urban policy issues in an accessible manner. The collaboration between the Wharton School and the Brookings Institution in this endeavor represents an effort to draw on resources and personnel in both academia and the policy community. We hope and expect that the journal itself will be of interest and use to an even wider audience, including policymakers and their staffs, private sector agents, journalists, students, and others.

Each volume of the journal will publish papers that are first presented at a conference and then revised extensively in response to reactions at the conference. The papers and formal discussant remarks presented in this inaugural issue are based on a conference held at Brookings on October 7 and 8, 1999.

The journal could not have been established without the efforts of many key people at each institution. At Brookings, President Michael Armacost has been an enthusiastic supporter of this project from the very beginning. Robert Litan, director of the Economic Studies Program, has encouraged the project at every turn. Bruce Katz, director of the Center on Urban and Metropolitan Policy, has been a tireless and vocal supporter of the journal and its goals and has helped provide significant financial support.

At Wharton, Peter Linneman and Joseph Gyourko, former director and current director of the Samuel Zell and Robert Lurie Real Estate Center, have supported this undertaking intellectually and financially from its inception. The dean's office has made its contribution by freeing some of Janet Rothenberg Pack's time to organize the annual conference and edit the volume. The Department of Public Policy and Management has in numerous ways encouraged Professor Pack's participation in this endeavor.

We are extremely grateful to Alice Rivlin, currently a senior fellow at Brookings and chair of the District of Columbia Financial Responsibility and

Management Assistance Authority, for delivering a stimulating after-dinner presentation. Her speech focused on the simple but beguiling question of what the District of Columbia could do to attract 100,000 new residents over the next ten years and stimulated a lively debate among conference participants.

Caleb Patten and Julia Niemiec at Brookings expertly arranged conference logistics. Amy Liu and Jamaine Tinker in the Brookings Center on Urban and Metropolitan Policy have provided outstanding assistance and guidance in establishing the journal and the conference.

We would like to thank the authors and discussants for taking special efforts to write their papers in a clear and accessible manner. The resulting papers make clear that one does not need to sacrifice analytical rigor in order to communicate research results in plain English.

# Editors' Summary

TWO BROAD PREMISES have guided the development of the Brookings-Wharton Papers on Urban Affairs. First, in recent years, the economic and social challenges of urban development have become increasingly significant. These challenges are associated with the enormous and long-term shift of population and employment from city to suburb and from the Northeast and Midwest to the South and West. Some of the major problems include economic decline in older cities; the interrelationships between urban development and crime, family structure, concentrated poverty, education, and employment; the erosion of urban tax bases; relationships between cities and suburbs; urban sprawl; and environment and transportation. Some of these problems can also be found in older suburban areas. Rapidly developing areas face some of the same issues and are trying to avoid others where possible. Because these problems are ubiquitous, and in many cases may be expected to become more severe over time, scholars and policymakers may be expected to devote increased attention and resources to these issues in the future.

Second, urban areas also face positive opportunities, including those created by radically changing technologies in communications, transportation, electronic commerce, and biotechnology. These developments could help provide solutions for problems in both older and more recently developed urban areas. They also provide new sources for growth and productivity improvement in older slow-growing urban areas, and the extension of growth and development to new areas. Many observers believe such technologies provide the key to the revival of older urban areas; others think they sound their death knell and will reinforce both suburbanization and the continued decline of older cities, as well as the continued movement of population and economic activity south and west.

These problems and opportunities create difficult intellectual challenges. The matters are often intertwined to a degree not found in other fields. Devising solutions to problems and developing ways to take advantage of opportunities for welfare-enhancing urban development may well require new data, new theory, and thinking that cuts across conventional disciplinary lines. The shortage of clear and systematic thinking on these issues and the lack of interplay between scholars and policymakers are serious obstacles to the implementation of effective urban research and policy development.

This journal aims to help fill the void. A central goal of the journal is to bring together scholars working on traditional urban problems, a broad range of scholars working in related fields with implications for urban areas, and policymakers. Many economists and researchers in other fields are currently working on subjects with important urban implications—poverty, education, health, transportation, employment, taxation, productivity, and other issues— but frequently do not identify their work as contributing to, or benefiting from, urban research. Thus another goal of the Brookings-Wharton papers is to help bring new ideas and new analysts into the urban arena by integrating this broader research into the urban-policy discussion.

The six papers in this inaugural volume exemplify these goals. The papers were presented at a conference held at the Brookings Institution on October 7 and 8, 1999, and attended by approximately forty-five scholars and policymakers. The papers are divided into two sets: a symposium on the past and future of urban research and policy, and general research papers on several urban or urban-related topics.

The symposium is an effort to take stock of the state of urban research and policy as this new journal is launched. Edwin Mills provides a thematic history of the development and achievements of urban economics over the past fifty years, and discusses the major unsolved and underresearched questions. John Quigley examines and evaluates the evolution of federal policy toward housing and urban development. Edward Glaeser sets out an ambitious future research agenda for urban economics, focusing specifically on the role of nonmarket interactions. Taken together, the symposium papers provide complementary and comprehensive views of where urban economics and policy have been and where they ought to be heading.

The other papers in the volume address important aspects of the urban economy: education, racial segregation, and federal housing policies. Jeffrey Grogger and Derek Neal provide new evidence of the ability of Catholic schools—the major source of private schooling for lower-income families—to improve the educational achievement of urban minority students. Ingrid Gould Ellen examines links between racial segregation and the incidence of low-weight births among black mothers. Richard Voith models the incentives for more restrictive zoning regulations that are created by federal tax policies that subsidize housing. These papers are indicative of the journal's efforts to take a broad view of the scope of interesting subjects for urban-economic analysis. In addition, they address some of the topics raised in the symposium as the appropriate focal points of future research.

Mills's paper is a wide-ranging discussion of the themes and topics that have dominated urban economics over the past fifty years. He begins by examining the definition, scope, successes, and failures of the field. He intentionally defines urban economics broadly and loosely, as analysis that has urban content and is economic in nature. The greater part of the paper is devoted to an examination of the progress and unfinished business in five core areas: the formation, size, and spatial distributions of urban areas; the spatial structure of urban areas; housing; transportation; and local governments. In each area, Mills argues that significant progress has been made, but that important problems remain unresolved. He provides numerous critiques of existing models and results, as well as suggestions for future research. Consistent with the important objective of this journal to link the best urban research with the major urban policy issues, Mills discusses the need for additional critical evaluation of housing programs, the investigation of innovative transportation policies, and a better understanding of local government policy formation. Finally, he provides some provocative views on the costs and benefits of urban sprawl.

Quigley's paper offers perspectives on selected aspects of the evolution of federal urban policy. His focus on federal policy toward low-income housing and urban renewal derives from the view that these two sets of policies are central to urban areas and have historically constituted the major portion of the federal urban policy agenda. Quigley delineates four periods in the evolution of housing policy: pre-1937, when little was done; 1937–62, when low-rent public housing owned and operated by government was the dominant policy; 1962–74, during which private entities began providing federally subsidized housing; and the period since 1974, when the link between the construction of new dwellings and subsidies toward low-income households was broken. He shows that the identity of the housing owner and the form of the subsidy are crucial elements of housing policy. From analysis of theoretical and empirical evidence, he concludes that subsidies provided in the form of housing vouchers work best. He also explores four phases in the evolution of federal urban development programs, with the phases distinguished by the objectives and resource-commitment levels of the programs and the incentives and flexibility given to lower levels of government. Quigley concludes that while the basic goal of housing policy—"a decent home" for all Americans—has remained remarkably constant over time, the level and structure of federal aid for housing has changed dramatically, and generally in positive directions.

Glaeser's paper makes the case that nonmarket interactions are crucial to understanding behavior in urban areas and that research on such topics should be a high priority in the future, noting that "only an economist could be surprised by such a deduction." Urban economists, with their attention already firmly focused on spatial analysis, are uniquely well qualified to examine nonmarket interactions, many of which have important spatial components. Glaeser goes on to explore several areas where nonmarket interactions are likely to play important roles in future urban analyses: the formation and flow of ideas and human capital, the role of peer and neighborhood effects, the importance of architecture, and the transmission of values. In each area, his analysis combines a review of what is known, some provocative facts to help stimulate new thinking, and informed conjectures regarding which factors will be important and productive focal points for future research. He then turns to the city of the future. Although urban areas have traditionally been thought of as facilitating production, Glaeser presents evidence and reasoning that cities will play increasingly important roles as centers of consumption in the future.

The poor performance of urban schools and students, and the resulting relatively low quality of the urban labor force, have been central explanations for the differential development of urban areas. Grogger and Neal provide new evidence on a long-standing issue: the impact of Catholic schools on student performance. While not obviously an urban question, the answer has an important urban twist. Specifically, the authors show that the generally positive effects of Catholic schools on educational attainment and test scores compared to public schools are due in large part to the impact on students in central cities in general and minority students in particular. The impacts on suburban students generally, and suburban white students in particular, are quite small or vanishing. Grogger and Neal also examine the supply of Catholic schools and show that between 1974 and 1994, the supply of such schools shrank in communities of all sizes but particularly in large cities. Thus Catholic schools are vanishing precisely in those places where they have the greatest differential impact on educational attainment. Finally, the authors discuss the relevance of this work for determining the impact of school-voucher programs and provide several qualifications regarding attempts to adapt their estimates for this purpose.

Ellen's paper provides new evidence on the effects of racial segregation in urban areas by considering its impact on the incidence of low-birth-weight children. She finds that in more racially segregated metropolitan areas, the difference in incidence of low-birth-weight babies born to black mothers relative to those born to white mothers is larger than it is in less-segregated metropolitan areas. Through a variety of tests, she concludes that segregation is a causal factor in determining birth-weight outcomes. She also shows that the influence of segregation operates largely through its effects on maternal behavior during pregnancy: alcohol and tobacco use are greater, and prenatal care is less frequent among black mothers in more racially segregated areas.

Voith examines the spatial implications of housing subsidies and zoning restrictions in theoretical and simulation models where city land is in fixed supply and suburban land is plentiful. Under the circumstances modeled, existing tax subsidies encourage high-income homeowners to locate in the suburbs. This pattern raises the benefits to suburban residents of enacting exclusionary zoning restrictions, thus amplifying the initial effects of the tax subsidies. Simulations suggest that interactions between tax subsidies and zoning restrictions can generate large shifts in the equilibrium allocation of low- and high-income residents between the city and its suburbs. The results suggest that differences in incentives created by public policies could be important determinants of the pace of metropolitan decentralization. In contrast, some observers have concluded that differences in preferences among households are the main driving force.

Much of the discussion at the conference focused on two recurring issues: urban sprawl or decentralization, and segregation, whether by income or race. Analysis of virtually every paper came back to, and hinged on, theories and evidence about the causes and consequences of these two phenomena.

The papers and conference discussions confirm that the problems of urban areas are neither simple nor short-lived. But they are not completely intractable either. The challenges presented by new opportunities to enhance urban development are ever-changing. The papers in this volume describe many of these problems and opportunities, indicate how urban economics has addressed them in the past, describe ways to address them in the future, and apply what is currently known to analysis of several important topics. It is our hope that the research in this inaugural volume provides a strong foundation for the evolution of thinking and policy on urban issues.

EDWIN S. MILLS
*Kellogg Graduate School of Management, Northwestern University*

# A Thematic History of
# Urban Economic Analysis

WHAT IS URBAN economics?[1] I will refrain from torturing myself with this issue. Any definition will be too wide for some and too narrow for others. My definition will be simple, but appropriate for my interests and background: urban economics is scholarly writing that has specifically urban content and contains specifically economic analysis. Everyone will notice that my definition leaves room for judgment, which I will exercise freely.

My concern, as the title indicates, is with themes and only incidentally with authors. I propose to ask: What subjects has urban economics been concerned with, and how have they changed through time? What has been the division of labor between theoretical and applied research? And most important, with what subjects has progress been made, and what significant problems are still outstanding?

Where does one look for urban economics publications? One journal, the *Journal of Urban Economics,* whose twenty-fifth birthday 1999 was, has exactly that title. Two or three other journals have those or similar words in their titles. Several scholarly journals are devoted each to housing, transportation, and analysis of local government, and each such subject has a continuum of journals and magazines that blend into trade publications. Per-

The author is indebted to Dennis Epple, Wallace Oates, and other attendees at the Brookings-Wharton conference for many helpful comments. This paper is dedicated to the memory of Stephen Mayo.
1. In this paper, I use the term "urban" to refer to a generic urban settlement. "City" is an urban place incorporated by government. "Metropolitan area" is a large urban area consisting of one or more cities, usually referred to as "central cities," and "suburbs" that are urban places, and may be cities, surrounding central cities in a metropolitan area. Terminology varies somewhat among countries, but I will use the above terms when they are good approximations, even when referring to countries other than the United States.

1

haps the most difficult distinction is between real estate analysis and urban economic analysis. Three or four scholarly journals are devoted to real estate and another three or four to housing and housing finance analysis. In addition, many journals are devoted to related subjects: urban planning, urban geography, regional science and economics, urban government, and so forth. Journals devoted to human resources, labor relations, poverty, and racial problems often contain urban economics articles. And of course urban economics research appears in general economics journals and in books, monographs, and reports of various kinds. Finally, as in the case of international capital flows, there is a home bias in a survey of urban economics. My home bias tells me that most urban economics is published in, or at least promptly translated into, English. But home bias is also geographical. Much urban economics is published in India, Japan, Korea, and other countries. One could certainly write a long survey of urban economics publications from or about India.

By definition, urban economics did not begin before economics, which I date with Adam Smith. In the nineteenth and early twentieth centuries, Johan Heinrich von Thünen, Walter Christaller, Henry George, August Lösch, and Alfred Marshall published more or less systematic urban economic analyses.[2] In the first half of the twentieth century, the list is long enough to require a separate survey of the period. This particular survey arbitrarily covers only the second half of the twentieth century. Another home bias is that, professionally, I have lived through that period.

Many fine economists have written on urban economics. Some have been part-time urban economists, many have been full-time. Among the part-time workers have been several Nobel laureates. Beyond doubt, urban economics has benefited greatly from the writings of its part-time participants. Simon Kuznets had many insightful observations about urban growth in developing countries. Gary Becker provided the first definitive analysis of the economics of discrimination. A paper by Robert Solow and William Vickrey, and one by James A. Mirrlees, are among the finest and most influential in urban economics. Solow has contributed three or four excellent papers to urban economics, but I believe that the Mirrlees paper is the only one he has written on the subject. Vickrey wrote many papers on urban transportation pricing and investment. Stretching the boundaries of the subject would permit inclusion of Paul Samuelson, whose analysis, certainly spatial if not urban, has

---

2. Smith (1776), von Thünen (1826); Christaller (1933); George (1874); Lösch (1954); Marshall (1920).

influenced urban research. Most recent is an important paper, I believe his first in urban economics, by Robert Lucas.[3]

Other urban analyses by Nobel laureates appear somewhat churlish to this reviewer. James Buchanan and Gordon Tullock advocated that entrance fees to urban areas be charged to migrants to compensate for the externalities they generate in urban areas. Migrants do not generate greater externalities than those born in urban areas. More important, externalities imply that governments have not gotten the prices right for urban transportation, polluting discharges, and other local issues; these problems should be attacked directly. Most important, large urban areas generate positive externalities, which are discussed later. And W. Arthur Lewis railed against infrastructure investments in large cities in developing countries, because high land values there made infrastructure excessively expensive, contributing to external debt. He failed to note that land rents are transfers, not resource uses; that land rents are high in big cities, at every stage of development, because land is productive there; and that infrastructure is justified to the extent that it increases land values by more than its cost. Infrastructure investments can, to an approximation, be financed by taxing the resulting increments in land values.[4]

## What Do Urban Economists Do?

Urban economists do what other economists do: theoretical and applied research. Theoretical analysis of urban resource allocation started in the 1960s with what is usually referred to as the Alonso-Mills-Muth model.[5] Early papers struggled to make sense of simple yet pervasive characteristics of urban areas: greater centrality of employment than of population, declining land values

---

3. Kuznets (1955); Becker (1957); Solow and Vickrey (1971); Mirrlees (1972); on urban transportation pricing and investment, notably, Vickrey (1963); Samuelson (1952); Lucas (1999).

4. Buchanan and Tullock (1962); Lewis (1978).

5. See William Alonso (1964); Edwin Mills (1967); Richard Muth (1967). A personal note: My first paper in urban economics, Mills (1967), which has received its share of plaudits, was written in the summer of 1966 while I visited the Rand Corporation. At that time, I had read several early applied studies, Alonso (1964), and a draft that became Muth (1967). I had never heard of von Thünen, the legitimate nineteenth-century precursor to the theoretical models of the 1960s. My immediate inspiration was Clark (1951) and, most important, Solow (1956). It occurred to me to make Solow's analysis reflect distance from an urban center instead of time. Add a reason for there to be a center and a representation of transportation costs, and the analytical results follow easily.

and population densities with distance from urban centers, and apparently universal flattening of density-distance functions as time passes and as one moves from small to large urban areas. Early theoretical models provided important and testable insights, some of which have withstood the test of time, but most of which were clumsy special cases. Compare any early theoretical paper with the abstract, general, and unified models in the survey by Masahisa Fujita or the surveys by Mahlon R. Straszheim, Konrad Stahl, and Jan Brueckner in volume 2 of the *Handbook of Regional and Urban Economics*.[6]

Until the late 1960s, there were few high-quality applied-research publications in urban economics.[7] A fine book on housing by Leo Grebler, David Blank, and Louis Winnick, and another by Margaret Reid, complete the list along with a few journal publications.[8] Much of the research until the late 1960s was financed by or undertaken at Resources for the Future (RFF).[9] During the early 1960s, RFF placed excessive emphasis on regional accounts, undoubtedly reflecting endemic faith in input-output analysis at the time.[10]

In the late 1960s the dam broke, and the quantity and quality of applied urban economic research increased quickly. Richard Muth's *Cities and Housing* was certainly the finest combination of theoretical and applied urban economic research prior to 1970.[11] Jerome Rothenberg first demonstrated appropriate welfare-economics evaluations of urban renewal, the most prominent government urban program of the time.[12] An idea of the increase in the quality and quantity of applied urban economic research from the late 1960s to the late 1970s can be obtained by comparing the survey edited by Peter Mieszkowski and Mahlon Straszheim in 1979 with the 1968 survey edited by Harvey Perloff and Lowdon Wingo.

The biblical generation since the late 1970s has seen a flood of publications on applied urban economic research. The growth rate can be ascertained by comparing the publications reviewed and referenced in volumes 2 and 3 of the *Handbook of Regional and Urban Economics*.[13] A guess is that lengthening bibliographies reflect not only growth in publications but also decreasing costs of computer-generated bibliographies. Specific topics are commented

---

6. Fujita (1987); Mills, ed. (1987).
7. See Goldstein and Moses (1973).
8. Grebler, Blank, and Winnick (1956); Reid (1962).
9. See Hoch (1969); Perloff and Wingo, eds. (1968).
10. See Hoch (1969).
11. Muth (1969).
12. Rothenberg (1967).
13. Mills, ed. (1987); Cheshire and Mills, eds. (1999).

on below. The growth in applied urban economics publications, which must have been close to a compound 10 percent annual rate, has resulted from obvious changes. First and foremost has been the decreasing cost of computing, especially since personal computers became available to almost every scholar during the 1980s. Closely related has been the dramatic increase in the quantity, quality, and availability of urban data. Better and more easily available econometric techniques and software have also spurred the revolution. A by-product that has frequently been referenced has been the rapid growth of publications coauthored by scholars in different institutions and countries, undoubtedly entailing economies of scale and scope. A corollary is that technological unemployment must have increased among research assistants; perhaps some of these individuals should be employed to verify published empirical results.

**Topical Survey**

Publications can be assigned to subject matter categories in many ways. I have compiled a classification of papers that appeared in the *Journal of Urban Economics* in 1978, 1988, and 1998. The first volume of the *Journal of Urban Economics* was published in 1974. The classification is in table 1. I believe that the nine categories are intuitively appealing and correspond to the way that urban economists tend to think about subfields in their specialty. The difficulty of classifying papers increases with the fineness of the categories. For that reason and because the total sample is only 129 papers, I have used the nine-subject classification. The only difficult task in my classification was assigning papers between categories 1 and 2. Many spatial analyses are primarily about housing and many housing analyses are also spatial. My classification has been subjective and some readers might classify some papers differently.

Several other comments can be offered. The number of papers per year in the *Journal* has increased only modestly, but the number of papers on similar subjects but in other journals has increased greatly. That is particularly true of housing, for which the number of outlets for scholarly papers has increased rapidly, but the same is true for "real estate," for which the number of high-quality papers and journals has also increased rapidly.

Category 8 includes all papers on relationships between an urban area and other places—for example, papers on rural-urban or interurban migration, or

**Table 1. Percent Distribution of Papers in the *Journal of Urban Economics* by Subject Matter, 1978, 1988, 1998**

Percent

| Topic | 1978 | 1988 | 1998 |
|---|---|---|---|
| 1. Spatial analysis | 30.8 | 22.7 | 8.7 |
| 2. Housing | 20.5 | 27.3 | 19.6 |
| 3. Government sector | 20.5 | 22.7 | 30.4 |
| 4. Labor, poverty, race | 10.3 | 4.5 | 13.0 |
| 5. Crime | 5.1 | 0.0 | 2.2 |
| 6. Transportation | 5.1 | 2.3 | 6.5 |
| 7. Education | 0.0 | 4.5 | 4.3 |
| 8. Interurban, rural-urban | 7.7 | 9.1 | 8.7 |
| 9. Developing countries | 0.0 | 6.8 | 6.5 |
| Total number of papers | 39 | 44 | 46 |

Source: Author's calculations.

papers on the size and spatial distributions of urban areas. Category 9 includes all papers on countries that are not members of the Organization for Economic Cooperation and Development (non-OECD). I put these in a separate category regardless of subject category because good papers on those countries have increased rapidly, although the *Journal* is not a primary outlet. The same is true of papers on transportation, crime, and education. Finally, I believe that the *Journal,* under both of its editors, has always welcomed submissions of papers, theoretical or applied, on all subjects that could reasonably be called urban economics.

The strongest suggestion in table 1 is that there is a trend away from spatial analysis. I believe this results from two causes. First is that the easy problems in spatial analysis, specifically the monocentric model, have been solved. Multicentric models are much more realistic but much more difficult. Second is the trend toward more and better applied papers referred to on page 4. Housing papers have been consistently numerous, despite the growth of competing outlets—again a tribute both to the importance of and interest in the subject and to the growth of applied work. Analyses of government behavior in urban areas, most but not all of these concerning local governments, have constituted the big growth sector in the table. The small growth of papers in category 4 surprised the author. The shrinkage of attention to crime probably reflects economists' overall attitudes. Good papers on economic aspects of education have certainly increased since the late 1970s, and many are published in other journals. Likewise, growth in the number of papers on developing countries probably reflects the rising quality of papers on the subject. Needless to say, my sample is too small for the results to be more than suggestive; better subject-matter analysis would require a survey of more journals, which would require a more subtle classification between urban and other papers and, for some journals, between economics and other specialties.

If one regards the distinction between categories one and two as arbitrary and adds the entries together, the percentage share declines from 51.3 to 50 to 28.3 during the twenty-year period. That decline is counterbalanced by a 50 percent increase in the share of papers related to government behavior and by modest increases in the shares of several other categories. What accounts for the increase in papers devoted to analysis of government behavior? Certainly not a decrease in alternative outlets available. Nor does the reason appear to be a dramatic increase in data available. Of course, more government data are available in electronic form, but that is as true of data related to the private sector. I believe the reason is a dramatic increase in analyses that relate to the positive theory of government. Many more economists now analyze how governments actually behave instead of ending papers with inane comments on "policy implications." At the local level, for example, governments have vastly overregulated housing and transportation for parochial reasons; yet until recently economists continued to identify "market imperfections" and to urge additional government intervention without asking whether the history of government involvement in such areas makes it likely that additional intervention will make things better or worse. Analyses of the motivation and behavior of government agents and the relations between government and private agents are the keys to progress in research on governments.

### Progress in Urban Economics

In this section I trace the development of several specific subjects of urban economic research. My goal has been to discuss important subjects on which there has been a substantial and persistent literature displaying a coherent line of development. In each subsection, I finish with my perceptions of important but inadequately studied topics.

Selection of topics is inevitably subjective, reflecting my reading, my interests, and my judgments, and probably reflecting some home bias.

8                              *Brookings-Wharton Papers on Urban Affairs: 2000*

*Formation, Size, and Spatial Distributions of Urban Areas*

This subsection reviews several closely related topics: why urban areas are formed, why they grow, rural-urban migration, and the size and spatial distributions of urban areas.

What is an urban area? In most countries, definitions are similar: a contiguous area with a population of at least 2,500 to 25,000 (occasionally 50,000) people in which a majority of resident workers are in nonagricultural sectors, and possibly having a minimum population density. An important peculiarity of U.S. data is that, although the minimum urban population is only 2,500 people and about 2 percent of workers work on farms, about 27 percent of the population of workers is rural. The apparent implication is that about 25 percent of workers are rural residents not working directly on farms. Furthermore, most of the 25 percent do not appear to be engaged in farm-related activities.[14] No other country appears to have a rural nonfarm workforce of 20 percent. The peculiar U.S. data are probably mostly illusion. Outside metropolitan areas, census employment data are provided by place of residence. In metropolitan areas, data are by both place of residence and place of work. We also know that a few more workers commute into than out of metropolitan areas on the way to work, but the difference is not large relative to the 20 percent of rural nonfarmworker residents. The reconciliation probably is that most of the rural and non–farm-resident workers commute to jobs in relatively small nearby urban but not metropolitan communities.

Why do urban areas exist? The simplest answer is the correct answer. Urban areas exist because proximity among diverse activities economizes on the cost of moving goods, people, and messages. This characterization covers early commercial urban areas, medieval fortress urban areas, medieval cathedral-based centers, and the largest metropolitan complexes in the late twentieth century. Even if scale economies internal to a single manufacturing plant justified employment of 2,500 workers, the location would not be an urban area unless commuting costs induced the employees to live close to the plant. Likewise, even if people's sole interest were in social interaction with each other, 2,500 people would not form an urban area unless social interaction were more costly at greater distances between residents. Alternatively, suppose that 2,500 fishermen who catch fish over a large part of the ocean live in a hamlet because it is at the best natural harbor in the region; then the reason for the urban cen-

14. U.S. Bureau of the Census (1992, table 17, p. 20).

ter is that the proximity of fishermen's residences near the harbor makes the costs of shipping fish from that place less than the costs of shipping them from scattered sites.

Works by the great urban historians Paul Bairoch, William Cronon, Paul Hohenberg and Lynn Lees, Adna Weber, Charles N. Glaab and A. Theodore Brown, and many others, as well as those by most modern urban economists, have all used this explanation of urban areas, mostly implicitly, but I have not seen a succinct statement.[15] Modern urban economists typically attribute the advantages of urban areas to economies of scale, scope, and agglomeration.[16] I have just shown that economies of scale, and by extension of scope, are not sufficient reasons for urban areas. Although much progress has been made during the last quarter century in understanding and measuring agglomeration economies, I believe it remains the great mystique of urban economics. The definition of *agglomeration economies* is economies from proximate locations or urban size that are external to individual firms. Thus agglomeration economies do not include economies of scale and scope, which are internal to firms.

Agglomeration economies is one of the few subjects in economics in which measurement preceded theory. Several imaginative measurements were made with U.S. data in the 1970s;[17] these have since been repeated with better data and estimation techniques for the United States and a few other countries.[18] Although data and conceptual approaches vary greatly, conclusions are remarkably uniform: each doubling of the size of an urban area increases total factor productivity by 5 to 10 percent. Although intuition suggests that there must be a limit to agglomeration economies, no careful study seems to have provided convincing evidence of a limit.

What could account for this almost incredible finding? Several sources have been prominently suggested. The economist Edgar Hoover suggested a probabilistic phenomenon: if employers' demands for similar kinds of labor are

15. Bairoch (1988); Cronon (1991); Hohenberg and Lees (1985); Weber (1899); Glaab and Brown (1967).

16. For a survey, see the paper by Randall W. Eberts and Daniel P. McMillen in Cheshire and Mills, eds. (1999, pp. 1455–92).

17. For references, see the paper by Eberts and McMillen in Cheshire and Mills, eds. (1999).

18. See Shukla (1996) for Indian estimates and for references to estimates for other countries. Agglomeration economies are mentioned in many studies of urban areas in developing countries, often as a catch-all phrase. Remarkably enough, World Bank (1999), devoted to "knowledge for development," does not mention the term.

only imperfectly correlated, proximate locations can reduce per-worker unemployment rates and hence competitive wage rates.[19]

This appears to be a reasonable source of agglomeration economies in that it does not result from scale or scope economies that are internal to particular plants, but after more than half a century I have not seen any estimation, and my intuition is that it is unimportant beyond an urban size of one or two million in population.

Urban economists' recent predilection is to attribute agglomeration economies to "nonexcludable public goods" (a redundancy) such as access to a large labor pool or capital market or to "infrastructure" such as roads, power, water supply, and sewage treatment. Access to large input suppliers may have the statistical advantage just discussed, but it is otherwise difficult to imagine how large input markets could be sources of market failure. Infrastructure is subject to scale economies but is certainly excludable. Governments pervasively underprice roads (see page 28) and most other products they produce, but metering by electronic means and pricing by fuel taxes or by metered travel are certainly methods of excluding "free riders" from use of such goods. Piped water, power, and sewage treatment are quintessential private goods. Fire protection can be priced by insurance, as health care typically is. The criminal justice system is almost inherently a public good, but evidence of substantial scale economies is scant. Education is excludable and is provided free of charge by governments mostly for equity reasons, and is priced at all levels by private providers. Local urban goods and services provided by governments may be underpriced and subject to scale or scope economies, but I am unable to identify any such services other than criminal justice that satisfy the technical definition of public goods.

The strongest case for a source of agglomeration economies is "knowledge spillovers." The concept was prominent in the work of Alfred Marshall, is often attributed to Jane Jacobs, and has recently been the subject of measurement.[20] Careful work requires a distinction between basic and applied research and development, spillovers being more effectively prevented (by patents, trademarks, company secrets, nondisclosure agreements, and other means) the farther toward the practical end of the spectrum one goes. One should also

19. Hoover (1948). Mills (1972) is sometimes given credit for this idea. Although I included Hoover (1948) in the chapter reading, I failed to include the acknowledgement, and the reference was omitted from later editions. I apologize.

20. Marshall (1920); Jacobs (1969); for recent surveys, see Helsley and Strange (1999) and the paper by Eberts and McMillen in Cheshire and Mills, eds. (1999).

distinguish between the generation and the application of new knowledge. Also important is the relationship, presumably complementary, between universities and industrial research centers. Nevertheless, the rapid growth of high-tech centers (most prominently Route 128, Silicon Valley, the Research Triangle, Austin, and Tsukuba in Japan) during recent decades provides a strong prima facie case that applied research and innovation benefit from proximity. It is worthy of note that all the above centers were on the peripheries of metropolitan areas when they started and that all reportedly have substantive interactions with nearby universities.

Of course, proximate locations of horizontally related firms do not prove that there is market failure. Urban firms are located near each other in many sectors (law, medicine, finance, advertising) in which no one suggests market failure. Firms locate near each other if some transactions benefit from proximity. That firms benefit from face-to-face communication accounts for extremely high densities of central-business-district employment, where land values may be at least an order of magnitude greater than their value twenty-five to forty miles away and no market failure is presumed.

An apparently unnoticed implication of agglomeration economies is that market forces result in metropolitan areas that are too small for social efficiency. If the most important source of agglomeration economies is technology concentrated on peripheries of metropolitan areas, the suggested government policy is subsidization of such firms to locate in distant suburbs!

My guess is that the most important reason for measured increases in total factor productivity with respect to urban size is unpriced and unmeasured inputs, namely time spent in commuting and other business travel. Of course, such travel is a business input and presumably affects input and output prices, but only a brave soul would expect that it would show up accurately in data on which urban productivity analysis is based. Presumably, message transmission is an increasingly important part of the urban transportation-communication syndrome. Message transmissions also cost money, but electronic transmission is increasingly both cheap and independent of distance in our knowledge-intensive economy. John Naisbitt and others have forecast an increasingly exurban economy as a result.[21] Jess Gaspar and Edward Glaeser have insightfully hypothesized that electronic and face-to-face communication are complementary as falling communication costs permit more information-intensive production.[22] For example, it seems highly likely that

21. Naisbitt (1994).
22. Gaspar and Glaeser (1998).

widespread use of telephone communication has promoted urbanization, including complementary face-to-face communication, during the last century. Furthermore, electronic communication has been important for thirty to forty years, and as yet there is no evidence that urban growth in the United States or elsewhere is off its long-term path. Finally, university administrations have shown little enthusiasm to encourage faculty to deliver electronic lectures from their Aspen retreats to students scattered worldwide.

My strong guess is that sufficiently fine measurement of input and output prices and quantities would show approximately constant total factor productivity with respect to sizes of urban areas with more than a few hundred thousand in population.

I would like to make three suggestions regarding future research on formation of urban areas and agglomeration economies. First, analysts must be more careful in their use of the term *public goods*. The term has a meaning. It refers to services that are nonexcludable and nonsatiable. Second, they must distinguish carefully between agglomeration economies and economies that are internal to plants and firms. Third and most important, they must think and estimate carefully regarding the kinds of technologies that are likely to generate significant underpriced external benefits from proximity.

Urban areas grow or shrink by three processes. The first is natural growth—the excess of births over deaths—of the urban population. The second is migration from rural areas, other urban areas, and other countries. The third—a significant part of urban growth in many rapidly urbanizing developing countries—is reclassification from rural to urban of places on the peripheries of urban areas as the density and occupational structure of the peripheral areas change.

Rural-urban migration has received far more study than the other two phenomena. Rural-urban is by far the largest kind of migration in most developing countries, whereas in many industrialized countries in which 70 to 80 percent of the population is urban, urban-urban migration is larger.[23] Much migration literature is country-specific. A voluminous literature has been produced on migration within India, for example. Generally speaking, fine studies have been produced on migration in many developing countries.[24] U.S. migration studies are too numerous to survey, but Michael Greenwood has been among

23. Substantial migrations, in many cases urban-rural, are the results of extreme violence and severe depressions. These events are ignored in this paper.

24. For surveys, see Stark (1991) and the paper by Charles M. Becker and Andrew R. Morrison in Cheshire and Mills, eds. (1999, pp. 1673–768).

the most productive economists who have written on domestic migration, and his *Migration and Economic Growth in the United States* reviews literature up to 1981.[25] A large literature on transatlantic migration exists. Transatlantic migration contributed greatly to both U.S. urban and rural growth in the late nineteenth and early twentieth centuries. The least studied transatlantic migration has been the slave trade.[26]

Although theoretical analyses of rural-urban migration have been published, most empirical studies are based more on common sense than on theory. Findings depend on data availability and on the fineness of studies. But most of the important causes of rural-urban migration appear to be common among times and places. Rural-urban migration is the property of youth. Many youth go to urban areas to pursue more or better education than is available in rural areas. Most do not return. Not surprisingly, the richest rural residents rarely migrate, but otherwise migrants span the income distribution from desperately poor to relatively well off. In many countries, young men migrate to urban areas and then, after they have completed their education and improved their living standards, marry women from their home regions and bring them to the city. An interesting aspect of migration, especially in low-income areas, is an informal contractual aspect. Male migrants may send remittances back to their rural families—sometimes because of loyalty, sometimes to retain informal rights to property or employment in case they want to return, sometimes as repayment for financial assistance provided by the family while they establish themselves in the urban area.

Comparison of rural and urban wage rates is complicated by the fact that urban living costs exceed rural living costs, but the range of goods and services available is much greater in urban than in rural areas. Benefit from the broader range of goods is the factual basis of the "bright lights" attraction of urban migrants. Rural wages are difficult to measure in poor countries because much farm production is consumed where it is produced, making valuation difficult. Unemployment data are predominantly urban in most countries, and are nearly meaningless in poor urban places because literal lack of earnings is life-threatening for the poorest people. Rural-urban migration has slowed

25. Greenwood (1981).
26. Between 1500 and 1825, approximately 11 million slaves moved from Africa, sometimes via Europe, to the Western Hemisphere, compared with about 2 million whites. The slave trade was by far the biggest trade flow of many European and American countries for three centuries. The slave migration was mostly, but not exclusively, rural-rural. The definitive study is Thomas (1993), see pp. 804, 805 for estimated statistics.

in many relatively high-income developing countries.[27] The countries that the
World Bank classified as upper-middle income had an average 73 percent urban
population in 1995.[28]

I have three suggestions regarding future research on U.S. migration: First,
researchers should perform all analyses in a simultaneous-equation framework,
because people attract jobs and jobs attract people. Second, they should distinguish carefully between amenities that are public goods (for example, good
weather) and those that are private goods (for example, golf courses). Benefits of public-good amenities have limited spatial effects and presumably are
capitalized in land values and thus have little effect on migration. This may
not always be the case, but researchers should make this distinction carefully.
Third, they would do well to read the paper by Joseph Gyourko, Matthew
Kahn, and Joseph Tracy in volume 3 of the *Handbook of Regional and Urban
Economics* before proceeding with further work.[29]

I conclude this subsection with brief comments on the size and spatial distributions of urban areas. When people migrate, they almost invariably go to
an urban area; they may also come from one.

Size and spatial distributions are of course related, as Paul Krugman has
emphasized.[30] A geographically small country heavily dependent on trade and
with only one fine natural harbor is likely to have a very different urban size
and spatial distribution than a large country with many harbors and a large
internal market, such as the United States. Likewise, a mountainous country
such as Japan is likely to have small urban areas in interior valleys and a few
large urban areas at natural harbors.

A cottage industry has grown in estimating the size distribution of urban
areas. Care must be taken in interpreting such studies, because some employ
city-size data, which for most of the twentieth century have had little to do
with sizes of generic urban areas. City data are better approximations to a metropolitan concept in some countries than in the United States, and no official
metropolitan data existed in the United States prior to 1940.

Although the first estimates appeared long before his work, George Zipf
clarified the rank-size rule for U.S. city-size distributions.[31] (A Pareto distribution with a unit exponent, it has the irresistible property that the $n$th largest

27. See the paper by Becker and Morrison in Cheshire and Mills, eds. (1999).
28. See World Bank (1999).
29. Cheshire and Mills, eds. (1999, pp. 1414–51).
30. Krugman (1993).
31. Zipf (1949). See also Rosen and Resnick (1980).

city has one-$n$th the population of the largest city, for all integer values of $n$ in the data.) Subsequent studies have shown that estimated parameters of the Pareto (or log-normal) distribution vary by country and by choice of urban unit (countries with fewer than about 15 million people are typically excluded from most estimates).[32] However, it is astounding that U.S. and other estimates, using the best available approximations to metropolitan areas, find the Pareto distribution with an exponent close to one to be a good fit with data between about 1800 and 1980. During that time, the U.S. urban population increased from about 6 percent to about 75 percent, industrialized massively, and bought or stole real estate that multiplied its size manyfold. Ingenious explanations have been put forward for a Pareto or log-normal distribution, some probabilistic and some economic, but the persistence of a near unit distribution parameter cries out for explanation.[33] Sukkoo Kim's recent computer analysis merits study and follow-on research.[34] I have seen only one paper on the social-optimum distribution of urban sizes: it is by Seong Hwan Suh, and is undeservedly neglected.[35] Uniform geography might contribute to a stable distribution of urban sizes over time, but U.S. geography has evolved dramatically since the early 1800s as boundaries have expanded westward.

There has been some speculation about the spatial distribution of urban areas.[36] The three metropolitan areas that have been the largest in the United States for many decades are spaced so that about a third of the population is located closest to each; Moscow and Vladivostok are at opposite ends of Russia; Bombay, Delhi, Calcutta, and Madras are geographically distributed about the same as the Indian population; and Canada's large metropolitan areas are distributed about uniformly along the inhabitable southern sliver of that country. (Why is there no large Maritime Provinces urban area?) Large urban areas do not like mountains or deserts and do like coasts and navigable rivers.

Analysis beyond these banal observations would require a careful model of the interactions between a metropolitan area and its surrounding countryside (central-place theory), the interactions with other nearby metropolitan areas, and many separate geographical characteristics. Such modeling might be great fun for computer enthusiasts, but I am not sure it has great social value. In principle, careful analyses of size and spatial distributions might shed

32. See the paper by Paul Cheshire in Cheshire and Mills, eds. (1999, pp. 1339–69).
33. See Gabaix (1999).
34. Kim (1999).
35. Suh (1991).
36. Lösch (1954); Hoover (1948); Krugman (1993). Again, see the paper by Cheshire in Cheshire and Mills, eds. (1999).

light on the determinants of economic growth. Governments influence urban sizes and locations. Undoubtedly, many national capitals are larger than social optima.[37] U.S. state and national capitals have been located on political considerations, many state capitals having been located simply to be near the state's geographic center. It has already been indicated that if agglomeration economies are real and substantial, some or all metropolitan areas are excessively small. Finally, some governments attempt to curtail growth of large metropolitan areas, especially by restricting migration of poor people.[38] It appears there have been few attempts to model influences of governments on the size and spatial distributions of cities.

*Spatial Structure of Urban Areas*

The spatial structure of urban areas refers to locations of various sectors within urban areas. The thirty-five-year history of this analysis is monotonic: going from simple and relatively unrealistic to complex and more realistic models.

The Alonso-Mills-Muth model is very simple and easily tested. It starts by assuming something that imposes centrality on the urban area, located exogenously at distance = 0. "Something" was sometimes thought to be a natural harbor, or a rail center, or a market, a place to which all the urban area's production had to be shipped for sale. Harbors are more or less exogenously located, but rail centers and product markets are endogenous (and not centralized)—and none of the three has served as a powerful centralizing force, at least in most urban areas, during most of the twentieth century. The assumption that all production had to be shipped to distance = 0 is really a deus ex machina to provide centrality. Production in the urban areas was assumed to be competitive, with a constant returns-to-scale, often Cobb-Douglas, production function. Producers located themselves endogenously and typically shipped their output to the deus ex machina at a constant transportation cost per unit mile. Labor, capital, and land were typically the inputs in production. Capital was purchased competitively from outside the urban area.

The urban area's labor market was competitive, and workers' housing was produced competitively, also with constant returns, and was located endoge-

---

37. See Glaeser (1998).

38 In Delhi, the only housing that the poorest quarter or third of the people can afford is illegal; thus poverty is criminalized and migration to the city discouraged. Delhi is not unique. The phenomenon dramatically illustrates the harm that can be done by excessively stringent land-use controls.

nously. Workers paid a constant per-mile commuting cost between home and work. Simple models did not have a production system for local transportation. The urban area's output was sold at a fixed price at the deus ex machina.

This canonical model generates several theorems about long-run equilibrium: production occupies contiguous space centered on the deus ex machina; land rent equilibrates to make producers' profits just zero, and rents decline monotonically with distance from the deus ex machina; a well-defined boundary exists between the production and residential areas; all workers occupy a contiguous residential area, are equally well off, with house rents and workers' density declining monotonically within the residential area, house rents decreasing with distance so as to offset increasing commuting costs; land rents are equal at the touching edges of the production and residential areas; the outer edge of the urban area is where residential land rents equal the rent of land in nonurban (presumably agricultural) use; and worker density and land rent functions flatten if the wage rate increases exogenously or if per-mile commuting costs fall. If the urban area is open, workers' common utility level equals that which can be obtained elsewhere; if the urban area is closed (with a locally exogenous worker population), then the common utility level is set by the model. Cobb-Douglas production functions and simple housing demand equations provide land-rent and density-distance functions that can be estimated.[39]

Complexity remains modest if several worker types with different competitive wage rates are introduced; the commuting system is assumed to require land, capital, and travel-time inputs; and a simple retail sector is introduced that can locate in the residential sector.

Estimates reveal some predictive accuracy of the simple models, at least at moderately high levels of spatial aggregation. Population density invariably falls with distance, as do house prices (and undoubtedly actual and imputed rents for equivalent houses), and the population density–distance function flattens if wages increase or if per-mile commuting costs fall, and, as simple models predict, high-wage workers live farther from the central business district than do low-wage workers. This is a good record of richness and accuracy for a simple model.

The greatest failure of the model is the predicted location of all businesses in contiguous space in the central business district (CBD). That prediction becomes less accurate every decade, and in the 1990s only about 10 percent of metropolitan-area employment was located in the CBD in many U.S. met-

---

39. See the paper by Jan Brueckner in Mills, ed. (1987).

ropolitan areas. In fact, I believe that the remarkable fact is not that the chimp types so badly, but that it types at all; the broad predictions from simple models remain more accurate than I would have expected, given the massive dispersion of employment in U.S. metropolitan areas and the pervasiveness in the United States of fragmented local government jurisdictions. The second greatest deficiency of the simple model is the absence of a government sector, discussed below.

Starting in the 1960s, dispersed employment was gradually introduced into metropolitan models. Rarely cited in recent years, computer simulation models provided the first important analysis. John Kain spearheaded that subsector.[40] Starting in the mid-1970s, dispersed employment was introduced in conceptual models that modified the above-described monocentric model. Michelle White dominated that subsector.[41] Early computer and analytical models simply introduced exogenously located employment subcenters scattered around the metropolitan area and away from the CBD. Investigation then centered on the effects of employment subcenters on residential locations and commuting. Still hardly studied is why subcenters form. Presumably the reasons have to do with exhaustion of scale, scope, and agglomeration economies in the CBD; residential suburbanization attracting employment to suburbs; decreasing costs of communication at considerable distances; and congestion, crime, taxes, and so forth in central cities. Even less studied is why subcenters locate where they do. Some were small urban areas before the metropolitan area spread out to engulf them, and subcenters grew there for reasons that put them there to begin with. Some affected and were affected by locations of transportation routes. Presumably there are other influences, such as locations of residences of desirable workers and business-friendly local governments.

A final comment is that identification of employment subcenters depends very much on the fineness of measurement. At a sufficiently gross density, only the CBD shows up. At a very fine density, dozens of subcenters show up in a large metropolitan area such as Los Angeles or Chicago.[42] The subcenter surrounding Chicago's O'Hare Airport has about the same employment as the CBD, but at lower density. Using a gross-density cutoff, only the CBD shows up; at a lower density, O'Hare appears; at a still lower density, two O'Hare subcenters appear.[43]

40. See the paper by John Kain in Mills, ed. (1987).
41. See the paper by Michelle J. White in Cheshire and Mills, eds. (1999, pp. 1375–410).
42. See Anas, Arnott, and Small (1998), and references therein.
43. See McMillen and McDonald (1998).

There has been an enormous literature on residential suburbanization, starting with the above-referenced deduction from the simple monocentric model that high-income residents are likely to reside farther from the CBD than lower-income residents and that high-income metropolitan areas are likely to have flatter residential-density functions than low-income metropolitan areas.[44] Most of the residential suburbanization literature has been written without regard for interactions between residential and employment suburbanization.

The central controversy in the population suburbanization literature has been the relative importance of basic economic causes (rising income, falling commuting costs, employment suburbanization, lower suburban taxes, and suburban land-use controls suitable to the wishes of high-income residents) compared with central-city social problems (racial discrimination, poverty, crime, poor schools).[45] There can be little doubt that both sets of causes are important; the difficult issue is how much. As in many applied economics specialties, an element of ideology affects this analysis. Those with great faith in markets tend to place greatest faith in the former category, whereas those with less faith in markets place greatest faith in the latter category. My home bias is certainly toward faith in markets.

That basic economic causes are at work is indicated not only by statistical studies of postwar U.S. suburbanization, but also by the fact that suburbanization has pervaded present OECD countries for a century or more and rapidly developing countries for most of the postwar years.[46] Most such countries have had few or no race-related central-city social problems that might cause suburbanization.

That racial and other central-city social problems are also important is also virtually certain.[47] Although racial discrimination has been illegal since the 1960s and is almost certainly less virulent in the 1990s than it was in earlier decades, only a braver person than I would claim that it no longer prevents suburbanization of blacks and Hispanics.[48] My judgment is that race is now a more important determinant of who suburbanizes than of how many people suburbanize. If discrimination prevents minorities from suburbanizing, more whites probably suburbanize than would have in the absence of discrimination.

---

44. For precise conditions, see the paper by Jan Brueckner in Mills, ed. (1987).
45. See Mieszkowski and Mills (1993) for a survey.
46. See Mills and Tan (1980) and references therein.
47. See Yinger (1995).
48. See Thernstrom and Thernstrom (1997).

Although claims that U.S. suburbanization is excessive have long existed, *sprawl* and *smart growth* have recently become political buzzwords. Anthony Downs has long been the intellectual leader of antisprawl advocates.[49] Remarkably enough, welfare economics and notions of the social efficiency of competitive markets are almost never mentioned in antisprawl literature. There is no reason to doubt that U.S. metropolitan land, housing development, housing, and housing finance markets are competitive. Instead, antisprawl writers simply point to the greater suburbanization of U.S. metropolitan areas than of those in Europe (and they occasionally point to even more pronounced centralization in Asia) as evidence of excessive U.S. suburbanization, lamenting congestion on arterial highways, auto pollution, and excessive disappearance of farmland into suburban developments. Benefits of suburbanization are almost never mentioned.

The farmland shortage claim cannot be taken seriously; agricultural surpluses have prevailed for several decades and are the likely future scenario. In any case, there is a market for land at urban peripheries and there is no reason to doubt that relative urban and rural prices can preserve farmland. Even at low suburban densities, urban densities exceed rural densities, so each rural-urban migrant results in a net increase in the rural land available for agriculture. Antisprawl advocates never point out that there is no intrinsic positive correlation between commuting distances and suburbanization. Although it has not happened in the United States, it would be easy to imagine a scenario in which suburbanization of employment and population reduced commuting distances (see page 28). Another false issue raised by antisprawl advocates is that suburbanization eats up excessive amounts of open space. The appropriate technique to preserve open space is for governments to buy land or development rights according to the wishes of voters to be taxed for the purpose. If governments simply prevent development by regulation, they impose the costs of open space on owners who are denied the right to develop their land. That procedure is likely to induce governments to preserve excessive amounts of open space. The Endangered Species Act is a contemporary example of the effects of governments imposing the costs of open-space preservation on landowners. U.S. metropolitan areas are indeed more suburbanized than those in most other countries. One reason is that the United States has large supplies of inexpensive rural land near most metropolitan areas. More important, most countries (all of northern Europe, all of East Asia, most of South Asia,

49. Downs (1994).

and Canada) place severe government restrictions on conversion of rural land to urban development. The result is certainly more compact urban areas; typically greater, not less, traffic congestion; and, never mentioned by antisprawl advocates, much more expensive housing. In Canada, which strictly controls metropolitan expansion, house prices (at least in Toronto and Vancouver) are 50 percent greater relative to residents' income than in the United States; in Europe and Asia, house prices are several times greater relative to incomes than in the United States.[50] It is difficult to imagine that U.S. antisprawl proposals could fail to raise house prices relative to income. My newspaper reading indicates that advocacy of suburban growth controls by political officials has already begun to strengthen the exclusionary proclivities of suburban governments.

Future research might begin to follow up on the fragmentary data now indicating that many minorities began to suburbanize in the 1980s. There are some key questions to be addressed: How many minorities have suburbanized? Which metropolitan areas have seen these changes? Which suburbs have seen the most increases, and for what reasons? Has minority suburbanization been a cause of the apparent increase in white settlements in central cities since the mid-1990s? If so, is it because Americans have become racially less tense, because central cities have become more attractive, or because there is no longer any place for whites to "hide"? It appears that job growth in central cities is not an important factor. The proportion of metropolitan jobs located in suburbs appears to have continued to increase, even during the rapid employment growth of the late 1990s.

### Housing

As was seen in table 1, housing has been a consistently strong interest of urban economists. The survey reported there far understates the volume of publications on the subject since many new scholarly journals, professional publications, and trade magazines have begun and expanded during the past thirty years. Between them, the Department of Housing and Urban Development and the Federal National Mortgage Association publish at least a half-dozen housing periodicals. Housing research is extensive not only in the United States but also throughout OECD countries.[51] There is also a vast hous-

50. See Malpezzi and Mayo (1997).
51. See the paper by Christine M. E. Whitehead in Cheshire and Mills, eds. (1999, pp. 1559–85).

ing literature related to developing countries. The World Bank has made progress in understanding even the chaotic housing markets in China and Russia.[52]

In the United States, housing is not only a crucial part of living standards and social status, but also is about half of the market value of privately owned produced fixed capital; it is a smaller part of fixed capital production since housing lasts much longer than most industrial plants and equipment.

Early housing research, such as the work of Leo Grebler, David Blank, and Louis Winnick, focused on time series and cross-sectional measurement of housing prices and quantities.[53] Margaret Reid provided the first sophisticated estimates of the income elasticity of housing demand.[54] Increasingly sophisticated estimates of price and income elasticities were published during the 1960s and 1970s.[55] Although estimates varied disturbingly, by the 1980s most specialists apparently believed that income elasticities were typically somewhat below one and price elasticities were somewhat above minus one-half.[56] These estimates can explain indications that for many decades a nearly constant fraction of income was spent on housing and that, as incomes have risen, housing prices rose somewhat faster than the overall price level. The persistent increase in the relative price of housing probably results from migration from cheap rural housing to expensive urban housing and from increases in urban land values as urban areas grow. It seems that construction costs have not risen faster than the price level. The massive worldwide data compilation under the direction of Stephen Mayo suggests strongly that housing-demand equation parameters vary little among countries.[57] Mayo and Stephen Malpezzi assume that income elasticities are close to one and that demand is price-inelastic, and analyze the dramatic differences in hous-

52. See the paper by Stephen Malpezzi in Cheshire and Mills, eds. (1999, pp. 1791–845).
53. Grebler, Blank, and Winnick (1956).
54. Reid (1962).
55. For a survey through the late 1970s, see the paper by John Quigley in Mieszkowski and Straszheim (1979).
56. See the paper by Christine M. E. Whitehead in Cheshire and Mills, eds. (1999, pp. 1559–85). The paper by Richard Voith in this volume cites evidence that the price elasticity of urban land is about −1.6. Muth (1969) and others have shown that reasonable estimates of the elasticity of substitution between land and structural capital in housing production imply that the price elasticity of demand for land might be an order of magnitude times the price elasticity of demand for housing. The Gyourko-Voith estimate appears to be consistent with this analysis. Indeed, the same analysis applied to business offices explains why the demand for proximity generates building heights and land values in CBDs that are one or two orders of magnitude greater than they are a few miles away. Yet office rents vary much less than proportionately.
57. See Malpezzi and Mayo (1997).

ing price-income ratios in terms of supply-side differences, especially government policies.

Housing is a complex and differentiated commodity. Although government and private housing price indexes have been compiled for decades, specialists have long known that they have been badly flawed. Hedonic analysis, applied in other areas much earlier, began to be applied to housing in the early 1970s.[58] The goal is to ascertain how house prices depend on house characteristics and how characteristics coefficients vary over time and space. An important issue is the extent to which characteristics coefficient differences result from differences in demand or supply. Dozens of applied studies have appeared in this and other countries.[59] I detect little tendency for estimates of characteristics prices to converge.

An alternative to hedonic indexes that has been analyzed during the 1990s is "repeat sales" indexes. In very large data sets compiled for secondary mortgage market securities, some dwellings sell two or more times. Assuming that the physical characteristics of a given dwelling do not change between sales, a precise price index can be estimated. (Many papers have appeared in the *Journal of Real Estate Finance and Economics* and in *Real Estate Economics*.) Repeat sales indexes pertain to time-series changes, but not to cross- sectional differences. An additional limitation is that second "sales" are frequently refinancings and resale "prices" are in fact appraisals.

It has long been recognized that dwelling prices are asset prices, whereas the cost of occupying a dwelling for a year is its rent or imputed rent or user cost. Dwelling prices are set by supply and demand and converge to land values plus depreciated current construction cost in the long run. Rents of rental dwellings are set by agreement between tenants and landlords, usually annual contracts but not infrequently unwritten agreements with no explicit duration. Imputed rent for an owner-occupied dwelling equals the sum of mortgage interest plus forgone returns on the owner's equity plus insurance, maintenance, and repair costs plus real estate taxes less the excess of the dwelling's value at the end of the year over its value at the beginning of the year. This equation appears in many articles in *Real Estate Economics* and other housing-related journals. Mortgage interest and real estate taxes are deductible for owner-occupiers who itemize, so their after-tax values are relevant. Long-run ownership costs also include the now negligible capital gains taxes on owner-occupied dwellings, and transactions costs ( financial and time costs) of buying and sell-

58. See Grether and Mieszkowski (1974).
59. See the paper by Stephen Sheppard in Cheshire and Mills, eds. (1999, p. 1595–632).

ing. Long-run costs of ownership include the present value of all such costs over the ownership period. If dwellings and people lasted forever, owner-occupants would be indifferent to exogenous marketwide house price increases, since capital gains would be offset by increases in imputed rents, other things equal.

Such data permit returns to owner-occupancy to be calculated ex post or to be forecast ex ante. Most calculations of returns to owner-occupancy overstate the after-tax returns because they fail to take account of the 80 percent phaseout on the federal tax form of deductions (and exemptions) for relatively high-income owners, to whom the deductions are ostensibly worth most. (Phaseout increases the effective marginal federal tax rate of many owner-occupiers with incomes between about $150,000 and $250,000 by about one percentage point.) Deductions associated with owner-occupancy are worth almost nothing to those with family incomes much over $200,000.

Neverthetheless, owner-occupancy is still a good investment for many high-income families because they have access to dwellings on which capital gains are substantial, to low-interest mortgages, and to optimal debt-equity ratios. Low-income families can obtain down payment assistance from government programs and government mortgage insurance, permitting owner-occupancy with virtually no equity. But deductibility is not worth much to families in the lowest tax bracket, and they typically lack access to dwellings with substantial capital-gains potential. Downside risk is negligible for low-income owner-occupiers because they can walk away from a dwelling whose value has fallen by, say, 5 or 6 percent, with little risk of pursuit by lenders or insurers, but with possible risk to credit ratings. Owner-occupancy is not very risky for families with annual incomes between about $50,000 and $150,000, if they can plan for long-term tenure and are sophisticated enough to refinance when interest rates fall and to optimize debt-equity status.

Deregulation, technology, and the secondary mortgage market (which has increased competition in mortgage origination by permitting entry of nondepository institutions) have made housing finance highly competitive, and it has been much studied, especially in the *Journal of Real Estate Finance and Economics*. The United States has as fine a system of housing finance as any country in the world. In most countries, governments restrict competition in mortgage finance. Some of the worst cases are in Asia, where governments restrict entry of private lending institutions and do not issue or permit modern mortgages, apparently to discourage diversion of savings from industrial investment to "unproductive" housing. India and Korea are examples.

I conclude with brief comments on housing supply.[60] Housing supply comes from the standing stock as owners put existing dwellings on the market, and from net additions to the stock. Net additions are mostly production less demolitions, but also include net conversion from nonhousing uses (for example, shops converted to dwellings) and net creation of dwellings from conversion of single-family to multifamily dwellings. Some demolition is intentional, as when land values rise and a single-family dwelling is demolished and replaced by a high-rise apartment. But most demolition results from fires, floods, earthquakes, arson, and so forth. Moves from one dwelling in the standing stock to another provide no net supply.

In the United States, no one has any market power over the standing stock of dwellings. Likewise, the construction industry is dominated by small firms. The largest national housing construction firms supply only a small percent of annual construction, and most housing is constructed by firms that build fewer than 100 dwellings per year. Entry is easy and many builders switch to repair, maintenance, and rehabilitation when the market for new dwellings is poor.[61] Over a period of a few years, housing supply is virtually perfectly elastic. Only two qualifications are needed. First, local governments restrict construction (see the discussion on page 31). Second, as urban areas grow, land prices and therefore housing prices rise. Thus the long-run industry supply of the stock of an urban area's housing is less than perfectly elastic, but prices of the flow of construction do not depend on the rate of construction in the long run.

Jerome Rothenberg and his colleagues provide detailed analysis of housing supply depending on assumptions made about the time of adjustment and how input prices vary.[62] The durability of housing makes supply elasticities asymmetric between increases and decreases. Absent delays imposed by the need to obtain local government approvals, substantial increases in housing supply can occur in a few months. Decreases, in contrast, depend on the age of the housing stock in question and may require many years. Decreases in demand result in intentional neglect and abandonment if costs of demolition and clearing exceed the value of the cleared land, as was common in poor neighborhoods in earlier decades.

Given that the United States now has quite good legal definitions of condominium property rights, rental versus owner-occupancy is almost entirely

60. See Rothenberg and others (1991) for a fine survey of the entire sector.
61. See Rothenberg and others (1991).
62. Rothenberg and others (1991).

demand-driven. The only important constraint is that governments sometimes prohibit conversion of single-family dwellings into apartments (or, equivalently, occupancy by people unrelated by blood or marriage) in neighborhoods of single-family dwellings. Such laws are frequently honored in the breach when economic conditions dictate multiple occupancy.

Beyond doubt, forty years of intensive research have improved understanding of markets for housing and housing finance. I can raise three issues for future research. First, at U.S. commuting costs, dwelling location hardly depends on work location within a broad range of distances and times spent commuting (see the discussion on page 28). My impression from the data is that commuting between similar subcenter suburbs is about equal in volume in both directions. What, then, do dwelling locations depend on? Two-worker families make a difference, but it is doubtful that this is the primary explanation, at least in large metropolitan areas.[63] Second: Why is housing development increasing in some central cities, certainly including Chicago? Is it because of the increasing numbers of suburban empty-nesters? Is it because of falling crime rates and improving amenities in central cities? A third area that cries out for study is manufactured housing. The term refers to any dwelling entirely or mostly produced in a factory and then moved to a site. It encompasses between 20 and 25 percent of annual housing production.[64] Most of these are similar to condominiums in that they are separately owned but located on sites that are owned by a landlord. As is the case in condominiums, rules are established that control housing-unit conditions and residents' behavior. This may result in low crime rates and low costs. This subsector is virtually unstudied by scholars.

### Transportation

As was shown in table 1, urban transportation economics has occupied a small but consistent fraction of papers in the *Journal of Urban Economics*. My judgment is that urban transportation economics publications have also been at a consistent volume in other outlets.

*The Urban Transportation Problem* is still the most important book ever published on the subject.[65] Its most important defect is a curious neglect of roadway congestion, which has been analyzed more than any other urban trans-

---

63. See Costa and Kahn (1999).
64. U.S. Bureau of the Census (1999, tables 1201, 1204) and *Housing Statistics of the United States* (1999).
65. Meyer, Kain, and Wohl (1965).

portation issue during the last quarter century or so. But it was the first publication to provide clear reasons for the suspicion, which still endures, that fixed-rail commuter systems should have only a very limited role in U.S. metropolitan areas.

I believe that the important issues related to urban transportation are by now well understood.[66] Functions are now known for estimating costs and benefits of alternative urban transportation investments, for estimating and analyzing congestion costs, in the long run and the short run, and even for estimating the relative wear and tear on roads by various kinds of vehicles. Alternative techniques of road pricing (electronic metering and charges for road use by time and place, fuel taxes, conventional and electronic tolls) have all been studied. A curiosity is that the United States retains high-transaction-cost tolls on roads built by taxpayers' money.

Only about 9 percent of metropolitan work trips are by public transit; about 83 percent are by private vehicle, and the remainder are by foot, bicycle, and so forth.[67] No careful benefit-cost study has indicated that benefits exceed costs of any postwar U.S. urban fixed-rail commuting investment (witness Baltimore, Atlanta, Dallas, Washington, San Francisco, and Los Angeles).[68] Both U.S. and World Bank studies for developing countries indicate that road investments have much greater benefits relative to costs.

Commuter bus services can be socially viable if they can provide frequent rush-hour service in suburban collection areas, high-speed express service on corridors, and good destination-area distribution. Those are stringent conditions, but they must be met if buses are to compete with cars in time and money costs. Privatization of bus services is resisted, even though private companies typically operate more flexibly and at lower cost.

There is strong opposition to the dominance of car-based commuting, and some of it is virulent.[69] Given U.S. suburban residential densities and the partially resulting origin-destination diversity, there can be little doubt that a dominant car-based system is privately and socially optimal. Opponents of our car-based system claim that low-density suburbs are in good part the result of auto commuting and that we should have made major investments in radial fixed-rail systems starting in the early postwar period. Many

66. See Small (1992) and the paper by Kenneth A. Small and José A. Gomez-Ibanez in Cheshire and Mills, eds. (1999, pp. 1937–90).

67. U.S. Department of Transportation, Federal Highway Administration (1993, table 2.5).

68. See Winston and Shirley (1998).

69. See Downs (1992) for a reasoned statement.

such advocates fail to realize that radial fixed-rail commuter systems encourage suburbanization, as London demonstrates. Some recognize the connection and advocate direct controls that would mandate high-density suburbs. Even those advocates fail to acknowledge the higher housing prices that would result.

Nevertheless, there can be no doubt that road use is far underpriced in U.S. metropolitan areas. Optimal congestion pricing would require much greater road-use fees.[70] Even if metropolitan road systems were optimized by modest highway construction in suburbs and much better traffic control systems in built-up areas (sequenced traffic signals, reverse-direction streets and lanes, much higher charges and more restrictions for on-street parking, much better traffic law enforcement), metropolitan road-use prices are much lower than roads' opportunity costs (current land values, replacement costs of improvements, operating costs, all converted to a vehicle-mile basis). In an optimized system with little congestion, I have estimated that fuel taxes should be perhaps 10 times their current level.[71] The result would be U.S. fuel prices comparable to those in much of Western Europe (about $3.50 to $4.00 per U.S. gallon). My estimate could easily be off by 25 percent in either direction. If fuel taxes were substantially increased, taxpayers would need to be assured of a decrease in or abolition of some other tax, such as the real estate tax, to avoid powerful opposition. (Fuel taxes could be partially refunded on the income tax to residents who neither live nor work in metropolitan areas.)

What would be the effect of much higher fuel prices? Certainly there would be less driving and less use of large vehicles. Undoubtedly there would be a reduction in frivolous driving and in the large amount of suburb-to-suburb commuting indicated by similar congestion levels in both directions on circumferential highways. Workers who work in suburb B but live in A would tend to move to B, and vice versa if A and B are similar, as many suburban communities are. I doubt that the wishes of public transit advocates for much denser suburbs and much greater reliance on public transit would be realized, and I believe that most urban economists oppose increases in regulatory controls on residential locations or densities.

There is no intrinsic connection between suburbanization and commuting. Employment suburbanization matched by housing suburbanization (in which workers lived near subcenters in which they worked) could result in shorter commuting trips than would be possible in a metropolitan area where employ-

70. See Small (1992).
71. See Mills (1998).

ment was mostly in the CBD. Higher fuel taxes would encourage such matching of worker residences and subcenters.

I can identify some connections needing further research. There are almost no studies of the response of car travel to fuel prices. A spurt of publications based on data from the gasoline crises in 1973 and 1980 was revealing, but recent studies are scarce. There is no doubt that the demand for urban car travel is inelastic with respect to fuel prices. Nevertheless, an increase in fuel prices to about two to three times their current levels might reduce urban car travel by 15 to 20 percent. Most of the reduced commuting travel would probably result from suburban workers' moving closer to work—to a considerable extent, they would be effectively swapping houses. Since commuting places the greatest stress on metropolitan road systems, research should focus there. To what extent and how quickly would owners substitute smaller cars and export their depreciated sport-utility tanks to Mexico? How many workers would move closer to work? How many would carpool or take transit modes to work? Would residential densities increase close to suburban subcenters? Would some CBD workers move to central cities?

The effects of increased road-use charges would inevitably interact with local-government land-use controls. Increased residential densities near work centers would depend on increased flexibility in land-use controls.

### Local Governments

As was shown in table 1, papers on local governments have become increasingly common in the *Journal of Urban Economics*. Undoubtedly, the volume of publications in other outlets has increased proportionately. Local public finance has been a specialty in economics for many decades, and many great economists have made perceptive comments on the subject. But postwar U.S. economic analysis of local government behavior can, with only moderate exaggeration, be said to start with Charles Tiebout's "Pure Theory of Local Expenditures," one of the most referenced scholarly papers written in the postwar period.[72] The fact that most of this section is about work based on Tiebout reflects a home bias, since Tiebout analysis is almost exclusively a provincial U.S. topic. It pertains to a system in which local governments, especially in metropolitan areas, are fragmented and largely independent of higher levels of government. Although U.S. local governments have no constitutional existence, in practice they have more independence to raise and spend money and

72. Tiebout (1956).

to regulate activities within their jurisdictions than have local governments in almost any other country. Big-city mayors who are believed to be able to influence the votes of their constituents in national elections also have strong influence in Washington.

The question that has dominated the analysis of local public choice in the United States for more than forty years can be stated simply: Are local governments socially efficient in a metropolitan area in which there are many local governments, people move freely among local jurisdictions, and local governmental taxes and expenditures are determined by majority vote of each jurisdiction's residents? A preliminary comment is that no one believes that a system of autonomous local governments is likely to engage in income redistribution that is optimal from the point of view of the entire society. That is why income redistribution should be, and largely is, financed by higher-level, mostly federal, government programs.

A fine survey, with a skeptical conclusion, appears in a paper by Stephen Ross and John Yinger in the *Handbook of Regional and Urban Economics.*[73] The champion of the view that fragmented local governments are likely to be socially efficient is Dennis Epple, ten of whose papers with various coauthors are referenced by Ross and Yinger; two other papers have become available only recently.[74]

Epple and his colleagues have produced variants of the following remarkable model: There is a fixed number of local governments in a metropolitan area, each with fixed but not necessarily equal land area. There is a fixed continuum of metropolitan-area residents' incomes, with fixed but not equal incomes before local-government taxes and expenditures, not dependent on community of residence. Residents have well-behaved utility functions in a composite good, housing, and local-government services. Residents take prices of housing, the composite good, and each community's tax-expenditure function parameters as fixed. Households are mobile among communities and locate where their utility is maximal. Tax-expenditure parameters are set by the median voter in each community. Communities are in equilibrium in that housing supply and demand are equated and no resident can obtain greater utility by a move.

Epple's theorem is that households sort themselves among communities in such a way that communities can be numbered so that a continuous segment of incomes is found within each community, the highest-income resident in

73. Cheshire and Mills, eds. (1999, pp. 2001–53).
74. Epple and Sieg (1999a) and (1999b).

one community and the lowest-income resident in the next are indifferent between residences in the two communities, and income levels ascend as one moves to higher-numbered communities. It does not seem to matter whether tax-expenditure functions are dependent on house values or are linear in income within each community (equals are treated equally within communities). Epple and his coauthors have ingeniously estimated and tested the model and find considerable consistency between facts and theory.[75]

One remarkable fact about the model of Epple and his coauthors is that, as in Tiebout's theory, there are no land-use controls in the model and dwellings are built to be optimal for residents who occupy them, yet no low-income free riders sneak across borders and pay low taxes levied on modest dwellings, receiving benefits from the richer community's generous spending. How many dozen papers on the Tiebout model assume the contrary?

The first thing to say is that this is an equilibrium model and no one believes that an entire metropolitan area is in residential equilibrium. But postwar suburbanization may be a move toward equilibrium. Second, what about central cities, which contain about one-third of the metropolitan population? Their income levels span the entire metropolitan distribution, although their mean incomes are typically lower than those of suburbs. High-income people have been moving from central cities for half a century, so perhaps equilibrium is on the horizon. But central cities do not fit easily into the Tiebout model. Third, if the Epple model tells the entire story, it is unclear why suburbs (and central cities) take land-use controls so seriously. Of course, jurisdictional locations do matter, and perhaps that is enough to invalidate the conclusions of the Epple model. In addition, even though equilibrium might not be much different if all jurisdictions dropped land-use controls, things might be much different if any single jurisdiction abandoned them. If that is so, land-use controls must have badly distorted resource allocation in metropolitan areas. One cannot attend many zoning hearings in high-income suburbs without concluding that keeping out the low-income hordes is really at issue. Again, things might be very different if all high-income suburbs abandoned controls simultaneously, but I do not think this is likely. Next to schools, land-use controls are the biggest political issue in some suburbs; they are fought over bitterly, with considerable expenditure of time and money.[76]

75. See especially Epple and Sieg (1999b).
76. See Fischel (1985).

Land-use controls stratify communities directly, according to housing demand, but also indirectly, according to income, family size, and race. Stratification has many faces. Children from low-income families probably perform worse if they live in neighborhoods that are predominantly low-income. In addition, low-income children are probably more expensive to educate than high-income children. Another aspect of the same syndrome (believed by some education specialists) is that children's success in school and in the workplace depends on their preschool environment. Residence in a neighborhood not dominated by other low-income residents may significantly improve the preschool environment of children from low-income families. Alternatively, it is possible that tension might result from neighborhood mixtures of incomes, family backgrounds, and races and that the outcome may be harmful to low-income children. Land-use controls also stratify residents by the propensity to commit crimes and by the frequency of teenage pregnancies. More mixing because of less zoning could affect such behaviors of any or all groups involved.

Dennis Epple and Richard Romano have recently applied the basic Epple model to the issue of school choice.[77] The main purpose of proposed educational voucher systems is to increase competition among schools for students in order to improve educational quality. Vouchers are likely to have that effect.[78] But vouchers also permit more stratification by student quality than is likely if schools have substantial monopoly power, as they currently have, at least in central cities. Epple and Romano show that stratification would be the likely result of almost any voucher system.

It is clear that zoning is the result not just of the median voter's preferences, but also of residents who vote and lobby, interacting with developers who lobby and make campaign contributions. Zoning almost certainly follows the market, at least when market forces are sufficiently strong. That may make resource allocation better or worse than it would be under the Epple median-voter model.

My guess is that land-use controls represent an important breakdown of the median-voter model. In many jurisdictions, owners of residences and businesses near a disputed property have a disproportionate effect on land-use controls on that property. Just as owners of expensive single-family detached dwellings go to great lengths to prevent rezoning of nearby property for high-rise apartment dwellings, even if it would be indisputably good for the entire

77. Epple and Romano (1998).
78. See Freeman (1999).

community, similar results occur if a business that would be good for the community tries to locate in a high-income neighborhood. In some jurisdictions, a city council member has a disproportionate influence on land-use controls within his or her district, and his or her reelection is not affected by those who do not live there because they have been zoned out.

Finally, this observer believes that Leviathan is at work to an unknown extent within local governments. Public school bureaucracies have undue influence on public school operations. Gangs that peddle illegal substances corrupt the criminal justice system. Contracting between local governments and private companies to haul waste and to build and repair buildings and streets is subject to corruption. Local government offices are overstaffed with political supporters of elected officials. Elected officials distort and hide facts from the electorate. (How else to account for massive cost overruns on virtually all government infrastructure projects?) The local criminal justice system is blatantly discriminatory against racial minorities.[79]

I have omitted private racial discrimination from the above examples because, although it is a violation of many state and local laws, it is primarily a federal matter.[80]

I propose a number of questions for future research. First: What exactly are the consequences of land-use controls, and how much waste do they cause? The above discussion has focused on housing, but similar analysis is needed for businesses. Small high-income suburbs sometimes permit almost no businesses. Everybody has cars, no residents need to work in the community, and it is little trouble to shop in a mall in a nearby community. I have nothing against malls in a country in which suburbanites own vehicles that are ideal for one-stop shopping and freight haulage. But if most suburbs zone out most businesses, the result is wasteful travel for shopping. Perhaps the median-voter model applies to business zoning, but I suspect that high-income suburbs are not only excessively homogeneous regarding race and income but also excessively exclude businesses. Second: Is there anything to my Leviathan story? No one can live long in Chicago, Philadelphia, Detroit, New Orleans, Washington, or many other U.S. central cities and believe that the local governments are producing the demands of the median voter at minimum cost. Why not? Are these cities too big? Are their residents so poorly educated that they cannot control their governments? Many characteristics of central-city governments appear to be impossible to explain, either by the Tiebout model

79. See Thernstrom and Thernstrom (1997).
80. See Yinger (1995).

or by any theory of rational social choice. Surely more research on how and why central-city governments allocate resources is close to the highest priority for economic research.

### How Far Have We Come? Where Are We Going?

I believe it is beyond dispute that urban economics has made progress on every major topic that has been addressed. We understand much better why and where urban areas form and grow. I have indicated important deficiencies in the analysis of what we refer to as agglomeration economies, but estimation and analysis are far ahead of where they were in 1960. The size and spatial distributions of urban areas have been studied intermittently, but further progress, especially related to the spatial distribution, will be difficult.

Analysis of the spatial organization of urban areas hardly existed in 1960. We now understand how and why suburbanization of residences and employment occurs. We still have much to learn about subcenter formation and growth, but important progress has been made.

Despite the careful work of urban economists on suburbanization, uninformed antisprawl proposals have swept the political scene since the late 1990s. Perhaps the proposals will fade, as the witch-hunt in child care centers did by the mid-1990s, but the potential for harm is enormous. Urban economists could undertake careful estimation of market failure related to suburbanization, of effects of government failures to "get the prices right," and of optimal government programs to ameliorate resource misallocation.

Understanding of urban housing markets is far ahead of its status in 1960. We now basically understand housing supply and demand and most basics of housing finance. We have much to teach governments in developing countries about the benefits of a modern housing finance system.

We still lack critical evaluation of government housing programs. I suspect that typical local-government land-use controls do more harm than good. Perhaps I am wrong, but estimates of benefits and costs of alternative control programs would be possible. Public housing is about the only government housing program that has been studied carefully, and it has been found wanting. Housing vouchers were studied carefully twenty years ago and were found to be preferable to all government supply-side programs;[81] but almost nothing has been written about them or alternatives for two decades.

81. See Bradbury and Downs, eds. (1981).

Urban transportation issues have been carefully studied. We know how to compute appropriate pricing and investment benefits and costs. Congestion and its pricing have been carefully studied. I do not believe that agreement is widespread with my belief that moderate road and traffic control investments and much higher fuel taxes would be better and vastly cheaper than sophisticated congestion pricing based on electronic metering. The issues could be studied.

The vast outpouring of literature has contributed much to our understanding of local governments. However close we may be to a Tiebout equilibrium, it is by now clear that powerful market forces propel at least suburban communities in that direction. The implication was formerly drawn forcefully that the ultimate result would be destitute and alienated central cities composed mostly of minorities. In the late 1990s at least some central cities—apparently those with relatively good governments—have begun to revive. Why? What should government do, or stop doing, to reinforce the process? Why do some central-city governments zone down or zone out high-rise residential and business developments? Congestion is the usual answer, but it is unlikely. Zoning out high-income high-rises induces more high-income residents to reside in suburbs, from which they commute to CBDs on congested arterials. Their employers also are likely to move, depriving the central city of both high-income residents and well-paid jobs. This pattern exists in Chicago. Is it common? Do central-city governments simply not understand the natural consequences of their actions, or is another motive at work?

## *Social Problems and Urban Economic Research: Three Proposals*

Some readers may be offended at my slight treatment in this paper of what I will call social problems in U.S. metropolitan areas and especially in central cities: poverty, crime, racial discrimination, and education. However they are designated, the most intractable colonial and U.S. social problems have revolved around the great American trauma of the last three or four centuries: racial relations. Whether justified or not, neglect has been intentional. First, adequate treatment would have made the paper much too long. Second, sociologists and political scientists have contributed more than economists to analysis of many social problems, and I am not competent to sort out economists' contributions or to survey the entire subject. Of course, economists have made important contributions to analysis of these social problems. However, at the risk of irritating colleagues, I venture the opinion that reading superb surveys such as that of James Q. Wilson and Richard J. Herrnstein or that of Stephan Thernstrom and Abigail Thernstrom leaves one with the impression that economists' contributions have been more slight than they should have been.[82] In this section I briefly propose three topics that I believe economists have a comparative advantage in analyzing.

Economists are the masters of quantitative benefit-cost analysis of government programs. One way to reduce crime is to decriminalize certain activities. In terms of the numbers of people involved, drugs are the prime candidate. Of the one percent of the U.S. adult population that is in prison, a larger number has been convicted of drug offenses than of any other crime. Some of those criminals could lead productive lives if drugs were decriminalized. Furthermore, decriminalization—presumably making drugs available on prescription—would reduce the profitability of sales efforts in marketing illegal drugs and might reduce consumption. Drugs probably provide a large part of the revenue of street gangs and help to corrupt the criminal justice system, as Prohibition did in the 1920s. International comparisons are never conclusive, but insight could be obtained from them. I do not have a firm opinion about decriminalization, but I believe that careful benefit-cost analysis could contribute to the debate.

A completely different social issue is projecting who would benefit from suburban growth controls. I argued on page 21 that the important effect would be to increase the relative price of urban housing by regulatory limits on supply. Existing owners would make capital gains when controls were instituted, but gains would be offset by proportionate increases in imputed rents, for them or their heirs. Older owners who would soon move to less-expensive housing even in the absence of controls would benefit, at least if they had no great concern for their heirs. That would seem to be a small consideration. Likewise, farmers or other owners of land on which housing development became illegal would suffer capital losses, of course offset by proportionate reductions in imputed rent unless they anticipated moves to urban areas. It is difficult to imagine a significantly important political group that could be mobilized to support proposed suburban growth controls. Why such controls exist in so many countries then becomes a mystery. Of course, governments confuse the issue by claiming land "shortages," apparently relying on citizens' lack of understanding of elementary supply and demand. Determining what groups might benefit from suburban growth controls is an issue in political economy on which economic analysis could shed light.

---

82. Wilson and Herrnstein (1985); Thernstrom and Thernstrom (1997).

A third example of a social issue to which economists should be able to contribute comes from James Heckman.[83] Education specialists have compiled increasingly strong evidence that preschool intervention is crucial if children from deprived backgrounds are to do well in school and in subsequent work experience. The claim is that unless children begin to develop cognitive, psychological, and social skills by about the age of six, later development of such attributes will be much more difficult. The subject cries out for benefit-cost analysis. The first issue is program design. Preschool programs are quite different interventions than reducing class sizes or introducing labs or computers in middle school. It is also important to design interventions so as not to violate rights of parents or children. The second issue is benefit-cost analysis of alternative programs or of no preschool intervention or of interventions in later secondary or postsecondary education.

*Forecasts*

I believe that in the near future urban economic research will move toward a general synthesis of how, when, and where subcenters form and grow, and how that process interacts with residential suburbanization and transportation improvements. The process can be accompanied by considerable reductions in commuting travel if governments take appropriate actions. Presumably such research will entail revival of interest in the type of large computer simulations that John Kain, Alex Anas, and others undertook in the 1970s and 1980s, but with much better data and theories and much more powerful computers. Such research may constitute a renaissance of urban spatial analysis in coming years.[84]

It is not difficult to predict that interest in urban governments will continue apace. It is dangerous to believe that a problem has been solved, but I believe that we now have the deepest possible conceptual understanding of the Tiebout model, thanks mostly to the work of Epple and his coauthors. Details of empirical estimation and testing can and will certainly continue to appear, but a key issue is simply how far toward a Tiebout equilibrium suburbs have progressed. More interesting, I believe, is how governments perform, and could perform, in distinctly non-Tiebout-like central cities. Am I correct in believing that central-city governments represent interests of constituents much less accurately than do suburban governments? If so, why? Most important, how much unde-

83. Heckman (1999).
84. See Anas, Arnott, and Small (1998).

sirable stratification has been strengthened by suburban land-use controls? Perhaps, to close on the most optimistic note possible, central city–suburban problems may be solved by continual out-migration of central-city minorities and in-migration of suburban whites, until by 2050 central cities and suburbs will be almost uniformly and fully integrated.

# Comments

**Dennis Epple**: When I was a Ph.D. student at Princeton University, the two faculty members whose work I found most exciting were Edwin Mills and Wallace Oates. It is an honor to share this forum with them.

Writing a history of urban economic analysis would be a daunting task for most of us, but Mills handles it with evident ease. He organizes research in urban economics into nine subject areas. It is an appealing classification that begins with the topic that unifies the field: spatial analysis. It includes eight other topics that divide urban research into relatively distinct subject areas: housing; government sector; labor, poverty, race; crime; transportation; education; interurban, rural-urban; and developing countries. The paper goes on to provide a concise summary of research efforts to date and highlights key remaining issues for research.

I like the paper very much. It not only provides a summary of the state of research, but also offers opinions about the issues within the research, pointing out where Mills thinks work is on target and, in some cases, where he thinks it is wrongheaded. The author has also been extremely modest in this history of research in urban economics, understating the central role that he has played in the field through his tremendous research contributions, his text, his role in founding and editing the *Journal of Urban Economics,* and his influence on his students and on virtually everyone else who has worked in the field. The editors of these new *Brookings-Wharton Papers on Urban Affairs* chose well in giving Mills the leadoff role to initiate the journal.

It might be helpful if I highlight some of the open research issues raised in the paper. The review begins with fundamental questions for the field of urban economics.

Why do urban areas exist? What is the reason for the measured increase in total factor productivity as urban areas increase in size? Mills's answer to the first question is that proximity economizes on the costs of moving goods, people, and messages. His conjecture regarding the second is that unpriced and

39

unmeasured inputs are the source of measured increases in total factor productivity as urban areas grow. The paper emphasizes in particular time spent in commuting and other business travel. This conjecture strikes me as providing a valuable focus for researchers looking to pin down the elusive sources of economies in urban areas. Mills also takes some stands about things that are probably not the source of increasing factor productivity, and he highlights key issues for this area, such as the importance of distinguishing between external economies and economies internal to firms.

The paper considers another question central to urban economics: What determines the size distribution of cities? Mills cites evidence of the pervasiveness of the rank-size rule within various countries and across countries for long periods of time. I find this particularly compelling because I know that Mills reads this literature with a skeptical eye. Indeed, I recall that some time ago he made the point that if you have two countries where the rank-size rule holds, then it cannot hold if the data for two countries are combined. The fact that this relationship is so robust over time and across countries makes it a central regularity that, as Mills says, cries out for explanation.

Regarding issues related to location within metropolitan areas and to the zoning activities of local governments, Mills takes to task those of us who neglect land-use controls in modeling household-location choices and local government tax and expenditure policies. He conjectures that land-use controls represent a massive breakdown of the median-voter process because residences and businesses near a disputed property have disproportionate influence on land-use controls for the property. He also expresses the view that the outcomes that result are often not the outcomes that are best when viewed from the perspective of the larger interests of the community. I wish I could say that I think his criticism is wrong, but, to borrow a phrase Mills uses elsewhere, it would take a braver person than I to assert that he is wrong about this. Several different researchers have taken a crack at modeling zoning from one angle or another. These efforts have produced models of zoning that generate many interesting insights. However, I do not believe that we have a good political-economy model of zoning. I have in mind the kind of model that can be made part of an analytic structure with which we can characterize the sorting of people among communities in metropolitan areas, or characterize the distribution of housing consumption across households and across communities.

The paper's discussion of the problem highlights the challenges for modeling. It is daunting to build a collective-choice model of how zoning is set.

One difficulty is in modeling the way that money and votes interact in determining political outcomes. This seems particularly important in conflicts between residents of a community and prospective developers. Residents have the votes, but developers and builders may be willing to spend a good deal of cash to influence political outcomes. It is hard enough to work with a model in which only one or the other force is present, but it is really challenging to devise sensible models that balance these very different forms of political activity. The other problem, as Mills notes, is that the traditional majority-rule model may not be very helpful if decisions about zoning for a parcel are dominated by owners of nearby parcels. In any case, I agree that models that characterize metropolitan equilibrium while neglecting zoning may be missing an important piece of the problem. Developing a model that responds to this challenge strikes me as an important item on the research agenda for urban economics.

A second topic that I want to comment on is stratification of the metropolitan population by income, race, and other characteristics. The paper discusses research focused on attempting to disentangle the relative importance of economic factors and central-city social problems in influencing suburbanization. Peter Mieszkowski and Edwin Mills have also developed this issue more fully in their paper reviewing this topic.[1] If I recall correctly, Miezkowski and Mills made the point that a key issue is whether central-city social problems are simply a consequence of the concentration of disadvantaged households or whether the concentration tends to foster increased social problems via peer effects.

I want to suggest that, for the same reason, stratification across municipalities in metropolitan areas and across neighborhoods within municipalities is also an important topic that needs more research attention. There are large differences in quality of local public services across municipalities in a typical U.S. metropolitan area. This is particularly so for education. In part, these quality differences can be traced to differences in spending levels. In the Chicago metropolitan area, suburban high schools spend a third more per pupil, on average, than do high schools in the city of Chicago. However, from a research perspective, I think a more important issue than spending differences is the effect of differences in peers. In the Chicago city schools, the average percentage of students from low-income households is 69 percent; the suburban average is 11 percent.[2] And these averages understate the concentration of disadvantaged students within many schools in the city. How

1. Mieszkowski and Mills (1993).
2. Author's calculations from Rodkin and Morton (1995).

much we worry about such stratification depends on the extent to which peer effects are important.

While the issue of peer effects is not new, there is a good deal of recent theoretical research that proceeds from the presumption that peer effects are important, including work by Roland Benabou, Steven Durlauf, Thomas Nechyba, and Richard Romano and me.[3] While research on local governments has emphasized the stratification that is induced by differences in expenditure across municipalities, peer effects can give rise to stratification even where there are no expenditure differences. Interesting empirical work by Sandra Black shows that housing prices differ across boundaries in urban areas that define which neighborhood school students may attend.[4] A paper by Daniel Aranson investigates whether stratification is lower where expenditure has been made more equal.[5] He finds a measurable reduction in stratification, but it is not large. Both of these findings are consistent with the idea that peer effects are a central force for stratification. But there are other potential explanations. The state-of-the-art empirical contribution on peer effects is the fine paper by William Evans, Wallace Oates, and Robert Schwab.[6] They show that peer effects in teen pregnancy and high-school dropout rates are significant when estimated in the usual way but disappear when one instruments using exogenous factors that influence peer-group composition. This certainly means that the standard method of estimating peer effects that neglects self-selection into groups will not do, and it highlights the importance of developing alternative ways of getting at the magnitude of peer effects.

The final issue I want to comment on is related to Mills's remarks about the likelihood that Leviathan is present to at least some degree. Mills observes, for example, that public school bureaucracies have undue influence on public school operations. I share this view. I think this is particularly true for central-city school systems, simply because a single bureaucracy typically has control over a substantial fraction of the schools in a metropolitan area. For example, a single district operates the sixty-three high schools in the city of Chicago. The ninety-five high schools in the surrounding suburbs are almost all single-school districts. The competition faced by the suburban schools must surely provide less scope for bureaucratic license than the city district can exercise via control of sixty-three high schools. Caroline Hoxby provides evidence

3. Benabou (1996); Durlauf (1996); Nechyba (forthcoming); Epple and Romano (1995).
4. Black (1999).
5. Aranson (1998).
6. Evans, Oates, and Schwab (1992).

that increased public school competition does indeed lead to lower per-pupil expenditures and improved educational outcomes.[7]

Mills also provides other examples, and I have one more to add to his list. I am increasingly struck by the amount of resources local and state governments in Pennsylvania spend in the name of economic development. I think much of the expenditure on economic development genuinely derives form a well-intentioned desire to foster economic growth. Expenditure on enterprise zones is a case of particular relevance for urban areas. It strikes me as an area that needs continuing research attention. One of the best empirical papers in this area is a recent paper written at Carnegie-Mellon by John Engberg and Robert Greenbaum.[8] They do a much more micro-level analysis than previous research, using restricted-access data files available through the U.S. Census Data Center. They find that spending on enterprise zones does indeed have a statistically significant positive effect on creation of new jobs. However, they find that there is a nearly identical and statistically significant reduction in old jobs, so net job creation is zero. This is a striking finding that points to the need for theoretical work and additional empirical work to try to understand better the circumstances in which enterprise zones may actually promote development and those in which they simply displace old jobs as they create new ones. There is also the related question of conditions under which enterprise zones would be a sensible policy even when they were not successful in creating net job growth in an area.

In closing, I want simply to reiterate that this is a fine paper. I highly recommend it.

**Wallace E. Oates**: Edwin Mills's paper provides a splendid history of research in urban economics. There is surely no more appropriate author for this paper: Mills is widely regarded as the father of urban economics, and the field bears his very strong imprint. Since I have not been very close to much of the recent research in urban economics, I have decided to take a somewhat different tack for my comments by offering some admittedly impressionistic observations on the evolution of the field over the past three decades. It is, in fact, something that I have puzzled over—and I will try to explain the nature of this puzzle and seek some help in understanding it. The discussion at the conference has been very helpful in clarifying several elements of the issue.

7. Hoxby (forthcoming).
8. Engberg and Robert Greenbaum (forthcoming).

To put the matter in perspective, I want to return to the period of the 1960s and early 1970s. This was a period in which two new fields emerged in economics, both of them as a result of the growing social consciousness in the 1960s. These two fields were environmental economics and urban economics. The former had its roots in the so-called environmental revolution with its widespread concern with pollution and general environmental degradation. It gave rise to a spate of new legislation—the Clean Air Act of 1970, the Clean Water Act of 1972, and a host of measures in subsequent years. Parallel to this, the new awareness and rising concern with urban problems likewise ushered in a variety of major new programs to address the decay of the cities: urban renewal programs, model cities, the war on poverty, and several others.

Associated with these concerns, new courses sprang up in the colleges and universities across the country in these two fields, at both the undergraduate and graduate levels. And economists working on these issues during this period often found themselves identified as either urban economists or environmental economists. Moreover, new journals emerged in both of these fields to offer outlets for ongoing research.

The thing that has struck me and that I have puzzled over is what has happened to these two fields in the 1980s and 1990s and why. It is my sense that one of the fields, namely environmental and natural-resource economics, has continued to expand with great energy and public attention, while the other, urban economics, has been less successful in maintaining its earlier momentum.

Let me begin by simply offering some casual evidence for this. First, during the past twenty years, urban problems have faded somewhat from the public view. This is most certainly not to say that these problems were successfully resolved by newly introduced policy measures. Far from it—but for whatever reasons these issues simply did not continue to engender the same level of public attention and concern. In contrast, environmental issues have continued to capture the public attention, both in this country and around the globe. The result has been an ongoing process of new legislation and policy measures aimed at a "sustainable world."

This divergence has also manifested itself in university curricula and academic research. One finds over this period an ongoing expansion of programs and courses in environmental studies. Economics departments in many universities now offer as a Ph.D. concentration the field of "environmental and natural-resource economics." And at the undergraduate level, programs of environmental studies (with environmental economics as one component) are ubiquitous throughout universities in this country.

In contrast, the interest in urban economics seems to have waned. Courses have disappeared in many universities. When, for example, I arrived at the University of Maryland at College Park in the late 1970s, we had a very active program of graduate study and research in the field of "regional and urban economics." There were many students taking degrees and writing dissertations in the field. But that is gone now. We still have an undergraduate course in urban economics, but there is little demand for courses at the graduate level. And my impression is that our experience at College Park is not atypical.

It is also my impression that there has been some difference in the expansion of research efforts. It seems to me that practically every time I turn around, I find a newly introduced journal in environmental and resource economics. This reflects to some extent the thriving and growing body of economists working in the field. Created in 1979, the Association of Environmental and Resource Economists (AERE) expanded rapidly to its present size of nearly 1,000 members with a very active sister organization (EAERE) in Europe. But—although there is still the splendid *Journal of Urban Economics,* initiated by Edwin Mills and now edited by Jan Brueckner—I do not have the sense that there has been the same proliferation of journals and research in urban economics that has occured in the environmental field.

I must be careful here. As the Mills essay makes clear, there has been a lot of valuable research going on in urban economics. Real advances have been made. And many urban economists have simply moved their base of operations to programs of management or finance, where their new home is often in "real estate economics."

Nevertheless, I think there is still some substance to my puzzle. It raises the intriguing question of why one field born of social concerns in roughly the same period has grown so much more rapidly than the other. I suspect that the answer lies largely in the extent of public interest and its manifestation in the form of monies to support research. On first glance, this may seem a bit strange. Urban problems certainly have not gone away. But somehow during the 1980s we turned our back on them; we simply chose not to pay a lot of attention to the problems of the center cities. There is some resurgence of concern at present, but the public attention that focused on urban issues in the 1960s and 1970s has apparently not sustained itself.

The visibility of and concern with environmental issues, however, has remained at a very high level, with lots of new legislation and public programs. Just why environmental issues have remained so visible and compelling while urban ones have not is an intriguing question. And I do not have a good answer to it. Perhaps it is, in part, the extent of exposure: nearly everyone has contact with the environment in one form or another—it affects high- as well as low-income families. One observer has suggested to me that the environmental movement sapped much of the energy that had been directed to the social concern with poverty and the cities. In her view, the advent of Earth Day in 1970 signaled the shifting of the focus of activist groups from problems of poverty to those of the environment. But we cannot simply wall off the problems in the center cities.

Some part of the answer to my puzzle may also lie in the intellectual evolution of the two fields. The theoretical core of urban economics was the elegant Alonso-Mills-Muth model of urban structure. This monocentric model provided a conceptual framework that generated a number of interesting and testable hypotheses. It provided a kind of intellectual focal point for the field.

But as Mills points out, as the field has evolved the model has manifested some serious limitations, both in theory and application. With the ongoing process of decentralization of employment in urban areas, the model has become a less apt description of urban structure (although, as Mills observes, it still retains considerable explanatory power). And efforts to extend the framework to provide a general treatment of metropolitan areas with multiple centers have not been very successful. In short, it seems as though the basic monocentric model, once its basic properties were thoroughly explored, simply played out as a source for further interesting work. It may be that the future of basic theory in urban economics will be of a nonspatial form.

My case here would be a stronger one if I could cite all the major theoretical advances in environmental economics that have maintained its intellectual vitality. Here I must hedge somewhat. The intellectual core of environmental economics was basically the theory of externalities, and that was worked out reasonably well early on. There has been important new work on methods for the valuation of environmental amenities—new ways to understand and measure people's willingness to pay for a cleaner environment. And during the 1990s there has emerged a challenging new literature on environmental policies in a second-best setting. The work of Lans A. Bovenberg, Lawrence H. Goulder, and others has led environmental economists to take a new, fresh look at some of the basic propositions.

But frankly I find it hard to ascribe the buoyancy of the field of environmental economists mainly to exciting new theory. I come back to the sustained social concern with environmental issues, which translates into funding for research (among other things). In fact, if one looks solely at the issue of global climate change, one finds virtually a whole industry in its own right. The vast commitment of public funds in the United States (and in other countries as well) to research on this potential threat has drawn many economists (and other scientists as well) into its study. Public attention and the stimulus for scientific work it provides, through funding and by engendering interest, constitute a powerful force with a profound impact on the portfolio of society's research efforts. It is my perception that this has worked in the favor of environmental and resource economics much more than of urban economics. But this tendency may be in the process of shifting back somewhat. We shall see.

## References

Alonso, William. 1964. *Location and Land Use: Toward a General Theory of Land Rent.* Harvard University Press.

Anas, Alex, Richard Arnott, and Kenneth A. Small. 1998. "Urban Spatial Structure." *Journal of Economic Literature* 36 (September): 1426–64.

Aranson, Daniel. 1998. "The Effect of School Finance Reform on Population Heterogeneity." Working Paper 98-11. Federal Reserve Bank of Chicago (March).

Bairoch, Paul. 1988. *Cities and Economic Development: From the Dawn of History to the Present.* University of Chicago Press.

Becker, Gary. 1957. *Economics of Discrimination.* University of Chicago Press.

Benabou, Roland. 1996. "Heterogeneity, Stratification, and Growth: Macroeconomic Implications of Community Structure on School Finance." *American Economic Review* 86 (June): 584–609.

Black, Sandra. 1999. "Do Better Schools Matter? Parental Valuation of Elementary Education." *Quarterly Journal of Economics* 114 (May): 577–99.

Bradbury, Katharine, and Anthony Downs. 1981. *Do Housing Allowances Work?* Brookings.

Buchanan, James M., and Gordon Tullock. 1962. *The Calculus of Consent: Logical Foundations of Constitutional Democracy.* University of Michigan Press.

Cheshire, Paul C., and Edwin S. Mills, eds. 1999. *Handbook of Regional and Urban Economics.* Vol. 3, *Applied Urban Economics.* Amsterdam: North-Holland.

Christaller, Walter. 1933. *Central Places in Southern Germany.* Prentice-Hall.

Clark, Colin. 1951. "Urban Population Densities." *Journal of the Royal Statistical Society* Series A, Part 3, 490–96.

Costa, Dora L., and Matthew E. Kahn. 1999. "Power Couples: Changes in the Locational Choice of the College Educated: 1940–1990." Working Paper 7109. Cambridge, Mass.: National Bureau of Economic Research.

Cronon, William. 1991. *Nature's Metropolis: Chicago and the Great West.* W. W. Norton.

Downs, Anthony. 1992. *Stuck in Traffic: Coping with Peak-Hour Traffic Congestion.* Brookings.

———. 1994. *New Visions for Metropolitan America.* Brookings.

Durlauf, Steven. 1996. "A Theory of Persistent Income Inequality." *Journal of Economic Growth* 1 (March): 75–93.

Engberg, John, and Robert Greenbaum. Forthcoming. "The Impact of State Enterprise Zones on Urban Manufacturing Establishments." *Policy Studies Journal.*

Epple, Dennis, and Richard E. Romano. 1995. "Public School Choice and Finance Policies, Neighborhood Formation, and the Distribution of Educational Benefits." Working Paper. Carnegie-Mellon University.

———. 1998. "Educational Vouchers and Cream Skimming." Mimeographed. Carnegie Mellon University.

Epple, Dennis, and Holger Sieg. 1999a. "Estimating Equilibrium Models of Local Jurisdictions." *Journal of Political Economy* 107 (August): 645–81.

———. 1999b. "The Tiebout Hypothesis and Majority Rule: An Empirical Analysis." NBER Working Paper 6977.

Evans, William N., Wallace E. Oates, and Robert M. Schwab. 1992. "Measuring Peer Group Effects: A Study of Teenage Behavior." *Journal of Political Economy* 100(5): 966–91.

Fischel, William A. 1985. *The Economics of Zoning Laws: A Property-Rights Approach to Ameran Land-Use Controls*. Johns Hopkins University Press.

Fujita, Masahisa. 1989. *Urban Economic Theory: Land Use and City Size*. Cambridge University Press.

Gabaix, Xavier. 1999. "Zipf's Law for Cities: An Explanation." *Quarterly Journal of Economics* 114 (August): 739–68.

Gaspar, Jess, and Edward Glaeser. 1998. "Information Technology and the Future of Cities." *Journal of Urban Economics* 43 (January): 136–56.

George, Henry. 1874. *Progress and Poverty*. Reprint. Doubleday, 1904.

Glaab, Charles N., and A. Theodore Brown. 1967. *A History of Urban America*. London: Macmillan Press.

Glaeser, Edward. 1998. "Primacy and Politics." Mimeographed. Harvard University.

Goldstein, Gerard S., and Leon N. Moses. 1973. "A Survey of Urban Economics." *Journal of Economic Literature* 43(1): 136–56.

Grebler, Leo, David Blank, and Louis Winnick. 1956. *Capital Formation in Residential Real Estate: Trends and Prospects*. Princeton University Press.

Greenwood, Michael J. 1981. *Migration and Economic Growth in the United States: National, Regional, and Metropolitan Perspectives*. Academic Press.

Grether, D. M., and Peter Mieszkowski. 1974. "Determinants of Real Estate Values." *Journal of Urban Economics* 1(2): 127–46.

Heckman, James J. 1999. "Policies to Foster Human Capital." Working Paper 7288. Cambridge, Mass.: National Bureau of Economic Research.

Helsley, Robert, and William Strange. 1999. "Innovation and Urban Development." Mimeographed. University of British Columbia.

Hoch, Irving. 1969. *Progress in Urban Economics: The Work of the Committee on Urban Economics, 1959–1968, and the Development of the Field*. Washington: Resources for the Future.

Hohenberg, Paul M., and Lynn Hollen Lees. 1985. *The Making of Urban Europe 1000–1950*. Harvard University Press.

Hoover, Edgar M. 1948. *The Location of Economic Activity*. 1st ed. McGraw-Hill.

*Housing Statistics of the United States*. 1999. Lanham, Md.: Bernan Press.

Hoxby, Caroline. Forthcoming. "Does Competition among Public Schools Benefit Students and Taxpayers?" *American Economic Review*.

Jacobs, Jane. 1969. *The Economy of Cities*. Random House.

Kim, Sukkoo. 1999. "Urban Development in the United States, 1690–1990." Working Paper 7120. Cambridge, Mass.: National Bureau of Economic Research .

Krugman, Paul R. 1993. "On the Number and Location of Cities." *European Economic Review* 37 (April): 293–98.

Kuznets, Simon. 1955. "Economic Growth and Income Inequality." *American Economic Review* 45: 1–28.

Lewis, W. Arthur. 1978. *The Evolution of the International Economic Order*. Princeton University Press.

Lösch, August. 1954. *The Economics of Location*. Yale University Press.

Lucas, Robert. 1999. "Externalities and Cities." Mimeographed. University of Chicago.

Malpezzi, Stephen, and Stephen K. Mayo. 1997. "Housing and Urban Development Indicators: A Good Idea Whose Time Has Returned." *Real Estate Economics* 25 (Spring): 1–11.

Marshall, Alfred. 1920. *Principles of Economics*. London: Macmillan.

McMillen, Daniel P., and John F. McDonald. 1998. "Suburban Subcenters and Employment Subcenters in Metropolitan Chicago." *Journal of Urban Economics* 43 (March): 157–80.

Meyer, John R., John F. Kain, and Martin Wohl. 1965. *The Urban Transportation Problem*. Harvard University Press.

Mieszkowski, Peter, and Mahlon Straszheim, eds. 1979. *Current Issues in Urban Economics*. Johns Hopkins University Press.

Mieszkowski, Peter, and Edwin S. Mills. 1993. "The Causes of Metropolitan Suburbanization." *Journal of Economic Perspectives* 7 (Summer): 135–47.

Mills, Edwin S. 1967. "An Aggregative Model of Resource Allocation in a Metropolitan Area." *American Economic Review* 57 (May): 197–210.

———. 1972a. *Urban Economics*. Glenview, Ill.: Scott, Foresman and Company.

———. 1998. "Excess Commuting in U.S. Metropolitan Areas." In *Network Infrastructure and the Urban Environment: Advancement in Spatial Systems Modelling*, edited by Lars Lundqvist, Lars Goran-Mattsson, and Tschangho John Kim. New York: Springer-Verlag.

Mills, Edwin, ed. 1987. *Handbook of Regional and Urban Economics*. Vol. 2, *Urban Economics*. Amsterdam: North-Holland.

Mills, Edwin, and Bruce Hamilton. *Urban Economics*, 5th ed. Harper Collins, 1994.

Mills, Edwin S., and Jee Peng Tan. 1980. "A Comparison of Urban Population Density Functions in Developed and Developing Countries." *Urban Studies* 17(3): 313–21.

Mirrlees, James A. 1972. "The Optimum Town." *Swedish Journal of Economics* 74 (March): 114–35.

Muth, Richard. 1967. "The Distribution of Population within Urban Areas." In *Determinants of Investment Behavior*, edited by Robert Ferber, 271–99. New York: National Bureau of Economic Research.

———. 1969. *Cities and Housing: The Spatial Pattern of Urban Residential Land Use*. University of Chicago Press.

Naisbitt, John. 1994. *Global Paradox: The Bigger the Economy, the More Powerful Its Smallest Players*. New York: Morrow.

Nechyba, Thomas. Forthcoming. "Mobility, Targeting, and Private School Vouchers," *American Economic Review*.

Perloff, Harvey S., and Lowdon Wingo, Jr., eds. 1968. *Issues in Urban Economics*. Johns Hopkins Press for Resources for the Future.

Reid, Margaret G. 1962. *Housing and Income*. University of Chicago Press.

Rodkin, Dennis, and Felicia Morton. 1995. "Charting a School's Course." *Chicago Magazine* 44 (February): 86–96.

Rosen, Kenneth, and Michael Resnick. 1980. "The Size Distribution of Cities: An Examination of the Pareto Law and Primacy." *Journal of Urban Economics* 8(2): 165–86.

Rothenberg, Jerome. 1967. *Economic Evaluation of Urban Renewal: Conceptual Foundation of Benefit-Cost Analysis*. Brookings.

Rothenberg, Jerome, and others. 1991. *The Maze of Urban Housing Markets: Theory, Evidence, and Policy*. University of Chicago Press.

Samuelson, Paul. 1952. "Spatial Price Equilibrium and Linear Programming." *American Economic Review* 42 (June): 283–303.

Shukla, Vibhotti. 1996. *Urbanization and Economic Growth*. Delhi: Oxford University Press.

Small, Kenneth A. 1992. *Urban Transportation Economics*. Chur, Switzerland: Harwood Academic Publishers.

Smith, Adam. 1776. *The Wealth of Nations*. Reprint. London: J. M. Dent & Sons, 1977.

Solow, Robert. 1956. "A Contribution to the Theory of Economic Growth." *Quarterly Journal of Economics* 70 (February): 65–94.

Solow, Robert, and William Vickrey. 1971. "Land Use in a Long Narrow City." *Journal of Economic Theory* 3 (December): 430–47.

Stark, Oded. 1991. *The Migration of Labor*. Cambridge, Mass.: Basil Blackwell.

Suh, Seong Hwan. 1991. "The Optimal Size Distribution of Cities." *Journal of Urban Economics* 30 (September): 182–91.

Thernstrom, Stephan, and Abigail Thernstrom. 1997. *America in Black and White: One Nation, Indivisible*. Simon and Shuster.

Thomas, Hugh. 1997. *The Slave Trade: The Story of the Atlantic Slave Trade, 1440–1870*. Simon and Schuster.

von Thünen, Johan Heinrich. 1826. *Der Isolierte Staat in Beziehung auf Landwirtschaft und Nationalökonomie*. Hamburg, Germany.

Tiebout, Charles. 1956. "A Pure Theory of Local Expenditures." *Journal of Political Economy* 64 (October): 416–24.

U.S. Bureau of the Census. 1992. *Residents of Farms and Rural Areas: 1990*. P-20 Series No. 457. Government Printing Office.

———. 1999. *Statistical Abstract of the United States: 1999*. GPO.

U.S. Department of Transportation, Federal Highway Administration. 1993. *Journey-to-Work Trends in the United States and Its Major Metropolitan Areas, 1960–1990*. GPO.

Vickrey, William. 1963. "Pricing in Urban and Suburban Transport." *American Economic Review* 53 (May): 452–65.

Weber, Adna. 1899. *The Growth of Cities in the Nineteenth Century: A Study in Statistics*. Cornell University Press.

Wilson, James Q., and Richard J. Herrnstein. 1985. *Crime and Human Nature*. Simon and Schuster.

Winston, Clifford, and Chad Shirley. 1998. *Alternate Route: Toward Efficient Urban Transportation*. Brookings.

World Bank. 1997. *World Development Report*. Oxford University Press.

———. 1999. *World Development Report: Knowledge for Development*. Oxford University Press.

Yinger, John. 1995. *Closed Doors, Opportunities Lost: The Continuing Costs of Housing Discrimination*. New York: Russell Sage Foundation.

Zipf, George Kingsley. 1949. *Human Behavior and the Principle of Least Effort: An Introduction to Human Ecology*. Cambridge: Addison-Wesley.

JOHN M. QUIGLEY
*University of California, Berkeley*

# A Decent Home: Housing Policy in Perspective

GOVERNMENT POLICIES directed specifically toward urban areas are certainly not a new idea. Indeed, two thousand years ago Caesar Augustus decreed a set of physical restrictions on Roman buildings and public infrastructure that affected the form and development of the city and whose effects are visible even today. Sets of policies intended to improve living conditions in the big cities were widely adopted in Europe during the latter half of the nineteenth century; the British Public Health Acts and the Salisbury Acts are but two well-known examples.

Urban affairs were, of course, a concern of the states and the cities they sanctioned since the beginning of this Republic. It was only after World War II and the end of the Great Depression, however, that direct urban policies were articulated by the federal government. The Housing Act of 1949 espoused the goal of "a decent home and a suitable living environment" for all Americans and provided the rationale for an ambitious program of urban renewal and slum clearance begun in the 1950s. The factors that ultimately led to the passage of the Housing Act included a severe nationwide housing shortage that continued long after the wartime victory. This shortage reflected the cumulative effects of the Great Depression, the explicit limitations on residential construction during the war, the postwar shortages of construction material, and the massive internal migration to the cities that had taken place during the war.

This paper reviews and analyzes American housing and urban development policy emanating from the landmark housing act enacted a half century ago.

The paper benefited from the written comments of Peter Chinloy, Bill Gale, Douglas Jones, Bruce Katz, Dick Netzer, Katherine O'Regan, Janet Pack, Eugene Smolensky, Michael Stegman, and William Wheaton. Tracy Gordon assisted greatly in the preparation of this paper.

53

Current U.S. policies and programs are directly descended from the 1949 Housing Act. From a broader viewpoint, housing and urban development is the most basic and durable aspect of national urban policy, and provides the spatial context within which other policies operate. The intra-urban distribution of population, the concentration of the poor, the distribution of work sites, housing quality, and tax bases are all directly affected by the substantial resources devoted to housing and urban development policy. These spatial relationships in turn have a profound effect on the economic health of the urban economy.

Other policies that entail substantial central government expenditures may also have important consequences for urban areas. For example, the federal tax code in its treatment of owner-occupied housing may substantially influence urban spatial structure, and the recent changes in welfare entitlements will surely affect the incomes and opportunities of the poor who live in central cities.[1] Yet neither of these policies is designed to pay attention to its distinctly metropolitan or urban impacts. Metropolitan areas are large, so most national policies do shape urban life in some way. Housing and urban development policies are directly intended to affect the residents of urban areas—and they do so in significant ways.

For the most part, this paper is an exercise in positive economics, indicating the course of urban policies, their economic rationale, and their economic consequences. Nevertheless, the paper also examines some normative issues and offers some evaluations.

### Federal Housing Programs for Low-Income Households

The history of housing programs for low-income Americans in the United States can be divided into four phases. During the first phase, from the founding of the Republic to 1937, the national government provided no support at all for low-income housing. Many crucial policy decisions about housing were taken under the new income tax law in 1913 and with the establishment of the Federal Housing Administration (FHA) in 1934. By increasing the demand for owner-occupied housing, both policies had important consequences for urban form. Neither these nor other national housing policies, however, were directed specifically toward those with low incomes. During the second phase, from 1937 to 1962, a single federal housing program subsidized poor house-

---

1. Gyourko and Voith (1999).

holds: low-rent public housing owned and operated by government agencies. The third phase, from 1962 to 1974, saw the first encouragement of private entities in the provision of federally subsidized housing for the poor. It was not until the fourth phase, beginning in 1974, that the link between the new construction of dwellings and the subsidy of low-income households was first broken.

Economists are quick to point out that public resources spent on low-income housing are small compared to the forgone revenues arising from the treatment of housing under the Internal Revenue Code. The imputed income an owner receives from an investment in owner-occupied housing has always escaped taxation. After passage of the Tax Reform Act of 1986 (TRA86), however, the treatment of imputed rent, local property taxes, and mortgage interest payments for homeowners has contrasted even more starkly with the tax treatment of other investment returns, other taxes, and other interest payments.[2]

Of course, most of these "subsidies" embedded in the tax code accrue to the wealthiest of households. It is estimated that these asymmetries in the tax code reduce federal revenues by almost $100 billion ($93.8 billion for fiscal year 1998), and that two-thirds of the benefits accrue to households in the top quintile of the income distribution.[3]

For the analysis of programs in each of the four phases, two important economic characteristics are salient: the *identities* of the owners and managers, and the *form* of the subsidy. For government housing programs, identity and form have been intimately interconnected. Each aspect matters in evaluating the economic incentives in these programs.

2. The treatment of investment in rental housing also contrasts more starkly with investment in owner-occupied housing after TRA86. The 1986 change in tax laws lengthened the depreciation schedule, required that a straight-line depreciation profile be used (instead of the more favorable Accelerated Cost Recovery System), increased the capital gains rate to 28 percent, eliminated passive loss deductions completely, and decreed a phaseout of existing programs within four years. These had the net effect of increasing the breakeven rents charged by landlords and reducing the profitability of rental housing.

3. The largest component of this total arises from the failure to tax the gross implicit rental income of owner occupants. The U.S. Congressional Budget Office (1996) estimates that federal tax revenues would increase by $40 to $50 billion if the mortgage interest deduction were eliminated, but this is surely a large overestimate since many owner occupants would simply reduce their reliance on mortgage debt finance in response to changes in the price of debt. See Follain and Melamed (1998). Federal efforts to increase homeownership through the FHA have been rationalized, in part, as a means to help lower-income households qualify for federal tax "subsidies."

*Public Housing: Government Ownership and Management*

For twenty-five years, beginning in 1937, low-rent public housing was the only federal program providing housing assistance to the poor. Indeed, it is still true that public housing provides shelter for more than 1.3 million U.S. households. Waiting lists for public housing accommodation are long—eleven months on average in U.S. metropolitan areas.[4] For the largest public housing authorities, current waiting times average almost three years.[5] Despite much criticism of public housing, there has always been excess demand at prevailing prices.

The first salient characteristic to consider is the *identity* of the ownership of public housing. For the first twenty-eight years of the program, all federally subsidized housing units were designed, built, and managed with direct oversight by local housing authorities. These housing authorities are established by local governments to operate within a single political jurisdiction or in groups of cities and counties. The local authorities issue long-term tax-exempt debt whose interest and amortization is guaranteed by an annual contributions contract with the U.S. Department of Housing and Urban Development (HUD). The proceeds are used to finance HUD-approved public housing projects.

The second salient characteristic to consider is the *form* of the subsidy. For the first thirty-three years of the program, essentially all the capital costs of public housing were borne by the federal government. Conversely, after the construction of public housing, local authorities were required to meet all subsequent operating expenses out of current rental income.

These two characteristics of the public housing program had far-reaching consequences. Control by local authorities meant that decisions about public housing were responsive to the political processes buffeting small units of government. Local governments, fearful that the availability of public housing would encourage an influx of the poor, could opt to not establish housing authorities, thereby preventing the building of public housing within their borders. The 1949 Housing Act, extending the public housing program originally enacted in 1937, included a requirement that local authorities' applications for funding be approved by local government. Moreover, any locality in which public housing was to be built needed a locally approved "workable program" for community development. This requirement was in force until 1969.

Local governments, fearful of neighborhood reaction to public housing, can also intervene in decisions about the design and location of facilities serv-

4. U.S. Department of Housing and Urban Development (1999c, p. 1).
5. Painter (1997).

ing low-income residents. Because public housing concentrates low-income households geographically, the program has been subject to intense political opposition.

The requirement that housing authorities cover operating costs from rent revenues, while the federal government finances all capital costs, led to predictable results still visible in the urban skyline of many cities. Subsidizing only capital costs made it economically rational for local authorities to design housing requiring additional capital up front as long as the design reduced subsequent operation and maintenance costs. High-rise structures, smaller windows, and smaller common areas were all predictable economic implications of the form of the public subsidy. The subsidy also increased the spatial concentration of program beneficiaries, typically the poorest households in the urban area. The federal government began contributing to operating costs in 1970, but the legacy of excessively capital-intensive design persists.

The efficiency costs of subsidizing input prices rather than output quantities is also worth pointing out. Even with very elastic substitution of capital for operating inputs in response to prices, this feature of program design ensures that the cost of the program to taxpayers exceeds the value of the additional housing produced. It is estimated that, as a result of the form of this subsidy program, taxpayer costs for public housing were about 40 percent greater than the value of housing produced.[6]

The requirement that operating costs be covered out of current revenues gave local authorities a Hobson's choice: to help those families most in need or to ensure the fiscal solvency of the agency itself. The Brooke Amendments of 1969 limited rents to 25 percent of income (this was increased to 30 percent in 1981), reducing wide disparities in rent burdens among public-housing tenants in different geographic areas. The amendments provided operating subsidies to local authorities and thus gave them greater incentives to serve a poorer clientele. But during the 1970s and 1980s, as local authorities permitted greater access to public housing for the very poor, rent revenues accruing to the agencies necessarily declined, and consequently the need for federal operating subsidies increased substantially. The solution to the Hobson's choice facing local authorities involved limiting the exposure to cost increases of local authorities but removing previous limits on the financial exposure of the federal government.

Some of the spatial and geographical problems encountered by local authorities, and tenants as well, were ameliorated by the Leased Housing (Section

6. Muth (1973).

23) program and the Turnkey program, both introduced as modifications to public housing in 1965. The Section 23 program provided more flexibility to local authorities, permitting them to rent privately owned dwelling units for occupancy as public housing. It reduced middle-class opposition to the geographical dispersion of public housing units, since public housing recipients could be anonymous renters whose bills were paid by local authorities. The anonymity of the program also benefited tenants, who were less easily identified as being "from the projects." The Section 23 program also helped to reduce the geographical concentration of public housing recipients.

The Turnkey program enabled private developers to propose construction of additional public housing with a particular design and price tag at a specific location. Choosing among locations proposed by others proved to be less politically contentious for local housing authorities than proposing them on their own initiatives.

Figure 1 summarizes the course of the public housing program during the postwar period. The program began with a substantial financial commitment, which was quickly scaled back with the outbreak of the Korean War. By the late 1960s, the program had been restored to the level contemplated in the original act. From a total of 830,000 units under public management in 1970, the number increased to almost 1.2 million by 1980. During the past two decades the size of the public housing program has scarcely grown. In 1998, there were just under 1.3 million units in the public housing inventory, down from a high of 1.4 million units in 1991. Since the early 1970s, half or more of the units added to the public housing stock have come from the leasing of existing units rather than the construction of new public housing projects.

With the aging of the public housing stock came the increasing need for substantial expenditures for rehabilitation and modernization. From 1980 to 1992, funds for modernization were allocated to local authorities as conditional grants (under the Comprehensive Improvement Assistance program). Beginning in 1992, this program was supplemented by disbursements under a formula taking structural conditions and management into account (the Comprehensive Grant program).

The Housing and Community Development Act of 1992 also authorized HUD to set aside up to 20 percent of development funds for major reconstruction of obsolete public housing projects. This assistance also comes in the form of conditional grants (under the Major Reconstruction of Obsolete Projects program).

**Figure 1. Summary of Public Housing Program, Fiscal Years 1949–98ᵃ**

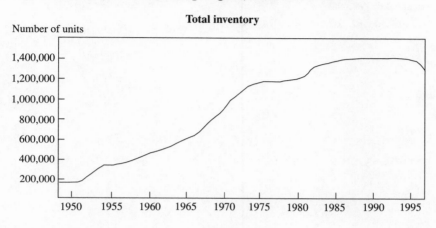

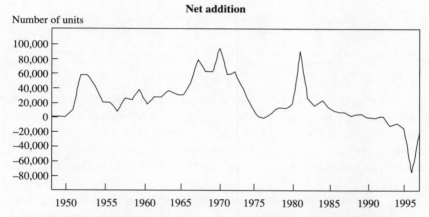

Sources: For FY1957–FY1998, U.S. Department of Housing and Urban Development, Office of Budget, "Annotated Tables for the 1998 Budget Process"; and Congressional Budget Office tabulations based on Congressional Justifications for the Department of Housing and Urban and Development. For FY1939–FY1956, National Association of Housing and Redevelopment Officials, *Housing and Community Development: A 50-Year Perspective.* (1985)

a. Units are number of subsidies outstanding at end of each fiscal year. FY1976 reflects subsidies outstanding at the end of the "transition quarter" (that is, September 30, 1976). Net additions for FY1998 are estimates only.

Since 1993, other HUD programs have provided grants and regulatory flexibility to local authorities to revitalize severely distressed public housing. For example, the HOPE VI program has funded planning, revitalization implementation, and demolition-only grants for public housing. Local authorities administer the program and can use these grants in conjunction with mod-

**Figure 2. HUD Expenditures on Operating Subsidies and Capital Fund,
Fiscal Years 1962–98[a]**

Real expenditures (billions of 1997 dollars)

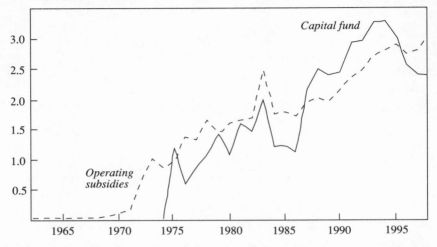

Source: U.S. Department of Housing and Urban Development, Office of Budget, "Annotated Tables for the 1998 Budget Process."
a. FY1976 includes outlays during the "transition quarter" from July 1, 1976, to September 30, 1976, annualized to reflect the
experience of four quarters only.

ernization funds or other HUD funds. They can commingle these funds with
municipal and state contributions, public and private. Figure 2 summarizes
information about HUD funds expended on operating costs and the rehabilitation of public housing projects. HUD currently spends about $3 billion
annually in operating subsidies and another $3 billion in rehabilitation (in 1997
dollars).

The most recent public housing programs are those encouraging private
ownership of individual dwellings. Enacted as part of the Cranston-Gonzalez
National Affordable Housing Act of 1990, the HOPE program provides funds
that nonprofit organizations, resident groups, and other eligible grantees can
use to develop and implement homeownership programs for the residents of
public housing units.

The endgame of the public housing program is not a pleasant sight. In the
new millennium no one would countenance the construction of high-density,
overcapitalized buildings, which would concentrate the most deprived households in particular urban neighborhoods. Yet the overhang from a half century
of public housing is a large stock of such buildings. Moreover, these buildings are deteriorating and many of them are functionally obsolete. There are

limits to the possibilities of converting this stock to mixed-use or home-ownership units, and the costs of rehabilitation are exorbitant.[7]

Yet it is worth emphasizing: this stock of public housing provides higher quality housing services to the lowest-income households than they could afford on the open market. At rents of 30 percent of household income, there is substantial excess demand by the poor for public housing.

### Private Suppliers

The 1960s saw the first efforts to subsidize low-income housing units that were not owned by an agency of government. As noted above, the Section 23 leased-housing program of 1965 allowed local authorities to contract with private-sector owners for units of public housing to be managed by the public sector.

At about the same time, beginning in 1961, a series of programs was initiated that invited greater participation by nonprofit and limited-dividend corporations, and ultimately by private profit-maximizing landlords.

These programs, including those with such colorful names as BIMR Section 221(d)3, Section 235, and Section 236, were short-lived in some cases. Several contained perverse incentives that led to escalating expenses and invited waste and fraud. Here are two examples:

The Section 236 Rental Assistance Act originally provided subsidies equaling the difference between one-fourth of tenant incomes and the amortization of construction costs for new low-income housing over forty years at market interest rates. In a period of rising interest rates, amortization costs increase much more than proportionately with interest-rate increases. Thus the annual subsidy due under the Section 236 program could simply explode.

The Section 235 Homeowner Assistance program required participants to pay a fixed percentage of their incomes for home purchase regardless of the selling price of the house they purchased (as long as it was appraised within general guidelines). Thus buyers had no real incentive to negotiate for lower prices or better terms, and honest appraisers had incentives to report the high-

7. Despite HUD's annual expenditures of roughly $6 billion on operations and maintenance, it is estimated that more than a million units of public housing are in jeopardy due to depreciation and undermaintenance. Stuart Gabriel reports that about 15 percent of all public housing units are in need of renovations costing $20,000 or more; more than $15 billion would be required to put the public housing stock in an "acceptable" physical condition. HUD currently reports that a fifth of all publicly subsidized units are not in "good condition." See Schnare (1991); Gabriel (1996); U.S. Department of Housing and Urban Development (1999a).

est value that could be justified. Dishonest appraisers had strong incentives to collude with sellers and report even higher values.

Table 1 provides a summary of the major HUD housing programs developed during the period of the Great Society.[8] With the exception of Section 235 and Section 312, these programs involved federal subsidies paid to private entities for the construction of rental housing for occupancy by low-income renters. By 1975, about 400,000 dwellings were subsidized under Section 236, and another 165,000 were subsidized by the rent-supplement program (which augmented the rental payments of households living in designated newly constructed dwellings).

Despite many problems in subsidy design, the new programs of the 1960s were real innovations in the course of U.S. housing policy. For the first time, federal government provision of low-income housing relied on units supplied by the private as well as the public sector. The owners and managers of units under these programs were private entities who would reap some of the benefits of increased productive efficiency.

These programs also freed subsidized housing provision for low-income populations from the threat of veto by local governments. By removing the requirement of a locally sanctioned "workable program" for community involvement, these programs increased the potential for some dispersion of low-income populations among urban communities. The liberalization of the "workable program" requirement did not come until 1969, however, and the programs—below-interest mortgages (BIMR), homeownership (Section 235), rental assistance (Section 236), and rent supplements—floundered well before President Nixon announced a moratorium on new obligations under these programs in his State of the Union Address in January 1973.

*Existing Housing*

Section 8 of the Housing and Community Development Act of 1974 opened the way for greater participation by private entities in the provision of housing for the poor. The act proposed federal funds for the "new construction or substantial rehabilitation" of dwellings for occupancy by low-income households. This project-based assistance was a logical extension of the rental programs introduced in the 1960s. HUD entered into

8. The table reports little information about subsidies under the short-lived BIMR Section 221(d)3 program, passed in 1961 but effectively scuttled when government accountants ruled that the present value of the program had to be charged as a public expense in advance of the housing services provided over the life of the project.

**Table 1. Summary of HUD Housing Assistance Programs, Fiscal Years 1967–98 (Excluding Section 8)[a]**

| Fiscal year | Total units | | | Net addition | | |
|---|---|---|---|---|---|---|
| | 235[b] | 236 | Rent supplement | 235 | 236 | Rent supplement |
| 1967 | | | 930 | | | 1,801 |
| 1968 | | | 2,731 | 3,454 | | 9,568 |
| 1969 | 3,454 | | 12,299 | 62,200 | 5,437 | 18,505 |
| 1970 | 65,654 | 5,437 | 30,804 | 139,178 | 26,885 | 26,982 |
| 1971 | 204,832 | 32,322 | 57,786 | 139,531 | 66,377 | 34,284 |
| 1972 | 344,363 | 98,699 | 92,070 | 67,307 | 92,562 | 26,114 |
| 1973 | 411,670 | 191,261 | 118,184 | 7,235 | 102,570 | 29,663 |
| 1974 | 418,905 | 293,831 | 147,847 | −9,990 | 106,529 | 17,479 |
| 1975 | 408,915 | 400,360 | 165,326 | −78,131 | 46,766 | 9,013 |
| 1976[c] | 330,784 | 447,126 | 174,339 | −37,970 | 96,234 | 5,569 |
| 1977 | 292,814 | 543,360 | 179,908 | −30,948 | 1,155 | −8,310 |
| 1978 | 261,866 | 544,515 | 171,598 | −26,679 | −3,055 | 7,293 |
| 1979 | 235,187 | 541,460 | 178,891 | −15,705 | −3,175 | −13,899 |
| 1980 | 219,482 | 538,285 | 164,992 | 21,057 | −1,079 | −7,213 |
| 1981 | 240,539 | 537,206 | 157,779 | 1,388 | −675 | −4,424 |
| 1982 | 241,927 | 536,531 | 153,355 | −12,155 | −3,062 | −76,436 |
| 1983 | 229,772 | 533,469 | 76,919 | −20,042 | −2,734 | −21,313 |
| 1984 | 209,730 | 530,735 | 55,606 | −9,259 | −2,757 | −9,995 |
| 1985 | 200,471 | 527,978 | 45,611 | −18,203 | 1,143 | −11,235 |
| 1986 | 182,268 | 529,121 | 34,376 | −22,889 | −947 | −10,889 |
| 1987 | 159,379 | 528,174 | 23,487 | −11,493 | 0 | −11 |
| 1988 | 147,886 | 528,174 | 23,476 | −6,922 | −174 | −3,476 |
| 1989 | 140,964 | 528,000 | 20,000 | −10,939 | 2,625 | 0 |
| 1990 | 130,025 | 530,625 | 20,000 | −5,195 | −2,510 | 0 |
| 1991 | 124,830 | 528,115 | 20,000 | −27,286 | −17,673 | 0 |
| 1992 | 97,544 | 510,442 | 20,000 | −2,281 | −337 | −730 |
| 1993 | 95,263 | 510,105 | 19,270 | −15,921 | −5,139 | −462 |
| 1994 | 79,342 | 504,966 | 18,808 | −4,220 | 3,387 | 2,052 |
| 1995 | 75,122 | 508,353 | 20,860 | −6,649 | −3,048 | 0 |
| 1996 | 68,473 | 505,305 | 20,860 | −7,663 | −11,184 | 0 |
| 1997 | 60,810 | 494,121 | 20,860 | −8,097 | −17,670 | 0 |
| 1998 | 52,713 | 476,451 | 20,860 | −9,189 | −29,793 | 0 |

Sources: U.S. Department of Housing and Urban Development, Office of Budget, "Annotated Tables for the 1998 Budget Process"; Congressional Budget Office tabulations based on Congressional Justifications for the Department of Housing and Urban Development; U.S. Department of Housing and Urban Development, Office of Policy Development and Research, *Annual Report on National Housing Goals*, 1972, 1975.

a. Entries represent the number of subsidies outstanding at end of the fiscal year.

b. Section 235 includes subsidies under original, revised, and restructured programs. Under the original program, lower–income households contribute at least 20 percent of their adjusted monthly income toward mortgage payments, with federal assistance payments making up the balance. Subsidies are not to exceed the difference between required payments and payments on a 1 percent interest rate mortgage. New contract approvals under the original program were discontinued in 1973. However, a 1975 court order mandated that the unused balance of contract authority under the original program be obligated for new commitments. Thus the program resumed in FY1975 in a revised form. In the revised program, participants contribute 20 percent of their adjusted income toward mortgage payments in addition to a downpayment of 3 percent of the cost of acquisition for a newly constructed or substantially rehabilitated unit. The assistance payment is based on the difference between the FHA maximum interest rate and the subsidy floor at the time of insurance endorsement. The Housing and Urban–Rural Recovery Act of 1983 authorized a restructured Section 235 program based on a ten–year interest reduction subsidy. Under the program, homeowners are required to contribute 28 percent of adjusted monthly income toward mortgage payments. Payments are based on the difference between the FHA maximum interest rate and the subsidy floor at the time of insurance endorsement.

c. FY1976 entry represents subsidies outstanding at the end of the "transition quarter" on September 30, 1976.

housing-assistance payments contracts for up to forty years with private suppliers, guaranteeing a stream of rental payments for the dwellings. Income-eligible households paid 25 percent of their incomes in rent (the portion is now 30 percent), and the difference between tenant payments and the contractual rate was made up by direct federal payments. Landlords received a reliable source of payment at an agreed-upon rule. (For newly constructed or rehabilitated units, agreements about the rental stream included provisions for its escalation during the contract period.) Moreover, landlords were able to shift the cost and risk of vacancies to the government. This program continued the advantages of the 1960s programs over the traditional public housing program. Section 8 involved private enterprise—nonprofit organizations and syndicates but also for-profit firms—in the building and management of low-income housing, and the program reduced the historical incentives for concentration of the poor in large projects.

In addition, a crucial modification to housing policy was introduced in Section 8: the restriction that subsidies be paid only to owners of new or rehabilitated dwellings was removed. An equally important modification permitted payments to landlords on behalf of a specific tenant rather than by a long-term contract with the landlord. Through these modifications, the project-based assistance program authorized under Section 8 came to be dominated by the tenant-based assistance program authorized under the same section. Under the tenant-based subsidies, HUD enters into an annual contributions contract with local authorities for program administration. Local authorities ensure that the low-income households assisted by Section 8 are income-eligible and that the housing units selected by assisted households meet minimum quality standards. Households receiving tenant-based assistance use the resources provided by HUD's annual contribution to lease dwellings from landlords of their choice (as long as the dwelling selected meets HUD standards and the owner agrees to participate in the program). Landlords receive HUD's currently published fair market rent (FMR) for the unit (FMRs are calculated by survey to be the fortieth percentile of the rent distribution).

The Housing Act of 1974 also set comprehensive income limits on eligibility for housing assistance across all federal programs. These limits were set at 80 percent of area median income. (This made almost 40 percent of the entire U.S. population eligible for assistance.) Other factors, however, made the effective targeting of public assistance somewhat narrower, with the lowest-income households residing in public housing and those with somewhat more resources residing in other programs.[9]

The targeting of federal housing assistance was again strengthened in the 1981 Omnibus Budget Reconciliation Act, which established eligibility for those entering federal housing programs at 50 percent of area median income, subject to a variety of exceptions.

Figure 3 summarizes the new units supplied by project-based assistance under Section 8 as well as the number of households assisted by the tenant-based demand-side program. As the table indicates, during the first few years of the program, the number of project-based subsidies (that is, units provided in newly constructed or rehabilitated dwellings) was about the same as the number of tenant-based subsidies (that is, the number of certificates outstanding). During the early 1980s, there was increased emphasis on new construction. By 1990 this had been completely reversed. There are now about 1.6 million households subsidized through Section 8 vouchers and certificates, while 1.4 million households are subsidized through the project-based program.

Note that the certificate program suffers from the same incentive problem as the Section 235 Homeowner Assistance program. Since the recipient pays a constant amount toward housing, and since the recipient is far better off with the certificate than searching for unsubsidized housing on the private market, he or she has little incentive to bargain for a lower price as long as the unit rents below FMR.

These incentives were changed by the more flexible "voucher" program introduced in 1987. Under this program, households in possession of a voucher may choose to pay more than the fair market rent computed by HUD for a particular dwelling, making up the difference themselves; they may also pocket the difference if they can rent a HUD-approved dwelling for less than the FMR.

In 1998, legislation made vouchers and certificates "portable," thereby increasing household choice and facilitating movement to other regions where employment opportunities may be greater. Also in 1998, the voucher and certificate programs were essentially merged; local authorities were permitted to vary their payment standards from 90 to 110 percent of FMR. The 1998

9. Indeed, several observers have cited the geographic isolation and unpleasant surroundings of public housing as factors "helping" to target assistance by discouraging all but the most desperate households from applying for assistance under the program. See Nelson and Khadduri (1992); Mayer (1995).

**Figure 3. Summary of Section 8 Housing Assistance, Fiscal Years 1976–98[a]**

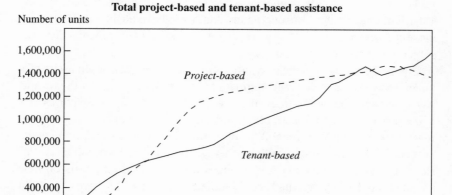

**Total project-based and tenant-based assistance**

Number of units

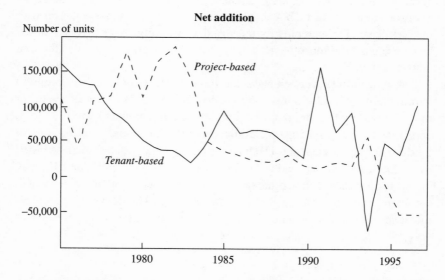

**Net addition**

Number of units

Source: Congressional Budget Office tabulations based on Congressional Justifications for the Department of Housing and Urban Development and on unpublished data.
a. Entries represent number of units eligible for HUD-assisted housing payments at end of fiscal year. FY1976 entry represents subsidies outstanding at the end of the "transition quarter" on September 30, 1976. Totals include Section 236 units also receiving Section 8 subsidies.

changes (in the Quality Housing and Work Responsibility Act) also sharpened the targeting of housing assistance. Three-quarters of all new vouchers had to be issued to those whose incomes are below 30 percent of local median incomes. All new vouchers were to go to recipients with incomes below 80 percent of the median income of the area.

With the unwillingness to appropriate new funding for public housing or for new construction under Section 8, additions to the stock of subsidized housing must rely almost entirely on used dwellings.[10] The cost advantage in producing low-income housing from the existing stock rather than by new construction is enormous. (This is something private suppliers of low-income housing have always known.)

Table 2 reports trends in new commitments by the federal government for rental assistance (across all programs) through new construction and through the existing stock of housing. Two trends are apparent in this summary. First, the distribution of newly subsidized units between newly constructed units and existing dwellings has changed markedly. In 1977, 66 percent of the newly subsidized units were newly constructed. By 1997, 72 percent of new federal commitments were made to existing dwellings. Second, the net number of new federal commitments for housing has plummeted. During 1977–79, the number of new commitments averaged 350,000 a year. During 1995–97, the number of new commitments averaged 48,500—a decline of 86 percent.

One way to illustrate the downward trend in incremental housing subsidies is to compare HUD's outlays and budget authority. Figure 4 presents trends in outlays and budget authority, in real terms, during the past two decades. Current outlays (that is, checks written on the U.S. Treasury in any year to subsidize tenants) are incurred as a result of budget authority previously or contemporaneously granted. Thus the sharp downward trend in budget authority is a reduction in the stock of funds that can be used to subsidize households in the future.[11]

The legacy of previous program commitments, of course, means that the current mix of housing subsidies includes a larger fraction of dwellings that were originally constructed for occupancy by subsidized low-income households. Table 3 reports these trends. During the last two decades, subsidized

10. The principal programmatic exception, the Low Income Housing Tax Credit (LIHTC), is discussed below.

11. This is subject to qualification; the accounting issues are somewhat more arcane but do not affect the point of the comparison. See U.S. Congressional Budget Office (1994) for a detailed discussion.

**Table 2. Net New Commitments Appropriated for Rental Assistance for All HUD Programs, Fiscal Years 1977–97[a]**
Numbers of units

| Fiscal year | New construction | Existing housing | Total |
|---|---|---|---|
| 1977 | 247,667 | 127,581 | 375,248 |
| 1978 | 214,503 | 126,472 | 340,975 |
| 1979 | 231,156 | 102,669 | 333,825 |
| 1980 | 155,001 | 58,402 | 213,403 |
| 1981 | 94,914 | 83,520 | 178,434 |
| 1982 | 48,157 | 37,818 | 85,975 |
| 1983 | 23,861 | 54,071 | 77,932 |
| 1984 | 36,719 | 78,648 | 115,367 |
| 1985 | 42,667 | 85,741 | 128,408 |
| 1986 | 34,375 | 85,476 | 119,851 |
| 1987 | 37,247 | 72,788 | 110,035 |
| 1988 | 36,456 | 65,295 | 101,751 |
| 1989 | 30,049 | 68,858 | 98,907 |
| 1990 | 23,491 | 61,309 | 84,800 |
| 1991 | 28,478 | 55,900 | 84,378 |
| 1992 | 38,324 | 62,595 | 100,919 |
| 1993 | 34,065 | 50,593 | 84,658 |
| 1994 | 29,194 | 66,907 | 96,101 |
| 1995 | 19,440 | 25,822 | 45,262 |
| 1996 | 16,259 | 33,696 | 49,955 |
| 1997[b] | 14,027 | 36,134 | 50,161 |

Source: U.S. House of Representatives Committee on Ways and Means, *Green Book 1998*; table 15-25. U.S. Department of Housing and Urban Development; and Farmers' Home Administration.

a. Net new commitments for renters represent net additions to the available pool of rental aid and are defined as the total number of commitments for which new funds are appropriated in any year. To avoid double-counting, these numbers are adjusted for the number of commitments for which such funds are deobligated or canceled that year (except where noted otherwise); the number of commitments for units converted from one type of assistance to another; in the FmHA section 515 program, the number of units that receive more than one subsidy; starting in 1985, the number of commitments specifically designed to replace those lost because private owners of assisted housing opt out of the programs or because public housing units are demolished; and, starting in 1989, the number of commitments for units whose Section 8 contracts expire.

b. Figures for FY1997 are estimates only.

units involving existing housing have increased almost tenfold, from 268,000 to 2.05 million. Subsidized units involving new construction have increased from 1.825 million to 3.3 million. By 1997, 40 percent of the dwellings subsidized by HUD for low-income renters made use of the existing stock of housing. Sixty percent involved new construction at the time of their initial occupancy.

The construction of new housing for low-income households has simply atrophied since the early 1980s, when the federal government curtailed the expansion of conventional public housing and new construction under Section 8. During this period, state and local governments continued several subsidy programs that relied on federal tax expenditures. State housing finance

**Figure 4. Outlays and Net Budget Authority for All Housing Aid Administered by HUD, Fiscal Years 1977–97[a]**

Billions of 1997 dollars

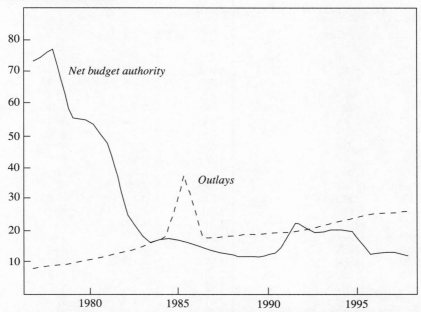

Source: U.S. House of Representatives Committee on Ways and Means, *Green Book 1998*; tables 15-27, 28, and 29.

a. All figures are net of funding rescissions, exclude reappropriations of funds, but include supplemental appropriations. Totals include funds appropriated for various public housing programs, including modernization of operating subsidies, drug elimination, and severely distressed public housing. Excludes budget authority for HUD's Section 202 loan fund and for programs administered by FmHA. Appropriations include $99 million, $1,164 million, $8,814 million, $7,585 million, $6,926 million, $5,202 million, $2,197 million, $4,008 million, and $3,550 million for renewing expiring section 8 contracts in 1989, 1990, 1991, 1992, 1993, 1994, 1995, 1996, and 1997 respectively. The bulge in outlays in 1985 is caused by a change in the method of financing public housing, which generated close to $14 billion in one-time expenditures. This amount paid off—all at once— the capital cost of public housing construction and modernization activities undertaken between 1974 and 1985, which otherwise would have been paid off over periods of up to forty years. Because of this one-time expenditure, however, outlays for public housing since that time have been lower than they would have been otherwise. Without this change, outlays per unit would have amounted to around $2,860. Figures have been adjusted to account for $1.2 billion of advance spending that occurred in 1995 but that should have occurred in 1996. FY1997 figures are estimates. FY1976 includes outlays during the "transition quarter" from July 1, 1976, to September 30, 1976, annualized to reflect the experience of four quarters only.

agencies, and in many cases local governments as well, issued tax-exempt bonds and used the proceeds for housing subsidies. These programs (and a variety of other private-purpose bond programs) were severely curtailed by the Tax Reform Act of 1986. As indicated previously, other provisions of TRA86 made investment in rental housing less profitable. TRA86 replaced these provisions, as well as the unlimited right of states to issue tax-exempt debt for housing subsidies, with a flat per capita tax credit for new low-income housing allocated to each state. These credits are administered by state agen-

**Table 3. Renter Households Receiving HUD Housing Assistance by Type of Subsidy, Fiscal Years 1977–97[a]**

Thousands of households

| Fiscal year | Existing housing | | | New construction | Total assisted renters[b] |
| | Household-based | Project-based | Total | | |
| --- | --- | --- | --- | --- | --- |
| 1977 | 162 | 105 | 268 | 1,825 | 2,092 |
| 1978 | 297 | 126 | 423 | 1,977 | 2,400 |
| 1979 | 427 | 175 | 602 | 2,052 | 2,654 |
| 1980 | 521 | 185 | 707 | 2,189 | 2,895 |
| 1981 | 599 | 221 | 820 | 2,379 | 3,012 |
| 1982 | 651 | 194 | 844 | 2,559 | 3,210 |
| 1983 | 691 | 265 | 955 | 2,702 | 3,443 |
| 1984 | 728 | 357 | 1,086 | 2,836 | 3,700 |
| 1985 | 749 | 431 | 1,180 | 2,931 | 3,887 |
| 1986 | 797 | 456 | 1,253 | 2,986 | 3,998 |
| 1987 | 893 | 473 | 1,366 | 3,047 | 4,175 |
| 1988 | 956 | 490 | 1,446 | 3,085 | 4,296 |
| 1989 | 1,025 | 509 | 1,534 | 3,117 | 4,402 |
| 1990 | 1,090 | 527 | 1,616 | 3,141 | 4,515 |
| 1991 | 1,137 | 540 | 1,678 | 3,180 | 4,613 |
| 1992 | 1,166 | 554 | 1,721 | 3,204 | 4,680 |
| 1993 | 1,326 | 574 | 1,900 | 3,196 | 4,851 |
| 1994 | 1,392 | 593 | 1,985 | 3,213 | 4,962 |
| 1995 | 1,487 | 595 | 2,081 | 3,242 | 5,087 |
| 1996 | 1,413 | 608 | 2,021 | 3,293 | 5,079 |
| 1997[c] | 1,465 | 586 | 2,051 | 3,305 | 5,120 |

Source: U.S. House of Representatives Committee on Ways and Means, *Green Book 1998*, table 15-26.

a. Data are for beginning of fiscal year.

b. Figures for total assisted renters have been adjusted since 1980 to avoid double-counting households receiving more than one subsidy.

c. FY1997 figures are estimates only.

cies (typically state housing finance agencies), which distribute credits among projects proposed by developers. Project eligibility requires that the rents charged for subsidized dwellings be no more than 30 percent of the incomes of households at 60 percent of local median income.[12]

These Low Income Housing Tax Credits (LIHTC) are used by developers in partnership with individuals and firms willing to invest capital in low-income housing in return for federal credits. Some of the investor capital is applied to "syndication costs," those costs required to make the business connection between investors and developers. The competitive returns required by investors are higher than treasury borrowing rates (since there is always some danger that a given project will fail, or that it will fail to qualify for tax credits).

12. See Wallace (1995).

**Figure 5. Economic Efficiency of the Low-Income Housing Tax Credit, Fiscal Years 1987–96**

Value per dollar of credit (dollars)

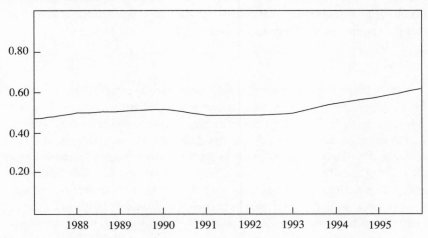

Source: Cummings and DiPasquale (1998, p. 46).

So in present-value terms, the tax credits represent more in lost federal revenue than an equivalent investment in housing through direct federal government appropriations. Estimates by Michael Stegman after the first few years of LIHTC experience suggested that the increased housing investment generated by the tax credit was only about half of its cost to the federal treasury.[13]

Recent research by Jean L. Cummings and Denise DiPasquale provides a somewhat more optimistic assessment.[14] Cummings and DiPasquale evaluated some 2,500 projects funded by the LIHTC during its first decade, confirming Stegman's estimates for the early years but also indicating an upward trend in the value of housing output per dollar of tax credit expended. Figure 5 reports their results, suggesting that the market for these credits has become far more competitive during the past decade. Still, in 1996, the evidence showed that a dollar of federal subsidy produced only about 62 cents in housing output.[15] The economic efficiency of the LIHTC is roughly the same as the public housing program.

13. Stegman (1991).
14. Cummings and DiPasquale (1998).
15. The figures reported by Cummings and DiPasquale represent the value of housing produced divided by the sum of the stream of tax credits incurred, rather than the present value of the stream. Thus they represent a slight underestimate of program efficiency. See Cummings and DiPasquale (1999).

The Low Income Housing Tax Credit appears to be a small program. The aggregate tax credit was set at $1.25 per capita each year and has been unchanged since the program was established in 1986. But each dollar of the tax credit represents a ten-year commitment of tax expenditures. This means that the annual cost of the program to the Treasury is about $3 billion.

## Summary

During the period since the explicit recognition of the goal of a "decent home" for all Americans, four important economic trends have emerged in housing subsidy programs. First, the locus of subsidy has changed from the dwelling unit to the household occupying the dwelling unit. Second, the type of property subsidized has changed from newly constructed dwellings to used dwellings that were originally constructed for higher-income households. Third, the ownership of subsidized dwellings has changed from agencies of the government to private nonprofit agencies, and increasingly to for-profit landlords. Fourth, there has been a downsizing of the relative commitment to housing programs in comparison to other objects of federal government expenditure.

During the 1970s, the Experimental Housing Allowance Program (EHAP), still the most expensive social experiment in history, provided subsidies based on a formula analogous to the current Section 8 rent subsidy rule. These subsidies were offered to all low-income households in two medium-sized metropolitan areas: Green Bay, Wisconsin, and South Bend, Indiana. EHAP also provided subsidies to a small number of households in Phoenix and Pittsburgh through a variety of more complicated formulas. These were intended to elicit the housing demands of low-income renters. The central findings of the experiments were that, first, income transfers and housing price reductions had modest but inelastic effects on the housing consumption of low-income households,[16] and second, marketwide subsidy programs had no perceptible effects on the price of housing suitable for low-income households.[17]

Almost two decades later, it appears that U.S. housing subsidies have grown to resemble more closely the modal experimental program evaluated by EHAP. Eligible households are offered the difference between the market price of "just standard" housing and 30 percent of income. To qualify, recipients must live in dwellings that pass a minimum standard. The one significant difference between the experimental housing allowance program as evaluated in the early 1980s and current policy is the extent of coverage. Under current

16. Hanushek and Quigley (1981).
17. Bradbury and Downs (1981).

**Table 4. Summary of Renter Households and Housing Market Needs, Fiscal Years 1973–97[a]**

Thousands

| Fiscal year | Renter households | Households in severely inadequate housing | Households paying 30–50% income | Households paying >50% income | Households in poverty | Total subsidized renters[b] |
|---|---|---|---|---|---|---|
| 1973 | 24,425 |  |  | n.a. | 4,828 | 1,356 |
| 1974 | 24,943 |  |  | n.a. | 4,922 | 1,551 |
| 1975 | 25,462 | 2,832 | 4,099 | n.a. | 5,450 | 1,717 |
| 1976 | 25,897 | 2,886 | 4,359 | n.a. | 5,311 | 2,067 |
| 1977 | 26,324 | 2,840 | 4,655 | n.a. | 5,311 | 2,092 |
| 1978 | 26,810 | 1,677 | 4,765 | 3,661 | 5,280 | 2,400 |
| 1979 | 27,174 | 2,621 | 4,790 | 4,620 | 5,461 | 2,654 |
| 1980 | 27,415 | 2,589 | 4,961 | 4,935 | 6,217 | 2,895 |
| 1981 | 28,709 | 2,882 | 5,399 | 5,455 | 6,851 | 3,012 |
| 1983 | 29,894 | 1,617 | 5,661 | 5,481 | 7,647 | 3,443 |
| 1985 | 31,736 | 1,108 | 6,739 | 6,128 | 7,223 | 3,887 |
| 1987 | 33,320 | 859 | 7,675 | 6,991 | 7,005 | 4,175 |
| 1989 | 33,734 | 1,587 | 6,983 | 5,187 | 6,784 | 4,402 |
| 1991 | 34,242 | 1,347 | 6,938 | 5,426 | 7,712 | 4,613 |
| 1993 | 35,184 | 910 | 7,163 | 5,948 | 8,393 | 4,851 |
| 1995 | 35,246 | 849 | 7,385 | 6,187 | 7,532 | 5,087 |
| 1997 | 35,059 | 1,072 | 7,264 | 7,359 | 7,324 | 5,120 |

Sources: U.S. Department of Housing and Urban Development, Office of Budget, "Annotated Tables for the 1998 Budget Process"; Congressional Budget Office tabulations based on Congressional Justifications for the Department of Housing and Urban Development; U.S. Department of Housing and Urban Development, Office of Policy Development and Research, tabulations of American Housing Surveys; American Housing Survey, Series H-150, various years; Housing Vacancy Survey, Series H-111, various years; March Current Population Survey, various years; U.S. General Accounting Office, Changes in Rent Burdens and Housing Conditions of Lower Income Households (Government Printing Office, 1985).

a. Prior to 1978, the American Housing Survey (AHS) did not report rent-to-income ratios beyond the 35+ percent category. Data on rent burdens and inadequate housing units prior to 1981 are taken from GAO (1985) and represent only households with less than 80 percent of median area incomes. AHS survey design and definitions of severe and moderate problems changed in 1985 so caution should be used in interpreting trends. Subsidized households include those in Public Housing, Section 8, Section 236, and Rent Supplement programs.

b. Number of subsidized households after FY 1980 reflects subtraction of units receiving more than one subsidy (that is, Section 236 projects that also receive either Rent Supplement or Section 8 subsidies).

housing policy, subsidies are given to only a fraction of qualifying households, and housing subsidies are rationed by queues.[18] For example, as reported in table 4, in 1997 there were about 7.3 million poverty households among the 35.1 million renter households in the United States. About 14.6 million households paid in excess of 30 percent of their incomes for rent, and about 7.4 million paid more than half of their incomes for rent. At the same time, about 5.1 million renter households received assistance under HUD programs. About 10 to 15 percent of the assisted households were not poor.

18. The effectiveness of the allocation of certificates and vouchers among metropolitan areas has recently been criticized by Scott Susin (1999), who argues that rents for low-income housing have risen more rapidly in cities with larger allocations of certificates.

In 1978 there were about 3.7 million renter households spending more than half of their incomes on rent. This was 1.5 times the number of subsidized rental households. In 1997 there were 7.4 million renter households paying more than half of their incomes on rent, about 1.4 times the number of subsidized rental households. In 1978 there were 2.2 households in poverty for each subsidized renter household; by 1997 there were 1.4 poor households for each subsidized renter household.

The limiting factor in improving the housing condition of most poor households is the federal budget devoted to existing programs. The economic effects of these programs are fairly well known and their costs can be fairly well calculated. There now seems to be consensus among professional economists and housing policy officials that a flexible shelter allowance program should be the backbone of housing assistance programs. This consensus was not achieved quickly. And, to be sure, the consensus does not yet extend to powerful congressional constituencies.

Finally, as indicated in table 4, deficiencies in the physical adequacy of rental accommodations have declined quite substantially, even in recent years. In 1978, it was estimated that 1.68 million renters, more than 6 percent of rental households, lived in severely inadequate housing. By 1995, the estimate was less than 850,000 households. Less than 2.5 percent of U.S. renters resided in severely inadequate housing (as conventionally measured by the U.S. Census Bureau). Increasingly, housing problems are those of rent burdens, not physical condition. Problems of rent burden are best addressed by the transfer of resources to those so burdened.

## Urban Development and Intergovernmental Fiscal Relations

As with housing programs, it is possible to distinguish four historical phases in postwar federal policies and programs for urban development, although the timing of these phases is less distinct. These phases are distinguished by the objectives of federal programs, the economic incentives provided to lower levels of government, the overall level of financial commitment, and the flexibility provided to localities. These four phases are the period of slum clearance (1949–62), the Great Society (1962–70), the New Federalism (1970–90), and the New Flexibility (1990 forward).

### Slum Clearance

The ambitious program of housing investment contained in the 1949 Housing Act included the template for a federal-local partnership for urban development—later termed *urban renewal*—and successively expanded in scope through the 1950s and 1960s. "Urban development" as envisioned in the 1949 act was quite clearly directed toward housing rather than some broader definition of development. The act authorized financial assistance from the federal government to a local agency for a "project," consisting of site assembly, clearance, site preparation, and final disposition for uses specified in an approved redevelopment plan. A "project" was defined to include an area that was "predominantly residential" either before or after redevelopment, and the project could not include construction or improvements of nonresidential buildings. The basic program was one of *slum clearance*, in which the federal government paid two-thirds of the net project costs as a matching grant to the local government. Indeed, the 1949 Act *required* the removal of one unit of slum housing for each unit of public housing constructed.

The slum-clearance aspects of the conditional matching grant program were weakened slightly when the name *urban renewal* was adopted in the 1954 version of housing act. The 1954 revision permitted 10 percent of federal capital grants to be used for nonresidential projects. However, these projects were eligible only if they contained substantial numbers of deteriorated dwellings or if the projects removed other substandard living conditions. By 1959 this exception had grown to 20 percent, and the requirement that a project area contain a substantial number of substandard dwellings was abandoned. It was not until 1969 that the act stipulated that a federally financed urban renewal project *could not* reduce the supply of low-income housing. During much of the heyday of urban renewal, it operated, by design, to remove units of low-cost housing from the inventory.

The inherent contradictions in programs aimed at destroying low-income housing and replacing it with housing that the previous residents could not afford were not well understood, at least initially. Ashley Foard and Hilbert Fefferman attribute the "predominantly residential" requirement in urban renewal legislation to the dominance of physical planners rather than social scientists among the early advocates of urban policy.[19]

By the early 1960s, it was clear that these urban investments would not be sufficient to attract back to the central city the white middle-class households that had been suburbanizing at a rapid rate during the postwar period. By this time, there was also fairly coherent theory suggesting that attracting large num-

19. Foard and Fefferman (1966).

bers of suburban households back to the city was infeasible without large and recurrent subsidies.[20]

### The Great Society

The first of the Great Society antipoverty programs, the Economic Opportunity Act (EOA) of 1964, included the Urban and Rural Community Action program (Title II) among a broad panoply of new initiatives.[21] With the establishment of the Department of Housing and Urban Development a year later, the concept of community action was expanded to the Model Cities program. As originally envisioned, a half dozen large urban centers would be chosen for intensive investment of public resources.[22] A task force appointed by President Johnson increased the demonstration tenfold to sixty-six cities. By the time legislation passed Congress (the Demonstration Cities and Metropolitan Development Act of 1966), a total of 150 cities had been chosen for the Model Cities program.

Cities chose to participate in the program through their elected officials, who promised that citizen participation would be widespread, that renewal projects would be comprehensive, and that coordination of public and private resources would be enforced. HUD committed funds for planning and subsequently for implementation in each city. HUD maintained overall supervision of the federal commitment to testing "whether we have the capacity to understand the causes of human and physical blight [and] the skills and the commitment to restore quality to older neighborhoods."[23] The model cities program survived for less than two and a half years before the newly elected president, Richard Nixon, began to dismantle it.

Although the ambitious urban development programs of the Johnson administration did not survive long enough to produce results that could be evaluated, the programs begun under the Great Society changed the nature of federal-local fiscal relations in a fundamental way. The 1960s witnessed a substantial reorientation of the system of fiscal federalism in the United States. Intergovernmental transfers and federal grants to state and local governments increased substantially. As figure 6 indicates, between 1960 and 1969 federal grants to lower levels of government more than doubled, increasing from

20. Alonso (1964).
21. The EOA Act included, for example, titles fostering small-business development, adult education, VISTA (the domestic Peace Corps), and, inevitably, a Rural Action program.
22. Haar (1975).
23. U.S. Department of Housing and Urban Development (1966, p. ii).

**Figure 6. Federal Outlays for Grants to State and Local Governments,
Fiscal Years 1960–2000[a]**

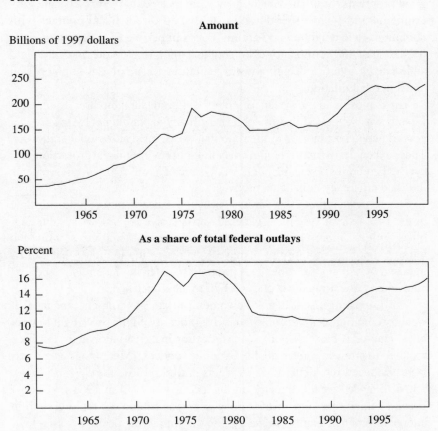

**Amount**

Billions of 1997 dollars

**As a share of total federal outlays**

Percent

Source: U.S. Office of Management and Budget, "FY2000 Historical Tables," table 12.1.
a. FY1976 includes outlays during the "transition quarter" from July 1, 1976, to September 30, 1976, annualized to reflect the experience of four quarters only.

$35.0 billion to $82.1 billion (in 1997 dollars). The expansion of federal grants continued apace until the "new federalism" initiatives of the Nixon administration were adopted in 1974. Between 1960 and 1974 intergovernmental grants increased from 7.6 percent of federal government outlays to 17 percent of federal outlays—while at the same time the Vietnam War was consuming major federal resources. During the period of "creative federalism" of the Johnson administration, the number of grant programs to local governments increased enormously. A total of 240 new categorical programs were enacted, including 109 separate grant programs in 1965 alone.[24] During this period, grant programs for urban development were created that bypassed state governments and local officials and established direct fiscal contact with community and neighborhood groups. For example, the EOA encouraged the formation of 850 community-action organizations to promote maximum feasible citizen input in deciding on expenditures for urban development and housing rehabilitation.

The explosion in the system of grants was predicated on three arguments. First, it was suggested that the objects of many expenditures by lower-level governments, particularly in metropolitan areas, have substantial spillovers. These expenditures may include transportation, environmental protection, and even expenditures on local schools.[25] A system of grants to urban governments thus had efficiency-enhancing motives.

Second, it was argued that vertical fiscal imbalance was more or less chronic in the U.S. federal system. A generally progressive federal tax system contrasts with the more regressive structure of state and local taxes, while the intrametropolitan mobility of taxpayers depresses the tax rates that can be imposed by urban governments. A program transferring federally raised revenue to city governments is one solution to the imbalance.[26]

Third, existing fiscal disparities among urban governments meant that wealthy communities were able to buy high-quality public services at low tax rates. Thus one object of equity was a reduction in the variation in the tax price required to produce a given quality of public services. (Models of this process were produced by Richard Musgrave as early as 1961; the *Serrano-Priest* school finance lawsuit, directly on this point, was filed in 1968.)[27] George Break claimed that "one of the strongest forces behind the rapid growth in intergovernmental grants" in the 1960s was simply the desire to assist low-income groups, expounding the proposition that a variety of local government programs should be thought of as merit goods, particularly those serving low-income groups.[28]

---

24. U.S. Department of the Treasury (1985, p. xxi).
25. George Break (1980) reviews many of the spillover arguments put forward in the 1960s by proponents of an expanded system of grants.
26. Heller and Pechman (1967).
27. Musgrave (1961).
28. Break (1980), p. 86.

## The New Federalism

After the election of Richard Nixon in 1968, the grant program, which had expanded so rapidly during the previous eight years, was increasingly called into question. The explicit and implicit incentives of categorical grants, seemingly capricious restrictions on the uses of grant funds, and the set of regulations governing federal grants were increasingly thought to have affected the behavior of recipients in arbitrary ways.

For example, the theory of fiscal federalism that had been developing over this period showed that matching grants from higher levels of government to lower levels were sufficient to internalize interjurisdictional spillovers in service provision in urban areas.[29] But, of course, the efficiency gains of these grants were dependent on the informed choice of a matching rate that correctly calibrated the spillovers of benefits associated with local spending. On this there was little evidence. There was even less evidence that the congressional sponsors of legislation (or their staffs) considered these issues in their choice of matching rates. Examples arose in which the same local expenditure on urban development could be justified under several grant programs at different matching rates.

The availability of categorical grants for some functions but not for others is premised on the theory that the federal government transfers resources in pursuit of its own national objectives. These objectives were questioned by many who also observed that local decisionmakers have better information about local costs and efficient production than federal grantors. Increasingly, a system of grants for some narrow and specific functions but not for others was questioned, as were federal preferences for capital spending rather than program operations.[30] Finally, the administrative difficulties in processing grant applications from nearly 40,000 units of general-purpose government were thought to encourage waste at the federal level and inordinate local attention to "grantsmanship."

The proposed solution to these inefficiencies was the program of General Revenue Sharing embedded in the State and Local Fiscal Assistance Act of 1972, followed soon after by the Community Development Block Grant pro-

---

29. See Oates (1972) for the definitive statement.

30. In much the same way as the original public housing program was criticized for encouraging the use of too much capital, so too were federal programs supporting mass transit criticized for encouraging overcapitalization of the transportation sector. The budgetary rationale for these capital subsidy programs was the same as that implicit in housing programs. Operating subsidies opened the way to increased federal liability in a way that capital subsidies did not.

gram (CDBG), Title I of the Housing Act of 1974. Like revenue sharing, CDBG grants were transfers of fixed resources to eligible jurisdictions (cities and suburbs with 50,000 or more people, and all urban counties) where the level of the transfer was determined by a congressional formula.[31] Recipient governments retained a high degree of discretion over the disposition of CDBG funds.

As enacted, the CDBG program replaced eight Great Society categorical programs that had been funded on a competitive basis, including the urban renewal and model cities programs; the open space, historic preservation, and urban beautification programs; and water and sewage treatment grants.

The CDBG funds are intended to foster "viable urban communities, by providing decent housing and suitable living environments and expanding economic opportunities principally for persons of low and moderate income."[32] Appropriated funds are intended to be used on local projects in which "maximum feasible priority" is given to the "benefit of low- and moderate-income families or in the prevention or elimination of slums or blight."

The program is thus the lineal descendant of the urban renewal program originally authorized in the 1949 Housing Act. However, the 1974 program differed enormously from the original urban renewal program in the discretion afforded recipient governments in planning their own expenditures.[33]

The CDBG program began with appropriations of $2.5 billion (in 1975 dollars), which increased steadily during the Ford and Carter administrations. (See table 5 and appendix table A-1.) In large part, these expenditures were financed by reductions in other federal grant programs. As reported in figure 6, aggregate grants in aid to state and local governments were declining during the mid- and late 1970s, in real terms. As a fraction of federal outlays, grant programs plummeted.

In any event, increases in funding for the CDBG program itself came to an abrupt halt with the inauguration of Ronald Reagan. During the Reagan administration, real expenditures on Community Development Block Grants declined

31. Some thirty percent of CDBG funds are distributed to smaller rural jurisdictions on a competitive basis, not by formula.

32. Connerly and Liou (1998), p. 64.

33. While retaining much local discretion, entitlement jurisdictions were required to make formal application for CDBG funds, justifying their proposed budgets until 1981. The Ford and Carter administrations differed somewhat in their interpretations of the congressional mandate. The former was more sympathetic to the expenditure of CDBG funds by local governments to protect their middle-class tax bases. See Peterson and others (1986, pp. 87–93). The latter increased HUD monitoring and oversight in attempts to target benefits to low- and moderate-income households.

**Table 5. Average Annual Growth in Community Development Block Grant Appropriations**

| Administration | Years | Average real growth (percent) |
|---|---|---|
| Ford | 1975–77 | 4.1 |
| Carter | 1977–81 | 5.1 |
| Reagan | 1981–89 | –6.5 |
| Bush | 1989–92 | 0.6 |

Source: Urban Institute, *Federal Funds, Local Choices* (Washington, November, 1994), pp. 2–4.

by more than 6.5 percent per year (and the Revenue Sharing program was eliminated altogether in 1985). CDBG funding remained stable during the Bush administration and has recently increased slightly. Urban development activities that are routinely funded by CDBGs include the acquisition and disposition of real property; the rehabilitation of residential and nonresidential structures; social service delivery systems; public works projects; and assistance to private businesses. Charles E. Connerly and Y. Thomas Liou report that the distribution of CDBG allocations across entitlement communities has stabilized, with about 40 percent of transfers spent by local governments for housing and housing rehabilitation.[34] The fraction spent on public works projects has declined to about 20 percent, while economic development and public services consume, respectively, about 13 percent and 10 percent of available funding. Evaluations by the Urban Institute suggest that the fraction of funds devoted to housing is somewhat larger. Statistical analyses of the funding choices made by grant recipients suggest that older central cities with larger populations and those with higher levels of urban "distress" spend considerably more of their urban development funds on housing and housing rehabilitation.[35] It is also reported that the geographic targeting of expenditures has declined over time, within recipient jurisdictions (as the locations in which expenditures are made have diffused) and across jurisdictions (as more communities have been made eligible for CDBG entitlements).[36]

34. Connerly and Liou (1998).

35. See Urban Institute (1994, ch. 4).

36. See Urban Institute (1994, pp. 2–7); Reischauer (1975). During the first two decades of the program, for example, the number of entitlement jurisdictions increased by almost 50 percent. There is surely a general lesson about the realistic possibilities for targeting expenditures in the U.S. political system. A program that began with six demonstration cities expanded to cover 150 cities authorized under the 1966 Model Cities Act. Similarly, 594 entitlement jurisdictions under the CDBG program grew to 889 over two decades. Note finally that the Senate and the House of Representatives never could agree on a common disbursement formula for General Revenue Sharing funds. Targeting is politically very difficult.

**Figure 7. Relative Importance of Community Development Block Grant Program, Fiscal Years 1975–92**

Percent[a]

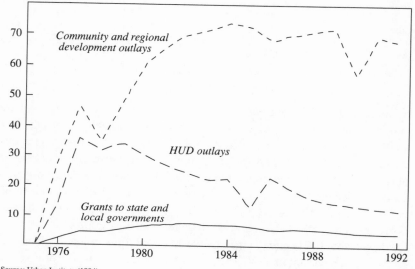

Source: Urban Institute (1994).
a. CDBG outlays as pecentage of outlays of a given type.

Over time, the relative size of these block grants as a fraction of HUD outlays has declined, from more than 30 percent in the 1980s to less than 15 percent in the 1990s. As indicated in figure 7 and appendix table A-1, however, CDBG funds are still the backbone of all federal expenditures on urban and regional development activities, constituting more than half of all these expenditures. As a fraction of all grants-in-aid to governments, CDBG appropriations are not large, and never constituted as much as 8 percent of the total.

*The New Flexibility*

As noted previously, federal grants as a percentage of total outlays declined precipitously during the Reagan years. The number of federal grant programs declined from 534 to 478 during the 1981–89 period. The decline was substantial in both project-based and formula-based grants. Since 1989, there has been a substantial increase in the number of discretionary grant programs, some of which serve urban development objectives.[37]

37. Appendix table A-1 provides more detail on the course of community development funding relative to other federal government expenditures.

The most important of these new programs are the Stewart B. McKinney Emergency Program, the HOME investment partnership program, and the HOPE VI program for public housing. Under the McKinney Act, funds are provided for emergency shelter, supportive housing, the rehabilitation of single-room-occupancy dwellings, and other programs benefiting the homeless. The HOPE VI program provides funds to local housing authorities to "transform" distressed public housing projects. As an operational matter, this typically involves the demolition of obsolete structures.

The HOME program provides formula grants to local governments and also provides lines of credit to participating jurisdictions. The program also disburses funds to each state government. Applications for assistance typically include proposals for site acquisition and improvement, demolition, and rehabilitation of public and privately owned housing. As a part of the HOME program, the Home Investment Partnership is designed exclusively to create or preserve low-income housing. Local jurisdictions must provide a 25 percent match for these block grants and must earmark 15 percent of program proceeds for nonprofit community housing development organizations.

The hallmarks of these programs are flexibility and local responsibility. Federal funds can be commingled with state and local resources, and can be used in partnership with not-for-profit participants. Increasingly, McKinney Act funds are used to contract with nonprofit providers of emergency services and shelter. HOME Act funds are used to provide incentives for nonprofit developers to provide housing affordable to those of low income. Units are often owned, developed, or sponsored by community-based nonprofit groups.

The increased flexibility is enhanced by the possibilities for coordination with the LIHTC program. In many states, the state portion of the HOME block grant is distributed by the same agency that distributes tax credits. Increasingly, projects for new affordable housing that involve tax credits also include gap financing using HOME funds and local contributions using CDBG grant funds. The remarkable thing about this increased flexibility is the extent to which program priorities and decisions are made by local rather than HUD officials and by members of nonprofit community organizations.

Table 6 indicates the funding for these grant programs sponsoring housing and urban development. Note that the HOME program is funded at about $1.2 billion per year. For completeness, the table also documents expenditures on the Urban Development Action Grant program.[38]

38. The UDAG program included only a modest housing component. It was principally focused on business development and rehabilitation or reuse of hotels or business property. See Rich (1992) for an extensive evaluation.

**Table 6. Summary of Grants Programs for Housing and Community Development, Fiscal Years 1979–98**
Millions of 1997 dollars

| Fiscal year | Urban Development Action Grants (UDAG) | Stewart B. McKinney emergency programs[a] | Revitalization of severely distressed public housing (HOPE VI) | HOME Investment Partnerships Program |
|---|---|---|---|---|
| 1979 | 158 | ... | ... | ... |
| 1980 | 439 | ... | ... | ... |
| 1981 | 661 | ... | ... | ... |
| 1982 | 651 | ... | ... | ... |
| 1983 | 727 | ... | ... | ... |
| 1984 | 701 | ... | ... | ... |
| 1985 | 741 | ... | ... | ... |
| 1986 | 675 | ... | ... | ... |
| 1987 | 500 | ... | ... | ... |
| 1988 | 293 | ... | ... | ... |
| 1989 | 313 | ... | ... | ... |
| 1990 | 257 | ... | ... | ... |
| 1991 | 151 | ... | ... | ... |
| 1992 | 59 | 86 | ... | 3 |
| 1993 | 57 | 89 | ... | 235 |
| 1994 | 36 | 94 | 1 | 847 |
| 1995 | 21 | 163 | 33 | 1,242 |
| 1996 | 28 | 312 | 113 | 1,234 |
| 1997 | 30 | 429 | 205 | 1,211 |
| 1998 | 6 | 574 | 233 | 1,266 |

Source: U.S. Office of Management and Budget, "FY2000 Historical Tables," table 12.3.

a. Stewart B. McKinney Programs include the emergency shelter grants program, supplemental assistance for facilities for the homeless, shelter plus care, Section 8 moderate rehabilitation single-room-occupancy program, and the innovative homeless initiatives demonstration program.

## Conclusion

During the half century since the passage of the 1949 Housing Act espousing the goal of a "decent home and a suitable living environment for all Americans," the shape of housing and urban development policy has changed radically. Programs in which the public sector owns and operates housing have been reduced in relative importance, and recently in absolute number (by 116,000 during the Clinton administration alone). The locus of responsibility for urban development activities, and for choices between housing and other development activities, has been returned to local decisionmakers. Many economists and policy analysts would applaud these directions.

The mix between project-based and tenant-based housing assistance projects has been changed to favor the latter. Many of the long-term contracts for project-based assistance entered into between HUD and the developers of new housing early in the Section 8 program will soon expire. Current monthly payments to landlords plus tenant contributions under these housing assistance payment contracts typically exceed HUD's estimates of fair market rents in the metropolitan areas in which these units are located.[39] Thus there is room for expanding the number of households served for the same program expenditure by shifting subsidies to tenant-based vouchers as project-based contracts lapse.

But there are other reasons for favoring the substitution of tenant-based for project-based subsidies wherever possible. For example, it is far simpler to phase out subsidies for those whose incomes have risen if these households are not required to vacate project-based dwellings to make room for other households. The subsidy can be transferred without incurring a residential move.

Even more important than this, however, is the greater possibility for dispersion of the poor throughout urban areas if poor households are subsidized regardless of their residential location choices. Careful research suggests that demand-side subsidies have only modest effects in decentralizing the urban poor.[40] Other research, however, indicates that there are substantial social benefits to even modest deconcentrations of urban poverty in big cities.[41]

These changes in program emphasis would make the existing housing subsidy program for low-income households approximate more closely the housing allowance experiments and demonstrations of the late 1970s. The only difference—and it is a major difference—is the universality of the program. A more effective program for assisting low-income households by substituting tenant-based subsidies for project-based subsidies under the Section 8 program would still be highly inequitable. Fifty years after the landmark Housing Act of 1949, the "housing problem" in the United States has been converted to an "affordability problem": at unsubsidized market prices, many poor households must spend large fractions of their low incomes on shelter. Few economists would prefer to subsidize landlords or to distort market rents in order to improve the lot of poor households—not when deserving households can be subsidized directly. It is clear, however, that a housing allowance for only *some* of the poor would be highly inequitable. A universal and fair program would require a much stronger political commitment than we have seen up to the present.

39. This is because it is far more expensive to create low-income housing through new construction than through depreciation. It also arises because rent escalation clauses favorable to landlords were negotiated ab initio.

40. See, for example, Straszheim (1981).

41. Summarized, for example, by O'Regan and Quigley (1999).

**Table A-1. Federal Outlays for Grants to State and Local Governments by Function, Fiscal Years 1958–98**
Millions of 1997 dollars

| Fiscal year | Transportation | Community and regional development | | Education, training, employment, and social services | Health | Income security | General government | |
| --- | --- | --- | --- | --- | --- | --- | --- | --- |
| | | Total | Community Development Block Grants | | | | Total | General revenue sharing |
| 1958 | 7,984 | 271 | ... | 1,891 | 930 | 11,516 | 654 | ... |
| 1959 | 13,566 | 432 | ... | 2,214 | 1,128 | 12,683 | 676 | ... |
| 1960 | 14,948 | 543 | ... | 2,617 | 1,067 | 13,134 | 822 | ... |
| 1961 | 13,275 | 756 | ... | 2,800 | 1,294 | 13,729 | 849 | ... |
| 1962 | 13,902 | 905 | ... | 3,220 | 1,786 | 14,944 | 900 | ... |
| 1963 | 14,831 | 1,186 | ... | 3,340 | 2,169 | 15,568 | 1,041 | ... |
| 1964 | 17,698 | 2,462 | ... | 4,020 | 2,567 | 16,550 | 1,195 | ... |
| 1965 | 19,241 | 3,018 | ... | 4,928 | 2,928 | 16,482 | 1,061 | ... |
| 1966 | 18,567 | 2,622 | ... | 11,778 | 5,312 | 16,324 | 1,204 | ... |
| 1967 | 18,283 | 2,573 | ... | 18,415 | 7,393 | 16,077 | 1,322 | ... |
| 1968 | 18,477 | 3,670 | ... | 22,010 | 11,520 | 17,830 | 1,439 | ... |
| 1969 | 17,956 | 4,273 | ... | 20,714 | 13,048 | 19,578 | 1,613 | ... |
| 1970 | 17,873 | 6,917 | ... | 24,938 | 14,958 | 22,521 | 1,861 | ... |
| 1971 | 18,318 | 7,962 | ... | 27,281 | 16,735 | 26,343 | 1,922 | ... |
| 1972 | 18,309 | 9,120 | ... | 34,262 | 21,725 | 32,678 | 2,111 | ... |
| 1973 | 18,189 | 8,919 | ... | 32,294 | 20,433 | 30,169 | 24,830 | 22,565 |
| 1974 | 16,325 | 8,356 | ... | 28,899 | 22,643 | 26,697 | 21,103 | 18,883 |
| 1975 | 16,747 | 8,116 | 109 | 34,650 | 25,160 | 26,708 | 20,197 | 17,506 |
| 1976[a] | 21,588 | 9,660 | 3,311 | 39,043 | 29,474 | 29,698 | 20,019 | 17,786 |
| 1977 | 21,076 | 11,418 | 5,305 | 40,006 | 30,739 | 32,158 | 24,306 | 17,162 |
| 1978 | 21,012 | 16,830 | 5,859 | 48,880 | 30,257 | 32,771 | 23,034 | 16,224 |
| 1979 | 23,708 | 14,404 | 6,856 | 48,256 | 31,183 | 31,970 | 18,293 | 14,853 |
| 1980 | 25,395 | 12,649 | 7,610 | 42,635 | 30,731 | 36,069 | 16,803 | 13,318 |
| 1981 | 23,877 | 10,909 | 7,200 | 38,253 | 33,659 | 37,432 | 12,323 | 9,151 |

| Year | | | | | | | |
|---|---|---|---|---|---|---|---|
| 1982 | 20,331 | 9,031 | 6,366 | 27,851 | 31,628 | 36,818 | 11,079 | 7,671 |
| 1983 | 21,271 | 7,996 | 5,727 | 25,985 | 32,590 | 39,896 | 10,540 | 7,435 |
| 1984 | 23,153 | 7,966 | 5,899 | 25,750 | 33,733 | 39,666 | 10,580 | 7,055 |
| 1985 | 25,371 | 7,788 | 5,694 | 26,576 | 36,472 | 40,502 | 10,200 | 6,838 |
| 1986 | 26,825 | 7,119 | 4,871 | 27,755 | 39,280 | 42,571 | 10,484 | 7,489 |
| 1987 | 23,839 | 5,983 | 4,192 | 26,360 | 41,631 | 42,346 | 2,826 | 107 |
| 1988 | 24,479 | 5,788 | 4,138 | 26,974 | 44,210 | 42,899 | 2,646 | [b] |
| 1989 | 23,526 | 5,273 | 3,816 | 28,459 | 47,476 | 42,096 | 2,853 | [b] |
| 1990 | 23,546 | 6,097 | 3,461 | 28,685 | 53,897 | 43,212 | 2,835 | … |
| 1991 | 23,363 | 5,035 | 3,507 | 31,306 | 65,735 | 45,798 | 2,621 | … |
| 1992 | 23,516 | 5,193 | 3,535 | 32,941 | 81,698 | 49,747 | 2,601 | … |
| 1993 | 24,760 | 6,293 | 3,552 | 33,500 | 88,486 | 52,194 | 2,367 | … |
| 1994 | 25,594 | 8,435 | 3,954 | 35,462 | 93,425 | 55,809 | 2,272 | … |
| 1995 | 27,158 | 7,614 | 4,563 | 35,939 | 98,561 | 58,052 | 2,287 | … |
| 1996 | 26,553 | 8,030 | 4,649 | 34,815 | 99,891 | 54,600 | 2,111 | … |
| 1997 | 26,846 | 8,161 | 4,517 | 34,735 | 98,974 | 54,965 | 2,153 | … |
| 1998 | 25,743 | 7,536 | 4,550 | 35,908 | 104,210 | 57,967 | 2,204 | … |

Source: U.S. Office of Management and Budget, "FY2000 Historical Tables," table 12.2.
a. FY1976 includes outlays during the "transition quarter" from July 1, 1976, to September 30, 1976, annualized to reflect the experience of four quarters only.
b. Indicates $500 thousand or less.

**Table A-2. Comparison of HUD Outlays with Total Assisted Housing Payments and Total Federal Outlays, Fiscal Years 1962–98**
Millions of 1997 dollars

| Fiscal year | HUD outlays on assisted housing[a] | Total HUD outlays | Assisted housing outlays as a percentage of HUD total | Total federal outlays | Total HUD outlays as a percentage of total federal outlays |
|---|---|---|---|---|---|
| 1962 | 795 | 4,042 | 19.7 | 522,706 | 0.8 |
| 1963 | 840 | −2,935 | (28.6) | 536,523 | −0.5 |
| 1964 | 689 | 348 | 198.3 | 564,503 | 0.1 |
| 1965 | 1,055 | 2,309 | 45.7 | 554,842 | 0.4 |
| 1966 | 1,057 | 11,317 | 9.3 | 613,420 | 1.8 |
| 1967 | 1,153 | 13,676 | 8.4 | 696,225 | 2.0 |
| 1968 | 1,219 | 15,867 | 7.7 | 758,369 | 2.1 |
| 1969 | 1,405 | 2,904 | 48.4 | 748,077 | 0.4 |
| 1970 | 1,733 | 9,451 | 18.3 | 760,331 | 1.2 |
| 1971 | 2,567 | 10,412 | 24.7 | 782,659 | 1.3 |
| 1972 | 3,418 | 13,014 | 26.3 | 833,881 | 1.6 |
| 1973 | 4,454 | 12,174 | 36.6 | 835,508 | 1.5 |
| 1974 | 4,676 | 14,785 | 31.6 | 832,989 | 1.8 |
| 1975 | 4,990 | 21,453 | 23.3 | 949,098 | 2.3 |
| 1976[b] | 5,348 | 18,129 | 29.5 | 1,011,133 | 1.9 |
| 1977 | 6,162 | 14,750 | 41.8 | 1,039,232 | 1.4 |
| 1978 | 6,934 | 18,190 | 38.1 | 1,090,796 | 1.7 |
| 1979 | 7,717 | 19,997 | 38.6 | 1,093,205 | 1.8 |
| 1980 | 8,833 | 24,836 | 35.6 | 1,152,454 | 2.2 |
| 1981 | 10,237 | 26,507 | 38.6 | 1,208,202 | 2.2 |
| 1982 | 11,551 | 25,573 | 45.2 | 1,252,026 | 2.0 |
| 1983 | 12,547 | 25,483 | 49.2 | 1,302,661 | 2.0 |
| 1984 | 13,554 | 25,740 | 52.7 | 1,315,936 | 2.0 |
| 1985 | 14,907 | 42,840 | 34.8 | 1,411,718 | 3.0 |
| 1986 | 14,704 | 20,705 | 71.0 | 1,450,446 | 1.4 |
| 1987 | 13,826 | 21,877 | 63.2 | 1,418,676 | 1.5 |
| 1988 | 14,981 | 25,694 | 58.3 | 1,444,214 | 1.8 |
| 1989 | 15,836 | 25,473 | 62.2 | 1,480,316 | 1.7 |
| 1990 | 16,624 | 24,765 | 67.1 | 1,538,888 | 1.6 |
| 1991 | 17,290 | 26,810 | 64.5 | 1,560,692 | 1.7 |
| 1992 | 18,217 | 27,993 | 65.1 | 1,580,612 | 1.8 |
| 1993 | 19,756 | 27,969 | 70.6 | 1,565,474 | 1.8 |
| 1994 | 20,990 | 27,990 | 75.0 | 1,583,049 | 1.8 |
| 1995 | 23,336 | 30,588 | 76.3 | 1,596,289 | 1.9 |
| 1996 | 21,546 | 25,815 | 83.5 | 1,596,317 | 1.6 |
| 1997 | 21,531 | 27,527 | 78.2 | 1,601,232 | 1.7 |
| 1998 | 20,429 | 29,763 | 68.6 | 1,627,206 | 1.8 |

Source: U.S. Department of Housing and Urban Development Office of Budget, "Annotated Tables for the 1998 Budget Process." U.S. Office of Management and Budget, "FY2000 Historical Tables," table 4.1.

a. HUD outlays on assisted housing includes outlays for public housing, Section 8, college housing grants, rent supplements, section 235, and rental housing assistance, and excludes rental housing development grant and rental rehabilitation grant outlays until FY1994. These programs covered FY1994 through FY1998.

b. FY1976 includes outlays during the "transition quarter" from July 1, 1976, to September 30, 1976, annualized to reflect the experience of four quarters only.

# Comments

**Michael A. Stegman:** John Quigley frames his historical analysis of American housing and urban policy in terms of the landmark Housing Act of 1949. He argues that this is an appropriate lens through which to view national urban policy because housing "is the most basic and durable aspect of national urban policy, and provides the spatial context within which other policies operate." I think this framework is too narrow. From the beginning, national urban policy has had much broader concerns than the programs that have emanated from the 1949 Housing Act. Robert C. Weaver, HUD's first secretary, argued that urban policy should focus on the problems of poverty and race by "putting a floor under income (especially for those with incomes too low even for our subsidized programs), breaking segregated residential patterns, increasing the citizen's role in decision-making, developing more effective instruments of local government, providing tax-sharing, or some other form of substantial financial aid to local governments." These, said Weaver, "are some of the major issues that the nation must tackle."[1]

An emphasis on race, space, and the spatial distribution of economic opportunities continues to preoccupy urban policymakers. For example, in his letter transmitting HUD's 1995 national urban policy report to the president, HUD Secretary Henry G. Cisneros says that "the polarization of urban communities—isolating the poor from the well-off, the unemployed from those who work, and minorities from whites—frays the fabric of our civic culture, and acts as a drag on the national economy. If we fail to address the problems of our cities, connecting residents of distressed neighborhoods with the jobs and opportunities of their metropolitan economy, we will not be able to compete and win in the global economy."[2]

1. Quoted in Zisch, Douglas, and Weaver, eds. (1969, pp. 87–88).
2. Transmittal letter from Henry G. Cisneros to the President, "Empowerment: A New Covenant with America's Communities, President Clinton's National Urban Policy Report," July 26, 1999.

Quigley's housing-centered analyses could have been better connected to urban policy had he chosen to examine the links between housing and other federal policy initiatives that affect cities, such as welfare reform. Because it has no explicit spatial concerns, Quigley chose to ignore welfare reform, but it is often the implicit spatial impacts of "nonurban" policies that have significant urban impacts. A recent report from the Brookings Institution Center on Urban and Metropolitan Policy, for example, indicates that many cities are having a harder time reducing welfare caseloads than other communities in their states, and that the greater the city's poverty and concentrated poverty, the slower the city's caseload decline relative to the state's.[3]

The housing-welfare nexus also illustrates why it is important for economists to pay careful attention to policy interdependencies. For example, according to Sandra Newman, about half of all families in assisted housing also receive welfare, and about a third of all welfare recipients also receive housing assistance.[4] Therefore it is virtually impossible to discuss low-income housing policy without taking account of welfare reform. Economists could help policymakers anticipate the implications of a time-limited cash assistance program's ramming headlong into a housing assistance system that remains a virtual lifetime entitlement for those who are fortunate enough to receive a housing subsidy. Economists who are evaluating the effectiveness of work incentives and liberalized asset limits on state efforts to move families from welfare to work could also help the housing community find cost-effective ways to eliminate the work disincentives built into the public and assisted-housing programs that cause rents to rise when unemployed residents go to work.

Even through a housing-policy lens, Quigley could have addressed the growing self-sufficiency movement within the assisted-housing realm, and whether the form of housing subsidy one receives might affect the likelihood of assisted household members finding work or increasing their work effort. For example, research in California by Paul Ong reveals that "residents with tenant-based Section 8 work considerably more than do those renting in the private market or residing in public housing. This finding holds after controlling for observable personal characteristics and accounting for income effects." Ong suggests that rather than being a statistical artifact or an effect caused by programmatic self-selection among applicants, the results are more likely the effects of Section 8's offering residential choice and mobility that improves opportunities for employment.[5]

3. Katz and Carnevale (1998, p. 1).
4. Newman (1999, p. 8).
5. Ong (1998, p. 775).

Quigley also understates the importance of recent changes in national housing policy by condensing his discussion of them into a very brief concluding section on "the new flexibility." While he touches upon the problem of expiring subsidy contracts, he fails to grasp the full significance of the fact that, according to HUD, "during the next five years, fully two-thirds of all project-based Section 8 will expire, totaling almost 14,000 properties containing 1 million subsidized housing units." As expirations increase, so does the risk of losing affordable housing. According to HUD, in 1998 more than 17,000 subsidized units in more than 300 properties left the project-based Section 8 program, more than three times the total from the year before.[6] Generally, owners who opt out can do so because they have good properties in good neighborhoods. The latest data show that 90 percent of subsidized units in properties whose owners say they will likely opt out are located in low-poverty neighborhoods, where good housing also brings better opportunity—more jobs, better schools, less crime.[7] I believe the spillovers from expiring contracts will dominate the housing policy debate for the next decade or more.

By lumping it into a brief section on "the new flexibility," Quigley understates the importance of the HOPE VI program, which was created in 1992 to radically transform the most severely distressed and obsolete public housing into dynamic mixed-income communities. Since its inception, Congress has appropriated more than $5 billion for HOPE VI, including $575 million in fiscal year 2000. When properly leveraged, HOPE VI becomes far more than just another public housing modernization program. "Used wisely," according to neighborhood developer Patrick Clancey, "a $25 million HOPE VI award can leverage another $75 million in private financing, equity investment, and local funds to spark comprehensive neighborhood revitalization."[8]

By limiting much of his analysis to matters that emanate from the 1949 Housing Act, Quigley fails to mention two critically important housing-policy-related developments. The first is the Community Reinvestment Act (CRA), passed in 1977, which requires regulated financial institutions to help meet the credit needs of their local communities.[9] Over time, the CRA has nurtured the creation of a new community-development lending industry that now features "a rich array of affordable lending programs that determine creditworthiness by nontraditional means—techniques that measure the cir-

6. U.S. Department of Housing and Urban Development (1999b, p. iii).
7. U.S. Department of Housing and Urban Development (1999b, p. vi).
8. Clancy (1999, p. 20).
9. "How Well Is CRA Doing?" National Community Reinvestment Coalition (www.ncrc.org/cra/how_dpoing.html. [December 22, 1999]).

92 Brookings-Wharton Papers on Urban Affairs: 2000

cumstances of underserved households more appropriately than established standards."[10] According to the National Community Reinvestment Coalition, since 1977 the CRA has encouraged banks and community organizations to enter into more than 370 agreements worth more than $1.05 trillion in reinvestment dollars for traditionally underserved populations.[11] The CRA has also helped create and sustain a national network of community-based housing development organizations that have become the backbone of the contemporary affordable-housing delivery system. It is this affordable-housing infrastructure, rather than that built in response to the 1949 Housing Act, that represents the future.

Quigley also ignores important policy developments in the secondary mortgage market that are critical to affordable housing. In 1992 Congress gave HUD the responsibility of regulating Fannie Mae and Freddie Mac, the two Government Sponsored Enterprises (GSEs) that help channel billions of dollars a year to the mainstream mortgage market. Through a new system of affordable-housing goals set by HUD, the legislation requires these financial giants to extend the benefits of the secondary mortgage market to tens of millions of low- and moderate-income families, first-time home buyers, and residents of underserved communities, who might not otherwise be able to buy a home.[12]

In late 1999 HUD raised the required percentage of mortgage loans for low- and moderate-income families that the GSEs must buy from the current 42 percent of their total purchases to a new high of 50 percent—a 19 percent increase—in the year 2001. Under the higher goals, Fannie Mae and Freddie Mac will buy an additional $488.3 billion in mortgages that will be used to provide affordable housing for 7 million more low- and moderate-income families over the next ten years, above and beyond the $1.9 trillion in mortgages for 21.1 million families that would have been generated if the current goals had been retained.[13]

10. Stegman (1999, p. 184).
11. "How Well Is CRA Doing?" National Community Reinvestment Coalition (www.ncrc.org/cra/how_dpoing.html. [December 22, 1999]).
12. U.S. Department of Housing and Urban Development, Press Release 99-131, "Cuomo Announces Action to Provide $2.4 Trillion in Mortgages for Affordable Housing for 28.1 Million Families," July 29, 1999, p. 2. This press release can be accessed at (www.hud.gov/pressrel/pr99-131.html).
13. U.S. Department of Housing and Urban Development, Press Release 99-131, "Cuomo Announces Action to Provide $2.4 Trillion in Mortgages for Affordable Housing for 28.1 Million Families," July 29, 1999, p. 1.

Community development finance has also been advanced through secondary market innovations. Recently, a number of securities backed by CRA mortgages have been brought to market by Wall Street investment-banking firms.[14] Though still a trickle, the securitization of affordable mortgage loans, made possible by developments in information technology that allow a more accurate pricing of credit risk, promises to increase home buying opportunities to even lower-income home buyers than those who benefit from mainstream GSE mortgage products. In short, with a decline in federal housing subsidies, it will fall to the secondary market and other private market institutions, in partnership with government, to meet the growing demand for affordable housing.

Quigley concludes his paper with a ringing endorsement of housing vouchers, a policy with which I generally agree. There are some problems with vouchers, however, that should concern housing and urban economists. One of them is the voucher utilization rates. HUD data suggest that around 15 percent of all households who receive vouchers return them to the housing authority unused because they cannot find housing that meets program standards in the time available to them.[15] Because a voucher can be a ticket out of a ghetto into a middle-class neighborhood with better schools and services, we should be concerned about the 15 percent of families who cannot use their voucher to find acceptable housing in the private sector. Research also suggests that success in using a voucher is not necessarily tied to market conditions or to the personal efforts of voucher holders, and that there exists something akin to a Section 8 submarket, in which landlords restrict the number of units available to voucher holders.[16]

It may be that problems with vouchers, combined with the prospect of continued hemorrhaging of Section 8 project-based units from the affordable housing inventory, make this an appropriate time to revisit the production issue.

**William C. Wheaton:** John Quigley's excellent paper on the history of U.S. housing policies characterizes the evolution of such policies as moving from a focus on projects to a focus on tenants. While this is undeniably true, I would characterize this same evolution more as a shift from a focus on places to a focus on people. I would further argue, in the tradition of political economy,

14. See, for example, Stegman (1999, pp. 184, 193–194).

15. U.S. Department of Housing and Urban Development (1995, p. 2).

16. Brian Maney and Sheila Crowley, "Scarcity and Success: Perspectives on Assisted Housing," draft paper prepared for presentation at annual conference of the National Low Income Housing Coalition, April 1999, p. 38.

that early U.S. housing policy probably was designed less to assist low-income people than it was to assist U.S. urban central cities. This is because it emerged in reaction to a *political* rather than *economic* need. Over time, the shift in policies toward people occurred not only because the original place-based policies were failing but also because of realignments in political forces. What I would like to do in this brief discussion is to outline the place-versus-people dilemma in U.S. housing policy and then compare this with the same issue in another policy arena, that of U.S. transportation policy.

*Housing policy: the evolution from place to people.* In theory, person-based policies are aimed at assisting selected categories of individuals—regardless of location. Hence they are "urban" in focus only indirectly, as the targeted group happens to live primarily in urban areas. From the 1930s through 1960, the majority of officially defined "substandard" U.S. housing actually existed in America's *rural* areas. If the housing acts of 1949 and 1954 were truly housing- or person-based, they would have targeted this category of residents equally with those in central cities. This was clearly not the case. Very few smaller impoverished cities had housing authorities, and almost no rural areas did. No: the acts probably had cities as their focus and simply chose housing as the primary object within cities to emphasize.

That cities mattered more than housing can also be seen in the timing of the subsequent CDBG programs. As public housing increasingly became an embarrassment and Washington shifted its focus toward tenant-based policies, it developed the CDBG program as a substitute (but still place-based) policy. Washington hoped that by broadening the focus of its policies to include other capital investments and public services, it could generate some success stories for its urban political constituency.

*Why places?* To understand the origins of U.S. housing policy, one need only remember that in the 1940s the vast majority of America's urban residents actually lived in central-city political jurisdictions. Furthermore, these jurisdictions had enormous political influence. It was not until 1980, for example, that the Illinois state legislature was finally controlled by a coalition of rural and suburban representatives rather than by those from the city of Chicago. How many national political elections prior to 1960 were strongly influenced by America's major central-city mayors?

As urban central cities increasingly developed social and fiscal problems such as white flight, suburban competition, and decaying infrastructure, they petitioned Washington to help them—first as places—and only secondarily as clusters of people. The emergence of U.S. housing policy resulted from this *political* need rather than from an articulated *economic* need by lower-income households.

Perhaps not surprisingly, American housing policy began shifting toward a more person-oriented approach at just about the same time that American suburbs began to wrest political power away from the central cities. Presuming that rural and suburban jurisdictions also supported the idea of a "decent home," they began to see not only that place-based policies were failing but also that a person-oriented approach was more likely to benefit their own residents as well. Washington needed to develop not only successful policies but also policies that were now more spatially neutral.

*The consequences of place- versus people-based housing policies.* Place-based housing policies focused largely on where problems were occurring and not as much on the processes that were creating them. In much of the early discussion surrounding the 1949 and 1954 housing acts, the belief was expressed that by building better housing a whole host of urban social problems, from crime to poverty, would be eradicated. The record, however, shows that most place- or project-based U.S. housing policies might actually have exacerbated these urban social problems.

Current research, including some of the work at this conference, suggests that the clustering of low-income residents, particularly in housing projects, may have increased not only current social problems but also the intergenerational transmission of these problems as well. In this sense, place-based policies created negative externalities that the later person-based policies have at least been trying to address. Early writing by British sociologists in the 1930s also suggested this, but it fell on deaf ears at the time of the creation of the U.S. housing acts. Large housing projects were what America's urban mayors wanted.

Politics as a process is inherently organized by geography (places) rather than by people or interest groups. Perhaps it is only natural that place-based policies emerged at a time when there was little political organization by lower-income social groups.

*Transportation policy: the evolution from people to place!* Housing is not the only sector to be subject to the dilemma of place- or person-based policies. I would argue that in transportation the evolution of policy occurred in the reverse order. In the early twentieth century, state and federal transportation policies largely involved the treatment of automobiles. It was decided to minimally tax both cars and gasoline (unlike policies in Europe) and to separately earmark these tax funds to build and maintain roads. In this regard, transportation policy was spatially ubiquitous or neutral. Highways were to be built wherever the population wanted to settle. Citizens in all locations were clamoring for more roads. This is why I would characterize U.S. highway planning as people- rather than place-oriented. Highways emerged more from an *economic* need by the citizenry and less from the *political* need of jurisdictions.

Over the years, transportation planning has been remarkably free of political influence. Not that roads do not occasionally get built in certain districts, but the civil engineering profession has kept quite tight control over highway development. Partly as a consequence of this technical focus, highway planning has *served* development—rather than being used as a tool to shape and *guide* development. The latter, of course, would be intrinsically very political. In this regard, highway planning never took on any *direct* spatial focus. To be sure, *indirectly* the policy of spatially ubiquitous roads did encourage suburban sprawl, assist rural areas, and hurt central cities.

By the 1970s the urban political lobbyists began to successfully plead their case, and the first clearly directed place-based transportation policy emerged: urban mass transit development. From 1880 to 1920 the early subway systems were largely developed and financed locally, but now the federal government has earmarked a large portion of the highway trust fund for the development of new rail transit systems. All these systems target central-business-district travel, are enormously expensive, and by and large have been significant failures in terms of ridership. Yet they continue to be planned and built in cities where there is little likelihood of economic success. Like early housing policies, the current round of transit funding has emerged to serve a political rather than economic need.

In the case of transportation policy, it has been argued that perhaps place-based policies *should* have emerged earlier. If a better mix of transit and highway infrastructure had more consciously tried to shape America's cities throughout the twentieth century, the externalities of congestion and air pollution might have been better controlled.

## References

Aaron, Henry. 1972. *Shelter and Subsidies*. Brookings.

Alonso, William. 1964. *Location and Land Use: Toward a General Theory of Land Rent*. Harvard University Press.

Bradbury, Katherine L., and Anthony Downs. 1981. *Do Housing Allowances Work?* Brookings.

Break, George F. 1980. *Financing Government in a Federal System*. Brookings.

Clancy, Patrick E. 1999. "Managing Change: A View from the Nonprofit Sector." *Journal of Housing and Community Development* 56(5): 20.

Connerly, Charles E., and Y. Thomas Liou. 1998. "Community Development Block Grants." In *The Encyclopedia of Housing*, edited by Willem Van Vliet, 64–65. Thousand Oaks, Calif.: Sage Publications.

Cummings, Jean L., and Denise DiPasquale. 1998. *Building Affordable Rental Housing: An Analysis of the Low Income Housing Tax Credit*. Boston, Mass.: City Research.

————. 1999. "The Low Income Housing Tax Credit: An Analysis of the First Ten Years." *Housing Policy Debate* 10(2): 251–308.

Foard, Ashley A., and Hilbert Fefferman. 1966. "Federal Urban Renewal Legislation." In *Urban Renewal: The Record and the Controversy*, edited by James Q. Wilson, 71–125. MIT Press.

Follain, James R., and Lisa Sturman Melamed. 1998. "The False Messiah of Tax Policy: What Elimination of the Home Interest Deduction Mortgage Promises and a Careful Look at What It Delivers." *Journal of Housing Research* 9(2): 179–99.

Gabriel, A. Stuart. 1996. "Urban Housing Policy in the 1990s." *Housing Policy Debate* 7(4): 673–93.

Gyourko, Joseph, and Richard Voith. 1999. "The Impact of Housing-Related Tax Expenditures on Urban Form." Unpublished paper.

Haar, Charles M. 1975. *Between the Idea and the Reality: A Study of the Origin, Fate, and Legacy of the Model Cities Program*. Boston: Little, Brown.

Hanushek, Eric A., and John M. Quigley. 1981. "Consumption Aspects of Housing Allowances." In *Do Housing Allowances Work?* edited by Katherine L. Bradbury and Anthony Downs, 185–246. Brookings.

Heller, Walter W., and Joseph A. Pechman. 1967. "Questions and Answers on Revenue Sharing." In *Revenue Sharing and Its Alternatives: What Future for Fiscal Federalism?* 111–17. Joint Economic Committee.

"How Well Is CRA Doing?" National Community Reinvestment Coalition. (www.ncrc.org/cra/how_dpoing.html. [December 22, 1999]).

Katz, Bruce, and Kate Carnevale. 1998. *The State of Welfare Caseloads in America's Cities*. Work in progress. Brookings Institution Center on Urban and Metropolitan Policy.

Mayer, Neil S. 1995. "HUD's First Thirty Years: Big Steps Down a Longer Road." *Cityscape* 1(3): 1–29.

Musgrave, Richard A. 1961. "Approaches to a Fiscal Theory of Political Federalism." In *Public Finances: Needs, Sources, and Utilization; A Conference of the Universities–National Bureau Committee for Economic Research*, 117–29. Princeton University Press.

Muth, Richard F. 1973. "Capital and Current Expenditures in the Production of Housing." In *Government Spending and Land Values: Public Money and Private Gain*, edited by C. Lowell Harriss, 65–78. University of Wisconsin Press.

Nathan, Richard P., and others. 1975. *Monitoring Revenue Sharing*. Brookings.

Nelson, Katherine P., and Jill Khadduri. 1992. "To Whom Should Limited Housing Resources Be Directed?" *Housing Policy Debate* 3(1): 1–56.

Newman, Sandra J. 1999. "Introduction and Overview." In *The Home Front: Implications of Welfare Reform for Housing Policy*, edited by Sandra J. Newman. Washington, D.C.: Urban Institute Press.

Oates, Wallace E. 1972. *Fiscal Federalism*. New York: Harcourt, Brace, Jovanovich.

Ong, Paul. 1998. "Subsidized Housing and Work among Welfare Recipients." *Housing Policy Debate* 9(4): 775.

O'Regan, Katherine M., and John M. Quigley. 1999. "Accessibility and Economic Opportunity." In *Transportation Economics and Policy*, edited by José A. Gomez-Ibanez and others, 437–68. Brookings.

Painter, Gary. 1997. "Does Variation in Public Housing Waiting Lists Induce Intra-Urban Mobility?" *Journal of Housing Economics* 6: 248–76.

Peterson, Paul E., and others. 1986. *When Federalism Works*. Brookings.

Reischauer, Robert D. 1975. "General Revenue Sharing—The Program's Incentives." In *Financing the New Federalism*, edited by Wallace E. Oates, 40–87. Johns Hopkins University Press.

Rich, Michael J. 1992. "UDAG, Economic Development, and the Death and Life of American Cities." *Economic Development Quarterly* 6(2): 150–72.

Schnare, Ann B. 1991. "The Preservation Needs of Public Housing." *Housing Policy Debate* 2(2): 289–318.

Stegman, Michael A. 1991. "The Excessive Costs of Creative Finance: Growing Inefficiencies in the Production of Low Income Housing." *Housing Policy Debate* 2(2): 357–73.

———. 1999. *State and Local Affordable Housing Programs: A Rich Tapestry*. Washington, D.C.: Urban Land Institute.

Straszheim, Mahlon R. 1981. "Participation." In *Do Housing Allowances Work?* edited by Katherine L. Bradbury and Anthony Downs, 113–40. Brookings.

Susin, Scott. 1999. "Rent Vouchers and the Price of Low-Income Housing." Working Paper 98–004. University of California, Berkeley, Program on Housing and Urban Policy.

U.S. Congressional Budget Office. 1994. *The Challenges Facing Federal Rental Assistance Programs*. Government Printing Office.

———. 1996. *Reducing the Deficit: Spending and Revenue Options*. GPO.

U.S. Department of Housing and Urban Development. 1966. *Improving the Quality of Life: A Program Guide to Model Neighborhoods in Demonstration Cities*. GPO.

———. 1995. *Tenant-Based Housing Assistance Works, Issue Brief*. March.

———. 1999a. *A House in Order: Results from the First National Assessment of HUD Housing*. GPO.

———. 1999b. *Opting In: Renewing America's Commitment to Affordable Housing*. April.

———. 1999c. *Waiting in Vain: An Update on America's Rental Housing Crisis*. GPO.

Urban Institute. 1994. *Federal Funds, Local Choices: An Evaluation of the Community Development Block Grant Program*. November.

Wallace, James E. 1995. "Financing Affordable Housing in the United States." *Housing Policy Debate* 6(4): 758–814.

Zisch, William E., Paul H. Douglas, and Robert C. Weaver, eds. 1969. *The Urban Environment: How It Can Be Improved*. New York University Press.

EDWARD L. GLAESER
*Harvard University*

# The Future of Urban Research: Nonmarket Interactions

MODERN GROWTH THEORY argues that intellectual spillovers—idea flows among individuals that are not mediated by the market—are a linchpin of economic progress. In Paul Romer's seminal work, endogenous economic growth requires increasing returns.[1] Without nonmarket intellectual spillovers or some form of externality, increasing returns and economic competition cannot coexist. In Romer's now canonical model of growth, idea flows are seen as the basis for economic progress; the robust relationship between human capital and economic growth has been taken as support for the importance of these intellectual spillovers.

Social capital theory argues that "social capital, connections, social networks are much more correlated with human happiness than is financial capital."[2] In large surveys such as the General Social Survey (GSS), measures of social connection (such as churchgoing or membership in organizations) are more strongly connected with self-reported happiness than income is. This body of research also claims that nonmarket social interactions (for example, membership in choral societies) are an important factor in determining the success of governments and societies at large. Social ties among individuals are thought to be critical in overcoming citizens' apathy and "making democracy work."[3]

These two large, separate literatures have independently concluded that nonmarket interactions are extremely important. Only an economist could be surprised by such a deduction. The tendency of economists to ignore these

---

1. Romer (1986).
2. Putnam (1999).
3. Putnam (1993).

interactions has led us to disregard critical segments of the economy. Over the next ten years, I believe that nonmarket interactions will be at the forefront of economic research.

There are isolated examples of research on nonmarket interactions in urban economics, including Alfred Marshall's famous analysis of human-capital transfers in agglomerated areas and Jane Jacobs's discussion of idea flows among innovators in cities. Work on ghettos and discrimination has indeed often addressed the existence of nonmarket interactions.[4] But traditional urban economics, such as research on real estate, has been primarily oriented toward the market.[5] Papers on local public finance often address externalities but treat them usually as mere assumptions and rarely in depth. Even the seminal work of Paul Krugman in part derives its strength from its ability to explain economic agglomerations without resorting to ad hoc external effects.[6]

### Nonmarket Interactions and Cities

Nonmarket interactions occur when one individual influences another without the exchange of money. The first kind of these interactions involves voluntary participation of both individuals. Neighbors' doing favors for one another is an example of this kind, and this fits our usual paradigm—there is a cost for one person and usually a benefit for another. In some circumstances, such interactions could be done through the market (that is, you could pay your neighbor every time he lent you his rake). These interactions do not involve cash, mainly because they are sufficiently small and sufficiently common that reciprocity saves transaction costs. Occasionally they are done out of altruism (for example, caring for a sick friend). In some cases there may even be a social stigma attached to using or accepting money for a particular service (for example, donating organs).

In dense urban areas, where the extent of the market is great, these interactions may evolve from nonmarket interactions into market interactions. For example, in a small town a relative may serve as an amateur nurse for a sick

---

4. Researchers in this area have emphasized ghetto residents' lack of informational access to mainstream society. Taste-based discrimination (as opposed to statistical discrimination) also reflects a nonmarket interaction in which proximity to one group appears to cause psychic harm to others.

5. Urban sociologists such as Wirth (1938) have given these interactions more attention.

6. Krugman (1991).

outpatient because professional nurses are rare. In a large city, this service might more commonly be performed in the context of a market.

The second kind of nonmarket interactions are classic externalities—for example, the positive effects of role models, or acquiring human capital through the observation of a neighbor's successes and failures.[7] In these cases, it takes effort to stop the interactions—that is, unless the influencing party specifically works to stop the other party from observing, the interaction will take place (at no cost to the influencing party)—so it is much less natural to imagine such interactions' being regulated by the market. Often physically proximate individuals create both kinds of nonmarket interactions with one another. For example, my research is improved by the work of my colleagues both because of the actions they take to help my work (reading my papers, talking to me), which impose costs on them, and because I learn by watching them do research.

Spatial proximity (and hence urban density) facilitates the first kind of nonmarket interaction, as proximity makes reciprocal relationships easier to start and maintain. The second kind of interaction even more strongly depends on spatial proximity. In many cases, these effortless transmissions of ideas and values depend on sight or hearing. Even if the affected person has not seen or heard the influential person himself, it is often true that he knows someone who has had this personal contact. Obviously, the ability to see or hear depreciates sharply with space.

Indeed, empirical evidence supports the idea that the effect of this proximity on nonmarket transactions is large. The work of Adam B. Jaffe, Manuel Trajtenberg, and Rebecca Henderson shows the extent to which patent citations decline with physical distance. Survey data show that the correlation between distance (measured in time to arrive) between friends and frequency of contacts is 64 percent.[8]

In nonmarket transactions (particularly of the second kind), individuals rarely receive the full social returns for their actions: these transactions are rife with externalities. When spatial distance deters standard trade, the increase in transport costs will only reduce market transactions that have social benefit equal to or less than those costs. Because of the externalities associated with nonmarket interactions, however, an equal increase in transport costs will reduce social interactions with social returns that may be much larger than the

7. See Wilson (1987).
8. Jaffe, Trajtenberg, and Henderson (1993); and author's calculations from the General Social Survey.

change in costs. This might explain why small differences in the architecture of work environments (the presence of an office lounge, the arrangement of offices in close proximity) might make a large difference to the overall quality of social connection in the organization.

Urban economics needs to increase its focus on nonmarket interactions because they are central to an understanding of causes and effects in cities. The example of Paul Krugman illustrates that a brilliant theorist can explain cities without addressing nonmarket interactions.[9] But it is less obvious to me why one would want to do so. The flow of ideas and values that occurs through face-to-face interaction may be the most interesting feature of cities. Furthermore, the market for space—that is, the real-estate market—also appears to be driven to a large extent by the relative presence or absence of particular forms of nonmarket interactions in different areas. Urban economics cannot continue to make progress toward understanding its basic issues, namely, the causes and consequences of human density, without learning much more about nonmarket interactions.

Since nonmarket interactions are so determined by space, and the spatial organization of economic activities is so determined by nonmarket interactions, the expansion of study into nonmarket interactions is naturally the province of urban economists. This paper first argues that space is crucial in understanding nonmarket interactions. I then identify areas that urban economics must explore in the future. I begin with idea flows and human-capital spillovers in cities. I then discuss peer effects and the importance of architecture. Next is a treatment of the transmission of values. I end by discussing the city of the future. Naturally, this essay is extremely speculative; I hope that there are many topics that will be explored by urban economists that I have not even identified at this point. Throughout this essay, I include empirical facts that are meant to be provocative.

## Why Are Nonmarket Interactions So Important for Urban Economics?

In this section, I try to make my case about the connection between nonmarket interactions and urban economics; we cannot understand cities and agglomerations without understanding nonmarket interactions. This connection also occurs because urban economists—specialists in the spatial

9. Krugman (1991).

organization of the economy—are particularly focused on the role of spatial distance, which is so important for nonmarket interactions.

### Why Study Nonmarket Interactions?

The central question of urban economics—namely, *Why do cities exist?*—can only be answered by understanding the effects of cities on their residents. And to understand what determines the demand for it, we must understand what urban density does. After all, people form cities because they prefer to live that way: alternative residential arrangements always exist. Only by understanding the positive and negative effects of urban areas can we both explain why cities exist and account for the rise of lower density alternatives to cities (suburbs, edge cities) that has marked the last half century.

The Krugman view of cities maintains that urban areas exist to minimize transportation costs between customers and producers for physical output. The downside of cities, according to this model, is that residents in large agglomerations are far from fixed agricultural resources. While there is certainly some truth in this model, Krugman himself argues that this model is more applicable to the nineteenth century than to the twentieth (let alone the twenty-first). As transport costs have fallen, cities have deindustrialized, and now have less manufacturing than the rest of the country. Lower transport costs mean that these linkages are not very important.[10] A working paper by Guy Dumais, Glenn Ellison, and Edward Glaeser has shown that indeed manufacturing firms do not locate themselves to be close to suppliers and consumers.[11]

Nonmarket interactions are not the only alternative explanation for why cities exist. Alfred Marshall emphasized the role of labor-market pooling in explaining industrial concentration. If firms locate near one another, then workers are insured against firm-specific risk. Firms that are spatially agglomerated may facilitate job shopping, as young workers move from firm to firm to find the best match for them.[12] Indeed, manufacturing firms do choose their location in large part to be close to other firms that use the same types of workers.

However, while this explanation along with transport costs for services can explain the existence of low-density edge cities, they cannot explain the exis-

10. Krugman (1991).

11. Dumais, Ellison, and Glaeser (1997). But Kolko (1999) shows that service firms still locate themselves, in part, to be close to suppliers and consumers. Indeed, cities are generally centers for such service firms. Certainly one benefit of urban residence is the elimination of transport costs for personal services that are difficult to transport.

12. Marshall (1890). Rotemberg and Saloner (1990) have argued that the agglomeration of firms also eliminates problems related to monopsony employers.

tence of dense downtowns or even the renewed interest in denser planned communities (such as Disney's much-studied Celebration). For labor-market pooling to work, workers must be able to change employers without changing residences. This does not in any sense require a dense downtown. A perpetual exurban sprawl works just as well. Employees just need many prospective employers within a reasonable commute.

Indeed, the twentieth century has seen a spreading of cities into lower-density suburbs and edge cities. This spread means that agglomerations are larger—Los Angeles is a lower-density city that creates proximity (at driving distance) to a truly immense number of consumers and producers. The average resident of Los Angeles in 2000 is both living and working within a lower density than an equivalent resident of New York (or most large cities) in 1900. Maybe dense downtowns are simply dinosaurs that are slowly going extinct. Perhaps the future of America lies in agglomerations like the suburbs and edge cities of Los Angeles, which radiate farther and farther out from a downtown of primarily historical interest. I do not think so. While populations of traditional dense cities have not been climbing, property values have been soaring. New York City does not seem like an obsolete agglomeration at this point. Nor does Chicago or Boston. Property values—the ultimate measure of demand for a location—in these areas are extraordinarily high.[13] These values do not just represent a general rise in asset values, as the central-city property values have seen a greater increase than property values in outlying areas. More technically, demand for the densest areas seems to be high.

The demand for dense areas seems particularly strong among the richest residents. During the 1980s the average income of people within three miles of the central business district (CBD) in New York, Chicago, and Boston rose 13 percent more than the average income of people living between three and ten miles from the CBD in the same cities.[14] Indeed, figure 5 shows that income declines with distance from the city center in several older cities when we consider only census tracts within three miles of the city center.[15] My presentation of these data is not meant to deny the fact that the prevailing pattern

13. Populations in New York City and Boston have tended to be stable, in no small part because of extraordinarily difficult zoning environments that make new construction extremely costly. A second reason that populations are stable in these areas is that success often means that the wealthy, who are often single or have small families, have been replacing poorer, larger families.

14. Author's calculations of the 1980 and 1990 U.S. Censuses.

15. In many of these cities, the richest census tracts in the metropolis are closest to the city center.

in the United States is that the rich suburbanize. Rather, my purpose is to suggest that cities continue to be attractive to the rich and that the demand for agglomeration is not clearly decreasing.

The new spate of moderate-density planned communities also suggests continued belief in the value of density. Walt Disney's Celebration is built in an area where land is cheap (certainly relative to large urban areas) and where more density has little effect on reducing commuting times. But Disney has created a "walking" town. The stated reason for this development is that high density would lead to more desirable social (nonmarket) interactions among neighbors. Disney's Celebration is in some sense the epitome of the building philosophy referred to as the "New Urbanism." The aim of this philosophy is to produce a comfortable community echoing the perceived neighborliness of a more bucolic past. (The fact that such a past may never have existed is irrelevant.) Lower densities and the greater transport costs facing interactions may be barriers to forming socially pleasant communities, and the planners of Celebration have structured their city accordingly. Of course, we have yet to see whether Celebration will be a long-term success, a model for successful communities elsewhere, or a brief aberration.

The continued preeminence of New York City and the design of Celebration both suggest that the demand for urban density is based on many factors beyond reduced transport costs for market transactions. New York City's growth is significantly based on the strength of the financial industry, which is crammed into two small areas of Manhattan. Physical transport costs are almost irrelevant in this industry—success in finance is based almost entirely on information. By locating in Manhattan, financial firms maintain their access to the continued swirl of information that surrounds the stock market. These information flows deeply concern a financial market, but they are themselves only rarely priced through a market (newsletters and illegally bought insider information are two forms of financial information that is traded). Less information-sensitive elements of the finance industry have left the city; the key to New York's continuing success is that financial firms are willing to pay extremely high costs to be close to this information. Of course, it is possible that electronic interactions will eliminate this role of cities, but as I have argued elsewhere, there are many reasons why this seems unlikely in the near future.[16] Most clearly, the high property values in Wall Street bespeak the continued demand for urban proximity.

16. Gaspar and Glaeser (1998).

Another benefit of urban density is the supply of social interactions outside the workplace. These interactions may, for example, be similar to those that seem to motivate the design of a planned community like Celebration. The designers of Celebration seem to be following the logic of Jane Jacobs, who argued that neighborhood liveliness and safety are desirable amenities that are created in part by neighborhood density.[17] Indeed, the demand for New York (or Paris, for that matter) comes in part from the remarkable social life that is possible in that city. That social life is a function, in no small part, of the population density within the city. Indeed, the fans of Haussmann's Parisian boulevards applaud the magnificent thoroughfares crowded with Parisians. Haussmann's detractors attack the empty wide streets away from the center city, which replaced an older, more human-scale city.

Of course, other forms of nonmarket social interactions are often cited as reasons for the decline of urban areas. Typically, crime and poor education are given as primary reasons for the flight of the middle class to the suburbs. Crime is clearly a nonmarket interaction. If we accept the view of James Coleman's report[18] (and hundreds of later studies) that peer effects are the most important ingredients of learning, then education should be seen as an example of cross-person information externalities. Just as we need to understand nonmarket interactions to understand the continued success of New York, we must understand nonmarket interactions to understand the exodus from less successful cities. Put another way, the strength of the suburbs comes (to some extent) from their ability to create positive nonmarket interactions.

### Provocative Facts: Happiness, Money, and Nonmarket Interactions

One of the facts that supports the contentions of social capital theory is that nonmarket interactions appear to correlate more with self-reported happiness than with financial well-being. In this brief empirical section, I report results from the National Opinion Research Center's General Social Survey on happiness and nonmarket interactions.[19] While there are doubts about what these self-reported happiness measures actually capture, the literature has tended to support the view that they have some meaning (even if they are not exactly equivalent to a utility level). The survey uses a one-zero variable, which captures whether individuals say that they are happy. A large number of the sample (88 percent) say yes to this question. Since there is such a small number of

17. Jacobs (1961).
18. Coleman (1966).
19. Data available at (www.norc.uchicago.edu/gss/homepage.htm [March 28, 2000]).

respondents who say no to this, we would not expect there to be very large coefficients.

Table 1 shows results from probit regressions. Coefficients are marginal effects of the variables based on the probit coefficients. The effect of income is large. A one-log-point increase in income (one standard deviation) raises happiness by 3.77 percent (about one-tenth of a standard deviation). The effect of education is also large: college graduates are 6.1 percent more likely to say that they are happy than high-school dropouts are. The effect of city size is small and driven mostly by people in the biggest cities. Holding everything else constant, individuals living in cities are less likely to say that they are happy.[20]

The one direct measure of a nonmarket interaction in this regression—marriage—shows a profound effect on happiness. The 5.8 percent increase in happiness for men associated with marriage suggests that marriage raises happiness more than income does. Although marriage is positively related to happiness, there is no way of knowing (without real exogenous variation) whether this represents happier people getting married or marriage creating happier people. This is generally true about most of the independent variables in this discussion, and this is why these facts are merely provocative rather than in any sense definitive.

The second regression shows that happy people are also those who say that they are more trusting and who are likely to think that others are fair or helpful. While there is no clear causal interpretation, this regression suggests a connection between happiness and one's social attitudes. The third regression shows that happiness is higher for people who socialize with friends, neighbors, and relatives. A one-standard-deviation increase in the variable capturing socializing with friends increases happiness by about one percentage point. It is also true in this data set that membership in nonprofessional organizations increases this happiness measure. The fourth regression shows the connection between self-reported church attendance and happiness. A one-standard-deviation increase in church attendance increases happiness by 2.5 percent.

The final regression shows the connection between one's happiness and the average level of self-reported happiness in a constructed peer group (people in the GSS who live in the same state and share one's education level). It appears that people who live around other happy people are also happier. While there are many issues in peer-effect regressions of this sort (which are dis-

---

20. Of course, unhappy people may choose to live in the largest cities. This result is robust if we control for how long the respondent has lived in the community.

*Brookings-Wharton Papers on Urban Affairs: 2000*

**Table 1. The Determinants of Happiness[a]**

| Variable | Happiness indicator (1) | Happiness indicator (2) | Happiness indicator (3) | Happiness indicator (4) | Happiness indicator (5) |
|---|---|---|---|---|---|
| Logarithm of income | 0.0377 | 0.0294 | 0.0386 | 0.0368 | 0.0378 |
| | (0.0026) | (0.0033) | (0.0034) | (0.0026) | (0.0026) |
| Less than 30 years old | 0.0538 | 0.0630 | 0.0468 | 0.0575 | 0.0531 |
| | (0.0065) | (0.0075) | (0.0086) | (0.0063) | (0.0065) |
| 30 to 39 | 0.0235 | 0.0294 | 0.0331 | 0.0277 | 0.0232 |
| | (0.0073) | (0.0087) | (0.0090) | (0.0071) | (0.0073) |
| 40 to 49 | 0.0546 | 0.0055 | 0.0106 | 0.0085 | 0.0051 |
| | (0.0082) | (0.0100) | (0.0102) | (0.0080) | (0.0082) |
| More than 60 | 0.0370 | 0.0211 | 0.0435 | 0.0344 | 0.0365 |
| | (0.0069) | (0.0091) | (0.0085) | (0.0069) | (0.0069) |
| Black | −0.0468 | −0.0207 | −0.0443 | −0.0598 | −0.0427 |
| | (0.0077) | (0.0088) | (0.0103) | (0.0081) | (0.0076) |
| Other race | −0.0188 | −0.0052 | −0.0395 | −0.0245 | −0.0168 |
| | (0.0139) | (0.0153) | (0.0211) | (0.0143) | (0.0138) |
| School dropout | −0.0353 | −0.0209 | −0.0355 | −0.0306 | −0.0336 |
| | (0.0064) | (0.0077) | (0.0081) | (0.0063) | (0.0064) |
| College graduate | 0.0261 | 0.0074 | 0.0283 | 0.0225 | 0.0256 |
| | (0.0060) | (0.0080) | (0.0077) | (0.0061) | (0.0060) |
| Married | 0.0371 | 0.0427 | 0.0366 | 0.0329 | 0.0373 |
| | (0.0072) | (0.0091) | (0.0095) | (0.0072) | (0.0072) |
| Male | −0.0197 | −0.0073 | −0.0243 | −0.0107 | −0.0198 |
| | (0.0074) | (0.0089) | (0.0097) | (0.0073) | (0.0074) |
| Married*male | 0.0215 | 0.0127 | 0.0303 | 0.01825 | 0.0216 |
| | (0.0089) | (0.0112) | (0.0110) | (0.0089) | (0.0089) |
| Logarithm of city size | −0.0034 | −0.0034 | −.0023 | −0.0025 | −0.0031 |
| | (0.0011) | (0.0013) | (0.0014) | (0.0011) | (0.0011) |
| Year | 0.0011 | 0.0017 | 0.0022 | 0.0013 | 0.0011 |
| | (0.0005) | (0.0008) | (0.0007) | (0.0005) | (0.0006) |
| Trust indicator | | 0.0279 | | | |
| | | (0.0067) | | | |
| Thinks people are helpful | | 0.0304 | | | |
| | | (0.0065) | | | |
| Thinks people are fair | | 0.0470 | | | |
| | | (0.0069) | | | |
| Socializes within community | | | 0.0054 | | |
| | | | (0.0014) | | |
| With relatives | | | 0.0055 | | |
| | | | (0.0018) | | |
| With friends | | | 0.0083 | | |
| | | | (0.0019) | | |
| With parents | | | −0.0007 | | |
| | | | (0.0013) | | |
| In the bar | | | −0.0038 | | |
| | | | (0.0018) | | |
| Attends religious institution | | | | 0.0249 | |
| | | | | (0.0024) | |
| Mean community happiness | | | | | 0.4675 |
| | | | | | (0.0974) |
| N | 17,216 | 10,450 | 10,208 | 17,091 | 17,216 |
| Pseudo $R^2$ | 0.0632 | 0.0848 | 0.0776 | 0.0725 | 0.0650 |

Source: General Social Survey (GSS), 1972–94.
a. Numbers in parentheses are standard errors.

cussed later), it certainly does not seem implausible that happiness declines when one has many market and nonmarket interactions with unhappy neighbors. This evidence is meant to be provocative rather than convincing, and to suggest the importance of nonmarket interactions, relative to wealth, in driving human happiness.

### What Urban Economists Can Bring to the Study of Nonmarket Interactions

I have just argued that urban economists must understand nonmarket interactions to understand why people organize themselves spatially into cities and suburbs. At the same time, I also believe that urban economists have particular skills that make them natural specialists in the field of nonmarket interactions. If economics as a whole increases its focus on intellectual spillovers and social capital, it is natural that urban economists should be in the vanguard of such movements. The nonmarket interactions that are of primary interest to the profession as a whole work poorly over long distances. As such, the spatial nature of these interactions means that spatial economists are particularly appropriate students of these effects.

In fact, proving the importance of these interactions requires a geographic focus. Estimation generally involves the assumption that these effects decay spatially. The general method of estimating peer effects involves studying whether behavior in the near neighborhood of particular subjects influences the subjects.[21] If we did not believe that peer influence depreciates over space, then this method of estimation would make no sense.

The underlying point is that many of the nonmarket interactions that are particularly interesting have very high transportation costs. Individuals who are far away from one another lose the ability to influence one another. In the realm of intellectual transfers, it is easy to transmit a particular piece of information. However, when two people are close to each other, they observe an infinitely larger amount of information by watching each other. In cases where people do not know what information they want to transfer, these effects become particularly important.

Added to the problem of high transport costs, it is also clear that most of the nonmarket interactions that we are interested in have substantial externalities. Given this condition, a small increase in distance may have profound social effects. In a market interaction, an increase in transport costs of X dol-

21. As we get more careful in our estimation, the urban economists' particular focus on endogenous choice of neighborhood becomes quite important.

lars will block transactions with social value of X dollars or less. Transactions that bring more than X dollars' worth of value will still take place.[22] With nonmarket interactions involving two individuals (or more), the total social gains may be equal to 2X (or more). So, for example, consider a social exchange that brings each participant 0.9X worth of utility. This exchange will be blocked if the costs of interacting equal X.

In many cases, the external benefits from nonmarket interactions are much higher than any of the benefits that accrue to any particular individual. For example, in the construction of a network formed of individuals, each person, by strengthening the connection between himself and his neighbors in the network, provides benefits to every other member of the network. As such, the gap between private and social benefits may be quite large. As I discuss later, this may explain why seemingly trivial differences in physical layouts seem to play a role in the formation of networks. A slight increase in transport costs can reduce everyone's investment, and if there are positive complementarities in investment, then these small changes in the costs of meetings can have a major effect on the functioning of the network. The classic claim is that the introduction of a coffee lounge can change significantly the interaction of an academic department.

## The Transfer of Ideas in Cities

I begin with two preliminary facts and then discuss the prospects for future research on the transfer of ideas in cities.

Figure 1 shows the relationship between urbanization and the level of development. There are very few variables that are as strongly correlated with a country's level of development as its level of urbanization. Naturally, this relationship levels off for very rich countries (where urbanization is close to complete). While there are a vast number of reasons for this relationship (for example, farming declines with development, and the ability to build cities is larger for richer countries), we still do not really understand why this relationship is so powerful.

---

22. In this case, I am only speaking about classic conditions in which there is one price. In a bargaining situation, it is easy to imagine cases where the social returns that are blocked by transport costs equal to X dollars are worth *more* than X dollars.

**Figure 1. Urbanization and Income across Countries**

Urbanization, 1990

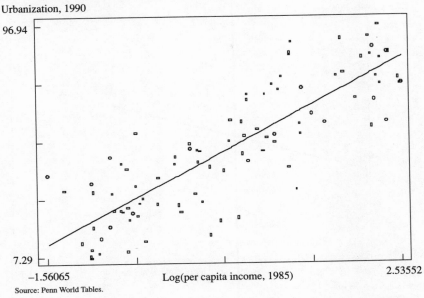

Log(per capita income, 1985)

Source: Penn World Tables.

Figure 2 shows the relationship between nonprimate urbanization in 1960 and later economic growth. Nonprimate urbanization denotes the share of the country's population that inhabits all cities except for the largest one. I eliminate the largest city because these cities tend to be political capitals that exist because of the tendency of nondemocratic governments to transfer resources to the capital.[23] The presence of a bloated primate city is not the sign of a healthy urban system. Interestingly, this figure shows a quite significant relationship between the initial level of urbanization and subsequent economic growth. Of course, one explanation for this relationship is the absence of other control variables (though this relationship does survive most basic controls). Alternatively, the presence of cities may be important for generating growth, perhaps through the generation of new ideas.

*Ideas and Cities*

At least since the contribution of Robert Solow, most economists believe that economic growth relies on technological change.[24] In the 1980s Paul

23. See Ades and Glaeser (1995).
24. Solow (1956). A prominent exception is the work of Young (1995), who argues that the growth of Singapore is best understood as the result of accumulation of physical and human capital.

**Figure 2. GDP Growth and Nonprimate City Urbanization**

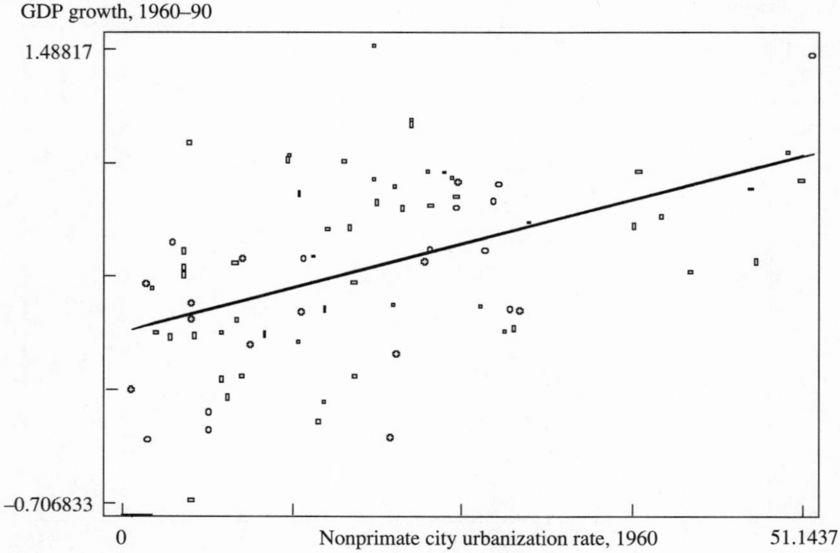

GDP growth, 1960–90

Source: Penn World Tables.

Romer argued that this technological change could only create endogenous growth if the benefits of new ideas are reaped by the entire society, not just by the innovator who created those ideas. To combine increasing returns with market competition, Romer required that the increasing returns occurred outside of each firm.

While Romer's paper is certainly theoretically correct, there are many cases where property rights over ideas appear to be respected. After all, patents are enforced. Why is the production of ideas not just like the production of any other commodity? Of course, technological ideas are probably the only items that can be termed a genuine public good. Private ownership and sale of new ideas is sure to be inefficient for this reason. But one could still imagine a world where each new idea was sold and the benefits generally reaped by its creator.

There are many reasons why this is generally infeasible. The market in ideas may function poorly since the transaction has already taken place by the time the purchaser knows what he is buying. By definition, the market for ideas is marked by asymmetric information. As such, ideas are occasionally kept private (for example, the recipe for Coca-Cola), but this is rare. More commonly, patents serve to protect certain uses of a particular idea. But just as the patent gives the idea's creator property rights over one use of the idea, the patent office makes sure that the idea itself becomes public information, and patents do not generally forbid uses of ideas in areas that do not compete with the original use of the idea. The fact that a market for ideas cannot operate efficiently means both that there will always be too little production of new ideas (since creators of new ideas rarely receive the full social returns of their innovations) and that ideas are rarely kept all that private. Since you cannot sell most ideas, you might as well give them away.

Robert Lucas linked this point with the ideas of Jane Jacobs on the transfer of knowledge in cities. While Alfred Marshall is really the pioneer of the view of the city as a place where knowledge is transferred (as I discuss in the next section), Jacobs deserves credit for putting together the view that ideas come from urban areas. In cities there are many ideas floating around, which makes imitation easier and news of breakthroughs more accessible. Jacobs's model emphasized that new ideas are generally combinations of old ideas. This model has recently been taken up by economists, including Martin L. Weitzman.[25]

Jacobs particularly emphasized the role of urban *diversity* in the formation of new ideas. One way to extend Jacobs's thinking is to say that the size of intellectual breakthroughs is a function of the distance between the old ideas that are combined. Thus a combination of two ideas that both come from nail manufacturing can produce a slightly better nail, but the combination of an idea from nail manufacturing with one from railroads can lead to the industrialization of the nail industry.

While Jacobs's ideas are appealing (and she cites enough examples to indicate that this process sometimes occurs and sometimes is important), without real empirical work in this area it is impossible to understand whether these effects are widespread or particular. Does Jacobs's famous story of the invention of the brassiere (which happened when a dressmaker used an idea from dressmaking in making lingerie) represent the norm, or is it an unusual example? It is an empirically difficult process to turn Jacobs's (or Marshall's or Lucas's) thoughts about the flow of ideas and growth into a body of facts that represents solid social science. First, we must understand the importance of idea flows for economic growth. Work of this kind is difficult, at both the national and the local level.

25. Lucas (1988); Jacobs (1969); Marshall (1890); Weitzman (1998).

The evidence for the importance of knowledge spillovers in growth at the national level is at best indirect. The Lucas endogenous-growth model focused on embodied human-capital spillovers rather than on disembodied ideas.[26] People have found evidence supporting this model by examining the connection between human capital and economic growth (or economic productivity). A very robust relationship between the initial levels of human capital and later growth at the country level[27] is the most direct piece of evidence, but clearly this is not strong evidence for the Romer view. Evidence on the positive effects of foreign direct investment may also suggest the role that idea transfers can play in growth. Again, this may or may not be evidence for the Romer viewpoint. Thus the critical theoretical insight of growth theory has almost no solid empirical foundations in international data.

The evidence at the subnational level is similar. There is a substantial connection between human capital at the city level and later growth. This fact appears to support the importance of idea transfers.[28] Naturally, there are many possible interpretations of these data, some of which do not relate at all to the existence of intellectual spillovers. In the next section I present two facts related to this question and suggest an alternative interpretation.

Other work has attempted to test indirect implications of the Jacobs viewpoint for local growth. In an earlier paper with my colleagues, we presented evidence suggesting that urban diversity and competition is good for growth.[29] J. Vernon Henderson, April Kuncoro, and Matt Turner suggest that the diversity-growth connection is far less clear.[30] In any case, suggestive evidence hardly constitutes a solid empirical foundation. Some researchers have looked for the level effects rather than the growth effects of knowledge spillovers. James E. Rauch shows that wages and rents are higher for individuals in high-human-capital cities (holding individual human capital constant).[31] Again, this is evidence for the Lucas model.

Given that idea transfers may be the linchpin of economic progress, it is clear that we need more than a few stories and some suggestive correlations. Urban economists should play a major role in providing this evidence. At this point, research must concentrate on more direct measures of innovations and

---

26. Lucas (1988).

27. Barro (1991).

28. For a longer perspective, see Glaeser, Scheinkman, and Shleifer (1995) or Simon and Nardinelli (1996).

29. Glaeser and others (1992).

30. Henderson, Kuncoro, and Turner (1995).

31. Rauch (1994).

idea flows. One example of such evidence is the work of Adam B. Jaffe, Manuel Trajtenberg, and Rebecca Henderson, which documents that patent citations are geographically determined. A patent is much more likely to cite another patent if that patent was taken out by someone living in the same area.[32] While this work is exciting, many of the most important innovations have nothing to do with patents, so this type of work can only capture a very small part of the overall growth process.

A second example of more direct work is the research done by David B. Audretsch and Maryann P. Feldman.[33] This work looks at new product innovations using a fascinating database. New product introductions are a more direct measure of intellectual progress than employment or population growth, but their work has not yet yielded truly direct evidence on idea flows. Thus we are lacking even the most basic evidence on the size and importance of these flows.

Ideally, we would want to know much more than this basic information. For example, we would like to quantify the importance of intellectual cross-fertilization versus direct idea flows. Is Jacobs right? Are the important ideas the ones that travel across goods and production processes? Or alternatively, do the important idea transfers all come from within one area of production? To some extent, patent-flow evidence can yield some information on this. For example, it is useful to know that the expected importance of an innovation (as measured by the number of citations a new patent will itself generate) is unrelated to the diversity of patents that the new patent itself cites, but we need to know more.

There is also an academic debate about the relative importance of embodied and disembodied ideas. Does the transfer of ideas mainly occur through libraries and through reverse engineering of new products (that is, using disembodied ideas)? Or do the important idea transfers occur because people in one firm move to another firm? The literature on Silicon Valley suggests the importance of intellectual transfers through workers' changing firms.[34] The answer to this question has great bearing on the future of cities. Since moving people spatially is much more difficult than moving products, the notion that idea transfers require people to move makes urban agglomeration more important.

---

32. Jaffe, Trajtenberg, and Henderson (1993).
33. Audretsch and Feldman (1996).
34. See Saxenian (1994).

**Figure 3. Population Growth and Human Capital**

Population growth, 1970–90

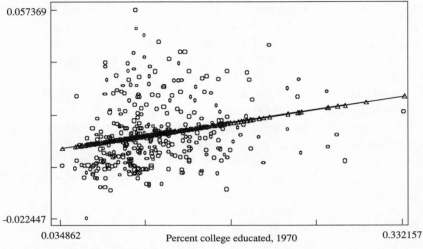

Source: Census of Population and Housing, 1970 and 1990.

Another critical question is the importance of industrial organization. Monopolies may be either good or bad for intellectual progress. Monopolies will tend to reap more of the social benefits from their innovations since they have fewer competitors who imitate them. Therefore it may be that monopolies invest more in idea production. Alternatively, competitive firms may have stronger incentives to invest. Certainly the empirical facts support the positive view of competition (more competitive areas or city-industries tend to grow faster), but the aggregate nature of this evidence means that it has many possible interpretations.

A final key issue is the role of the Internet. Will it become the primary field within which ideas are moved, or will physical space retain its importance? Again, this is an area of critical importance for the future of the city that needs research.

## Formation of Human Capital

Figures 3 and 4 show the relationship between growth at the county level and the initial percentage of college-educated people in that county. Figure 3 measures growth in terms of population growth. Figure 4 measures growth in

**Figure 4. Housing Price Growth and Human Capital**

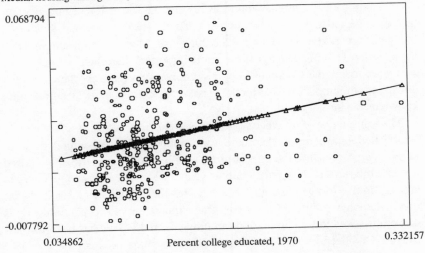

Median housing value growth, 1970–90

0.068794

-0.007792

0.034862                    Percent college educated, 1970                    0.332157

Source: Census of Population and Housing, 1970 and 1990.

terms of growth in self-reported housing values. In both cases, there is a robust positive relationship between growth and the initial level of human capital (correlation coefficients are 23 and 25 percent for housing and population growth respectively). These are among the few reliable data about the factors that predict growth at the city, county, or metropolitan-area level.

One interpretation of these data is that better-educated cities produce more innovations and that these innovations in turn attract workers in the future. Alternatively, cities with more educated workers may generate human-capital spillovers that become more valuable over time. As skills have become more important since 1975, it is not surprising that people are now willing to pay more to live in cities that have high-skilled populations. This occurs because people learn from one another, and will learn more when the people around them have more human capital.

Alfred Marshall introduced the idea that learning from neighbors is one reason why industries agglomerate. He argues that in dense agglomerations "the mysteries of the trade become no mystery but are, as it were, in the air."[35] Marshall's ideas ring true to anyone who has ever learned from phys-

35. Marshall (1890).

ical neighbors, either in a classic mentoring relationship or through less formal mechanisms.

Marshall's idea of intellectual transfers and the formation of human capital are connected to the large literature in education research, which documents that peers are more important than anything else. Most research suggests that the benefits of having better peers are more important than class size or teacher salaries. Indeed, the Coleman Report's emphasis on the importance of peer effects was the empirical basis for the massive experiment in social engineering known as busing.

The importance of intellectual transfers in the urban context is less clearly established. I have argued that there is an increase in human-capital accumulation in cities because the age-earnings profile is steeper in urban areas and because migrants receive only small wage increases when they come to urban areas. Migrants' wages rise only over time, but these wage increases stay with them when they return to rural areas. One explanation of this phenomenon is that cities speed the accumulation of human capital.[36] This has been formalized in a model in which learning is faster in cities because the speed of interaction with neighbors is faster there.[37] Again, this is at best indirect evidence for the presence of such transfers.

One critical question is whether these transfers are really nonmarket interactions. When students learn from teachers whom they pay, this is clearly a market interaction. When workers learn from one another within a firm, the firm presumably sets wage scales so as to compensate the teachers and charge the learners. Of course, there is surely some learning that occurs outside of firms, and in many cases firms may not have the wage flexibility to appropriately price the transfer of human capital. Within private schools, at least, the transfer of human capital can also be priced. Schools may charge lower tuition to students who are likely to give human capital and higher tuition to students who are likely to be big acquirers (at least this is a reasonable facsimile of the logic behind college scholarships). Marshall's theory may have been appropriate for an era when connections among firms and workers were weak at best. In the modern corporate era, however, the importance of nonmarket human-capital spillovers is perhaps small.

In this case, we are lacking both direct and indirect evidence on the size and nature of these interactions. There are many forms of indirect evidence that are valuable. The location of industries and people in principle provides

36. See Glaeser and Mare (forthcoming).
37. Glaeser (1999).

evidence about these effects. One of my recent papers shows that human-capital-oriented individuals usually choose to live in cities.[38] But do people choose urban areas on the basis of what they are going to learn? Do firms locate in areas where it is likely that their workers might learn from other workers outside of their firm? We do not even know if the age-earnings slope is steeper in higher-human-capital areas.

Presumably much of the nonmarket human-capital acquisition that is of interest to urban economists occurs for individuals before college, and outside of school. Certainly, parents care about the pool of children that their progeny will interact with both inside and outside of school. Indeed, there is a significant body of anecdotes about children from ghetto environments who, despite going to elite high schools, ended up in jail or dead because of interactions with peers in their own neighborhood.

Again, as valuable as this sort of anecdotal evidence can be, we need much more rigorous evidence on the nature and magnitude of human-capital spillovers. The best form of evidence would connect the acquisition of measurable skills with the presence of these skills in the physical neighborhood. For example, if skill as a computer programmer increased with randomly assigned exposure to other programmers, this would be good evidence for this theory. Of course, this evidence would only confirm the importance of this type of phenomenon in a particular context. Given the rising importance of skill accumulation in the economy and our beliefs about the impact of these skills on growth, the importance of studying how people learn from their peers is high. We know that little about wages can be explained either by measures of innate ability or by formal measures of schooling levels. It seems likely that the bulk of the heterogeneity across individuals has to do with the skills that are acquired outside of school.

These issues also relate to the costs of ghettos to minority youths. The traditional spatial-mismatch hypothesis tended to focus on the physical transport costs of segregated minorities getting to jobs. The modern literature argues that the costs of ghettos lie in human-capital accumulation.[39] According to the skill-accumulation view, there are no benefits that accrue to firms that would move into a ghetto. This model suggests that ghetto residence can be the result of parents' choices in which human-capital accumulation losses for their chil-

38. Glaeser (1999).
39. The traditional view was hard to reconcile with free choice of location by both adult minorities and firms.

dren in ghettos are weighed against lower housing costs in those areas.[40] If ghettos are bad because skills are not accumulated there, proper measurement of neighborhood effects on human-capital accumulation is one part of understanding the negative effects of ghettos on their residents.

## Peer Effects and Transfer of Values

In some circumstances, human-capital transfers are called peer effects, especially when they relate to the transmission of values. If crime, drug use, and unplanned pregnancies relate to these types of effects, then understanding these effects is crucial for improving conditions in low-income areas. This idea has long tenure in the economics literature. John Kain suggested that one reason ghettos are harmful for African Americans is that information is not exchanged between young people and working, successful mentors.[41]

For the purposes of this paper, I first duplicate the traditional form of estimating peer effects. The basic methodology involves regressing an outcome on the average level of that outcome among a peer group. The General Social Survey does not really provide information about a peer group, but within its primary sampling units, samples are fairly geographically concentrated. The methodology for sampling means that a surveyor goes to an area and then proceeds geographically through the area until he or she has acquired the right number of responses. While at that point in the survey it is not clear who lives in the geographic area, the data show who is in the same metropolitan area during the same year. For these groupings there is a reasonable chance that these respondents live close to one another. Thus I create an admittedly false peer group composed of those subjects from the same metropolitan area who were surveyed during the same year. In the better work on peer effects, peer groups will be identified more accurately.[42]

In table 2, I examine a variety of outcomes for which it is reasonable to expect there to be peer effects. In forming the peer group average, I naturally exclude the subject. I also control for a battery of reasonable personal attributes that might plausibly lead to a spurious correlation between individual behavior and the behavior of peers.

---

40. Inner-city neighborhoods also attract the poor because residents do not need to own cars. See Glaeser, Kahn, and Rappaport (1999).

41. Kain (1968).

42. See, for example, Case and Katz (1991).

The four variables that I consider are membership in organizations, socializing within the community, drinking, and being in favor of racial exclusiveness. In the case of the last variable, I examined whites alone. There are several explanations regarding peer effects for the different variables. The first two variables are presumably standard network variables. When other members of your community are members of an organization, the social network is denser and you may want to join more organizations yourself. Naturally, it takes two to socialize, so we expect there to be a positive relationship between one person's socialization and his or her neighbor's socialization. The stories that lie behind the peer effects for drinking and racist opinions are somewhat different. In these cases, I would imagine that transmission of values across peers is likely to be the most powerful mechanism inducing correlation across these variables.

In table 2, regressions 1–4, we find a positive correlation between peer outcomes and individual outcomes. The two network variables have very similar coefficients. An increase by one in the community average of the variable raises individual outcomes by about 0.4. The taste-for-racial-exclusion effect is larger. The peer effect on drinking is largest.

There are two major sources of bias for these variables. The first source of bias is location-specific omitted variables (for example, a drinking ban) that induce correlations between peer outcomes. The second source of bias is that peers elect to be near one another and that there is significant correlation in unobservables among peers. In principle, the first problem can be mitigated through instrumentation strategies. The second problem is best handled with a natural experiment over neighborhoods like "Moving to Opportunity" (discussed below).

The general instrumental-variables strategy is to use average exogenous characteristics of peers to instrument for the average endogenous characteristic that is used in the regression. In a study by Anne C. Case and Lawrence F. Katz, parental characteristics are used to instrument for children's characteristics.[43] This approach will be a problem if we believe that the exogenous characteristics may themselves have a direct effect on outcomes. Nevertheless, in regressions 5 to 8, I show results using this somewhat problematic methodology. In this case, I use the average marital status, years of education, age, and income of the peer group as instruments for the dependent variable.

In three of the four cases, the peer effects remain significant. In most cases, standard errors increase. Because of the uncertainty over specification, it is

43. Case and Katz (1991).

**Table 2. Peer Effects and Individual Outcomes**[a]

| Variable | Any membership (1) | Socializes within community (2) | Drinks (3) | For racial exclusion (4) | Any membership (IV)[b] (5) | Socializes within community[b] (6) | Drinks (IV)[b] (7) | For racial exclusion (IV)[b] (8) |
|---|---|---|---|---|---|---|---|---|
| Intercept | -1.4588 (0.2077) | 2.8570 (0.2579) | 0.6321 (0.0583) | 0.2074 (0.0956) | -0.8884 (0.2258) | 1.5310 (0.6867) | 1.3887 (0.1004) | 0.1871 (0.0992) |
| Logarithm of income | 0.2708 (0.0199) | -0.0718 (0.0226) | -0.0492 (0.0047) | -0.0157 (0.0092) | 0.2911 (0.0204) | -0.0582 (0.0236) | -0.0061 (0.0022) | -0.0162 (0.0092) |
| Less than 30 years old | -0.2747 (0.0603) | 0.5377 (0.0664) | -0.1184 (0.0143) | 0.1754 (0.0258) | -0.2923 (0.0612) | 0.5276 (0.0670) | -0.1222 (0.0147) | 0.1757 (0.0258) |
| 30 to 39 | -0.2669 (0.0581) | 0.1650 (0.0646) | -0.9135 (0.0137) | 0.1381 (0.0250) | -0.2957 (0.0590) | 0.1631 (0.0650) | -0.0962 (0.0141) | 0.1385 (0.0250) |
| 40 to 49 | -0.1200 (0.0620) | 0.0169 (0.0687) | -0.0545 (0.0147) | 0.0858 (0.0268) | -0.1407 (0.0629) | 0.0240 (0.0692) | -0.0524 (0.0151) | 0.0858 (0.0268) |
| More than 60 | 0.0872 (0.0597) | 0.2301 (0.0661) | 0.0436 (0.0141) | -0.0135 (0.0259) | 0.0776 (0.0606) | 0.2326 (0.0665) | 0.0490 (0.0145) | -0.0130 (0.0259) |
| Black | 0.1770 (0.0503) | 0.1365 (0.0584) | 0.0639 (0.0119) | | 0.1140 (0.0518) | 0.0899 (0.0628) | 0.0929 (0.0126) | |
| Other race | -0.1885 (0.0916) | -0.1586 (0.1116) | 0.1081 (0.0217) | | -0.2674 (0.0936) | -0.1929 (0.0497) | 0.1326 (0.0224) | |

| | | | | | | | | |
|---|---|---|---|---|---|---|---|---|
| School dropout | -0.5301 | -0.0106 | 0.0569 | -0.0995 | -0.5586 | -0.0292 | 0.0752 | -0.0966 |
| | (0.0429) | (0.0487) | (0.1021) | (0.0196) | (0.0442) | (0.0497) | (0.0105) | (0.0200) |
| College graduate | 1.0275 | 0.1485 | -0.0119 | 0.2086 | 1.0643 | 0.1531 | -0.0166 | 0.2067 |
| | (0.0432) | (0.0490) | (0.0102) | (0.0192) | (0.0442) | (0.0493) | (0.0105) | (0.0193) |
| Married | -0.1116 | -0.2928 | 0.0638 | -0.0024 | -0.1183 | -0.2944 | 0.0819 | -0.0017 |
| | (0.0387) | (0.0434) | (0.0092) | (0.0173) | (0.0393) | (0.0437) | (0.0096) | (0.0173) |
| Logarithm of city size | -0.0355 | -0.0289 | 0.0030 | 0.0123 | -0.0346 | -0.0197 | -0.0061 | 0.0106 |
| | (0.0081) | (0.0092) | (0.0019) | (0.0038) | (0.0082) | (0.0102) | (0.0022) | (0.0044) |
| Any membership (community mean) | 0.4197 | | | | -0.0196 | | | |
| | (0.0257) | | | | (0.0679) | | | |
| Socializes within community (community mean) | | 0.3974 | | | | 0.1628 | 0.7316 | |
| | | (0.0290) | | | | | | |
| Drinks (community mean) | | | 0.8431 | | | | 0.3840 | |
| For racial exclusion (community mean) | | | | 0.5452 | | | | 0.6077 |
| | | | | (0.0956) | | | | (0.0911) |
| $N$ | 10,194 | 11,502 | 10,198 | 3,886 | 10,194 | 11,502 | 10,197 | 3,886 |
| Adjusted $R^2$ | 0.1649 | 0.1649 | 0.2501 | 0.1537 | 0.1411 | 0.0279 | 0.2096 | 0.1532 |

Source: GSS, 1972–94.

a. Numbers in parentheses are standard errors.

b. Columns 5 to 8 include community means for age, income logarithm, marital status, and years of education as instrumental variables.

almost certainly true that the standard errors in this approach understate the true degree of uncertainty about the parameter estimates. Nevertheless, these coefficients seem statistically sizable and probably do reflect the existence of real peer effects for these variables. As this discussion ties to emphasize, understanding the spatial organization of individuals becomes critical for the identification of peer effects.

Individuals may learn skills from their neighbors, but they also learn values and many other things. The peer-effects literature has focused more on negative peer interactions (drug use, out-of-wedlock births, crime) than on learning skills. These interactions may occur because of transfers of knowledge—for example, one person telling a neighbor how to buy drugs—but it seems more likely to me that these interactions occur because of the transfer of values. In other words, an individual is more likely to think that drug use is acceptable if he or she sees physically proximate friends also using drugs.

There has been a significant literature testing for the presence of this form of peer effect by examining the correlation of one person's behavior and the behavior of physically proximate friends. Case and Katz show a correlation among peers for a wide range of behaviors.[44] Katherine O'Regan and John Quigley use tract-level data to show how peer behavior in a person's tract influences his or her own behavior.[45] In my paper with Bruce A. Sacerdote and José A. Scheinkman, we argue that the extremely high variance in crime rates over space can best be understood as evidence for the presence of social interactions that create covariance among individuals in propensity to commit crimes.[46]

As mentioned above, all of this research is problematic because of the choice of neighborhood. If there is a correlation in intrinsic individual attributes within neighborhoods that occurs because of endogenous neighborhood choice, then the above phenomena would appear without the presence of peer effects. Indeed, William Evans, Wallace Oates, and Robert Schwab claim that properly dealing with the endogeneity of peer groups eliminates one study's estimate of peer effects.[47]

The best piece of work in this literature is a paper by Lawrence Katz, Jeffrey Kling, and Jeffrey Liebman.[48] They use the "Moving to Opportunity" experiment, a randomized study in which some people are induced to move

44. Case and Katz (1991).
45. O'Regan and Quigley (1996).
46. Glaeser, Sacerdote, and Scheinkman (1996).
47. Evans, Oates, and Schwab (1992).
48. Katz, Kling, and Liebman (1999).

out of high-poverty areas. They find that male children who move into low-poverty areas are much less likely to have disciplinary problems. They also find that depression and asthma decline for those who leave the ghetto. The important element of this research is that it provides a situation in which seemingly identical families are randomized into different neighborhoods. While this offers a means of cleanly estimating neighborhood effects, since many attributes of neighborhoods (beyond peers) differ, the experiment does not really pin down peer effects. To truly estimate peer effects, one would need an experiment where individuals were randomized among groups where only peers differed.

But beyond the simple measurement of peer effects, the goal must be to determine the channels through which these peer effects operate. Different channels tend to imply radically different policy responses. For example, if studies proved that peer effects work primarily through information, then policy actions could be aimed at providing *different* information. If peer effects work through preference formation, then policy alternatives become much more difficult and one must consider fairly massive education projects to changes these preferences.

Furthermore, the information-versus-preferences question may imply a different kind of need for policy intervention. If individuals are taking actions because their preferences lead them in that direction, then there is no a priori need for policy intervention (except for the externalities related to the actions). If individuals are taking actions because their peers have given them misinformation, then the individuals can themselves be made better off by information-based policy interventions. My own suspicion is that most peer effects work through preferences rather than information, but this opinion is based on very little data.

It would be difficult to distinguish the various channels through which peer effects operate without special surveys. Knowledge can presumably be elicited by surveys. Preferences are harder to measure, but techniques are being developed that involve using real-stakes games that may permit the measurement of factors such as risk aversion and time preference, two types of preferences that may possibly be influenced by peer effects.

These techniques involve confronting subjects with real choices involving monetary costs and benefits. For example, time preference is measured by testing a subject's willingness to forgo cash today relative to cash in the future. The taste for vengeance is measured by putting subjects in a situation where they have been wronged and then measuring their willingness to pay in order

**Table 3. City Size and Social Capital**[a]

| Variable | Cities with population over 1 million | N | All other U.S. cities | N |
|---|---|---|---|---|
| Number of organization memberships | 1.5027 (1.8779) | 728 | 1.7039 (1.7949) | 10,850 |
| Number of close friends | 4.9753 (6.6838) | 81 | 7.5980 (11.04) | 1,346 |
| Frequency of visits to friends | 4.0821 (1.4215) | 73 | 4.0448 (1.5033) | 1,272 |
| Trust indicator | 0.321 (0.467) | 1,737 | 0.423 (0.494) | 23,040 |
| Thinks people are fair | 0.483 (0.500) | 1,687 | 0.625 (0.484) | 22,895 |

Source: GSS, 1972–94.
a. Entries are sample. Numbers in parentheses are standard deviations.

to punish the individual who has done them wrong. Taking experiments to neighborhoods to measure preferences is one possible new route for empirical work in this area.

## Social Capital

Table 3 shows the connections between city size and five different measures of social capital. The first column shows the means of the variables for people who live in cities with more than one million inhabitants. The second column shows results for people who do not live in cities with more than one million people.

The first measure reflects the number of types of nonprofessional organizations to which the respondent belongs.[49] This is among the most standard measures of social connection. This measure is 1.5 for people in big cities and 1.7 for people outside big cities. This difference is quite statistically significant, but the economic significance is not huge.

The second measure is the self-reported number of close friends. This number is 7.6 outside of big cities and 5.0 inside big cities. This different is significant both statistically and economically. People in big cities appear to have fewer people that they refer to as close friends. Of course, given the ambi-

49. Thus people who are members of fraternal organizations only, but are members of five such organizations, will have a value of one for this variable. Unfortunately, the General Social Survey does not allow us to count the total number of organizations to which an individual belongs, only the number of *types* of organizations.

guity over what a close friend is, this variable is difficult to interpret. The third variable reflects the frequency of visiting one's closest friend. Here there is a difference between the big cities and elsewhere, but the difference is small.

The fourth and fifth variables reflect self-reported measures of trust and how fair one believes others to be. In other research, I have found that these variables are more correlated with one's own trustworthiness than with one's tendency to trust others.[50] In many cases, these variables are much higher outside big cities, where people appear to be more trusting and more likely to think that others are fair. Perhaps this reflects the greater presence of opportunistic behavior in cities.

These topics bring us to the next area of major research for urban economists: social capital. The literature that has followed Putnam in studying social capital has been among the most prominent in economics.[51] In this paper, I use the term *social capital* in Putnam's sense to refer to networks. This literature has argued that the level of social connection among individuals can play a major role in government efficiency,[52] economic growth,[53] and happiness itself.

Very little in this literature has suggested that there is a connection between space and social capital, except insofar as the substantial differences across different areas are a major topic of research. There is a rich sociological literature that seeks to explain the effects of urban density on the degree of connection among individuals.[54] Yet economists have barely studied the topic.

One specific topic for research is the connection between cities and network formation. The raw correlations mentioned above have been observed, but very little is known about why big cities apparently have less organization membership than smaller towns. It seems entirely possible that urban residents simply form different types of networks. On the other hand, cities may genuinely have less membership because opportunism is more common in urban areas. If cities facilitate social flight, then it may be easy for urbanites to behave opportunistically and escape punishment. This may cause a level of misbehavior that stymies that growth of social capital. Good research on the role that cities play in creating social connection appears to be important.

An even more broad-ranging topic is the more general connection between physical space and the formation of social connection. It is obvious (but hardly

50. Glaeser, Kahn, and Rappaport (1999).
51. Putnam (1993).
52. Putnam (1993); LaPorta and others (1997, 1999).
53. Knack and Keefer (1997).
54. See Wirth (1938).

proven scientifically) that spatial organization plays a major role in determining the social connection of neighborhoods and offices. The New Urbanism, which provided the philosophical basis for Celebration, takes as given the point that medium-density areas, not low-density areas, will lead to more connection and better networks. Of course, the New Urbanism is presently a philosophy, not a proven viewpoint. It may well be that Celebration will be no more successful in forming a spatial utopia than many earlier exercises.

Given the previous discussion of urban social problems, it seems surprising that higher density is thought to increase social connection, but it is likely that the New Urbanists have in mind a nonmonotonic relationship between social connection and density. At low levels of density, social networks cannot exist because transportation costs between people are too high. At high levels of density, individuals do not form bonds because they are too mobile and find it too easy to take advantage of one another and just move on. According to this view, the optimal level of density for the generation of social capital is somewhere in between the low density of rural areas and the high density of New York City.

In spite of these raw correlations, next to nothing is known about the role that density really plays in the forming of networks. At best, the relationship between city size and memberships has been established, and this may be a reflection of selection into cities, not the effect of cities. More important, even if a true relationship between city size and social capital is observed, how this relationship actually operates remains a mystery. My hope is that future urban economists will be able to understand more clearly how density effects network formation.

### Architecture

Table 4 shows the relationships between living in apartment buildings and a few related outcome measures. I divide the population into three groups: those who live in single-family dwellings, those who live in multifamily dwellings with fewer than five units, and those who live in apartment groups with more than five units.

The first three rows look at the connections between apartment dwelling and socialization with friends and neighbors. Individuals who live in apartments are much more likely to socialize with their neighbors than individuals who live in single-family dwellings. However, this socializing appears to drive

**Table 4. Building Structure and Social Connection[a]**

| Variable | Lives in single-family dwelling | N | Lives in multifamily dwelling with fewer than 5 units | N | Lives in multifamily dwelling with more than 5 units | N |
|---|---|---|---|---|---|---|
| Socializes with friends | 3.9926 (1.5975) | 10,443 | 4.2839 (1.6281) | 2,205 | 3.9420 (1.7606) | 466 |
| Socializes with relatives | 4.5216 (1.6056) | 10,440 | 4.3852 (1.6656) | 2,204 | 4.3447 (1.6557) | 467 |
| Votes in local elections | 0.7143 (0.4518) | 1,369 | 0.5445 (0.4988) | 303 | 0.5365 (0.5017) | 82 |
| Meets local representatives | 0.3499 (0.4771) | 1,383 | 0.2574 (0.4379) | 303 | 0.2650 (0.4440) | 83 |
| Afraid to walk alone at night | 0.4027 (0.4904) | 10,543 | 0.5051 (0.5000) | 2,215 | 0.6866 (0.4643) | 501 |

a. Entries are sample. Numbers in parentheses are standard deviations.

out socializing with relatives. The effect of apartment size on socializing with friends appears to be nonmonotonic; dwellers of smaller multifamily units are most likely to socialize with friends. These results are robust and become strong to the inclusion of control variables (such as income, education, and family structure) and are not just the result of richer people living in houses.[55]

The next two variables look at the connection between housing structure and local politics. It appears that individuals in apartment buildings are less likely to work to influence local politics. They are also less likely to vote in local elections. Interestingly, apartment buildings appear to build some forms of social capital (the connections among neighbors), but they reduce the amount of involvement in local politics.

The final variable shows the connection between apartment dwelling and fear of crime. The connection is strong and positive. Victimization data suggest that this fear has at least some basis in fact. Surveys routinely show that residents of multifamily dwellings are much more likely to be victimized (in street crimes, not in burglaries).[56] For some reason, the presence of single-family detached dwellings seems to be negatively correlated with criminal victimization. These results are true if we control for a wide set of individual characteristics and available neighborhood variables.[57]

One important relationship is the connection between social capital and density. However, there are many other ways in which physical space could relate to the formation of social networks. The existence of public spaces is often said to play a major role in creating interactions, especially among people who do not have natural reasons to interact. These public spaces may be traditional squares or piazzas. They also may be commercially handled coffee shops and bars. In the latter cases, nonmarket interactions are mixed with market transactions (for example, a bar owner is able to charge more for drinks because he offers a meeting place).

Housing infrastructure may also be important. Since owners of single-family units generally do not delegate their relationships with neighbors or the government, they may tend to develop stronger networks than residents of multifamily units. In large apartment buildings, the owner or the co-op board will take on the work of dealing with neighbors and the public sphere. This could in principle lead to a less-connected citizenry. My own work in this area

55. As shown in Glaeser and Sacerdote (1999).
56. For details, see Glaeser and Sacerdote (1999).
57. Of course, it is always possible that the connection between building size and crime may be spurious. Since we cannot control for everything, it is always possible there are other features of the neighborhood that cause street crime.

has not tended to find such clear effects, but there are many limits to the preliminary work that I have done.

More generally, although urban economics has addressed the distribution of individuals across cities and within cities, it has said almost nothing about the physical architecture of urban areas. Casual observation suggests that the physical environment in which we live can play a major role in determining our social connection, vulnerability to crime, and perhaps even our overall level of utility. Yet economists have made few attempts to study the impact of physical buildings.

A barrier to such work is the absence of evidence on physical infrastructure. At best, standard data sets only tell us the smallest facts about the places in which people live. There are very few data that give a detailed picture of the physical environment surrounding people. The best data on physical environment (the American Housing Survey) have so few questions on outcomes that it is impossible to apply it to many architectural questions. A major step forward would be to ask a much wider range of survey questions during at least one year of that survey.

## Political Economy, Altruism, and Crime

Table 5 shows the connection between city size and attitudes toward redistribution. Again, I have divided the sample into those living in cities with more than 1 million inhabitants and those living in smaller areas. In this case, I consider variables relating to support for redistribution.

The first column shows that people in big cities are more likely to support the presence of a social safety net. This is a general phenomenon that holds with many variables asked in greater numbers of years. People in large cities tend to favor higher levels of redistribution and to say that the government is spending too little. This holds even if the sample is restricted to only the wealthier residents of the city, and if controls are introduced for income and other variables. The second row simply reminds us that urbanites are much more likely to be Democrats. Again, this holds true even if only the wealthier urban residents are studied. The third row shows that white people in large cities are less likely to object to a family member's marrying a black person. It appears that urban residents are more likely to be sympathetic to other races and more likely to support transfers to the poor. The fourth row shows that urban residents are much more frightened. As I discuss below, one reason that

**Table 5. City Size and Opinions**[a]

| Variable | Cities with population more than 1 million | N | All other U.S. cities | N |
|---|---|---|---|---|
| Agrees with government social welfare | 0.8589 (0.3503) | 78 | 0.7259 (0.4462) | 1,277 |
| Voted for Democrats in 1988 | 0.6338 (0.4830) | 183 | 0.3681 (0.4823) | 3,420 |
| Objects to a family member marrying a black person | 0.3428 (0.4780) | 70 | 0.5951 (0.4910) | 1,240 |
| Afraid to walk alone at night | 0.6896 (0.4629) | 915 | 0.41137 (0.4921) | 12,344 |

Source: GSS, 1972–94.

a. Entries are sample. Numbers in parentheses are standard deviations.

urban residents might be more likely to support transfers to the poor is that they believe these transfers will make crime less likely.

One possible explanation for the concentration of poverty in America's cities is that urban governments appear to be more supportive of the poor than the governments of suburbs. This support shows up in public housing, health, and redistribution expenditure. Suburbs show their lack of support with zoning laws and perhaps also through policing strategies that are less sensitive to poorer citizens. There are many possible explanations for the differences between city and suburb governments. City governments have fixed resources to tax, so it is possible to redistribute in the city. Suburbs have less market power, and attempts to redistribute simply lead to a quick exodus of the wealthy. Cities have fewer homeowners, and homeowners have the strongest incentives to fight antipoverty redistribution.

Most important for our purposes, it appears that cities also have voters who are more likely to believe in spending on the poor. There are two natural explanations for this phenomenon. First, urban proximity among the rich and the poor may lead to greater altruism of the rich for the poor. Second, urban proximity among the rich and the poor may lead to greater fear of crime by the rich. The desire of the urban rich to redistribute may simply be a response to greater fear of criminal activity and the belief that redistribution may reduce the incentives to engage in crime.

Understanding criminal behavior has been a major topic of research for economists. But there has been less spatial analysis of crime than is still needed. Indeed, little is really known about the effects of spatial organization on criminal behavior, despite anecdotal information on concepts like defensible space and aggregate studies like my own on the connection between crime and city size. Elsewhere, I have tried to connect criminal behavior with architecture. But there is very little direct evidence on the way that urban density affects the nature of criminal activity. Pressing questions include both how physical structure determines crime and why crime is so much higher in cities.

Far more adventurous is the attempt to understand how spatial proximity affects altruism and other behaviors. A pathbreaking work in this area is by Erzo Luttmer, who shows that proximity to welfare recipients of one's own race tends to increase support for welfare. Proximity to welfare recipients of another race tends to decrease support for welfare. While this work is important, it is also very indirect. Essentially, Luttmer regresses survey evidence on support for welfare on metropolitan-area segregation measures.[58]

There are several ways in which this work might be improved. First, more tangible outcome measures might be substituted for a survey question about support for welfare. Questions about charitable giving might be helpful. Experimental evidence on the willingness to forgo cash if it is given to the poor might be useful. Second, the work could contain better measures of the spatial proximity among the rich and the poor, and this proximity would ideally be the outcome of exogenous variation, not endogenous location choice.

These topics are extremely important, and they may require further collaboration between economists and the social psychologists who have made more thorough studies of the formation of preferences. Ideally, this is another area in which urban economists will extend their reach. Without work of this kind it will be impossible to fully understand the political economy of cities (or nations, for that matter).

### The Consumer's City

In this section, I briefly discuss the future of the city and nonmarket interactions.

Figure 5 shows the relationship between distance from the central business district (CBD) and the logarithm of median income for four traditional metropolitan areas by census tract within three miles of the CBD. For all four of these metropolitan areas this relationship is strongly negative. Richer people live closer to the CBD. This relationship levels off and then disappears farther away from the CBD.

58. Luttmer (1998).

**Figure 5. Income and Distance from the Central Business District (CBD) in Boston, Chicago, New York, and Philadelphia**

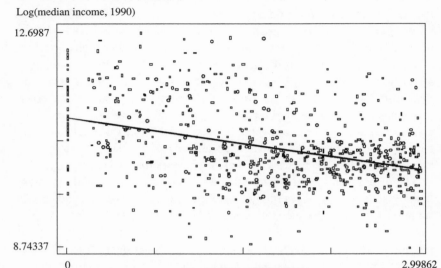

Source: Census of Population and Housing, 1990.

In figure 6, I show the relationship between the change in income and distance to the CBD for the same subsample of U.S. tracts. There is a significant positive relationship between income growth and proximity to the CBD. This relationship is strongest in New York City and Chicago in the 1980s.

The previous fact shows that richer people moved closer to the center of cities in the 1980s. The popular press appears to suggest that this trend has, if anything, increased in the 1990s. The *Boston Globe* repeatedly reports on new urban homesteaders—wealthy people choosing, because of the attractions of urban life, to move into gentrifying downtown areas that were previously much poorer. (Of course, these media blasts must be taken with significant skepticism.) While the mainstay of New York City's resurgence is the financial industry, a second factor is the strong appeal of New York as a center for consumption.

If the productive edge in cities weakens, then it may be that this role of the city as a center for consumption may be the driving force for urban growth in the future. Given the increasing wealth in America, this force may not be a bad one to rely on. If city living is a luxury good and rich Americans are get-

**Figure 6. Income Growth and Distance from Central Business District in Boston, Chicago, New York, and Philadelphia**

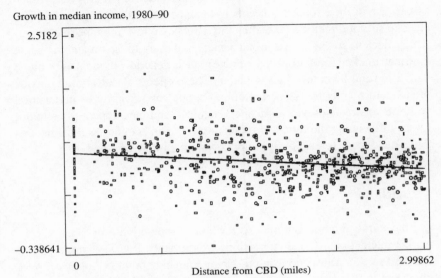

Growth in median income, 1980–90

Source: Census of Population and Housing, 1980 and 1990.

ting richer, this may continue to cause urban renaissances throughout the country.

These cities are not attracting the rich because of cheaper manufacturing goods. There are little differences in these prices over space, and generally the large land costs involved in retail trade in cities mean that traded goods are usually more expensive in cities. The amenities of urban life do often come from less expensive and more available services in cities. There already exists a rich literature on the role of urban markets in increasing the division of labor and the range of available products. These standard market forces are one reason why cities are appealing as centers for leisure activities. Public amenities such as museums and theaters are another classic market-related reason for the popularity of some cities.[59] Indeed, some cities are attempting to use big infrastructure projects as attempts to increase their desirability as consumption centers.[60]

59. To the extent that these institutions have large fixed costs, big-city crowds enable these more impressive institutions.

60. We still do not know if these will be generally successful, or what is needed to make such projects work.

It also may be true, however, that density itself is attractive. Gary Becker has argued that restaurants attract customers because of their crowds as much as because of their food.[61] It seems to be appealing to many people to live close to (if not directly on) bustling city streets. Young single people in particular flock to cities because urban density makes for thicker matching in the marriage market. Finding an appropriate mate is generally thought to be much harder in rural Iowa than in Manhattan. These effects of density fall outside of standard market transactions (although they can certainly be understood with the apparatus of neoclassical economics), and they appear to be major forces influencing the future of urban areas. Urban economics must try and understand these forces if it is to understand the future of cities.

## Conclusion

I have argued that economics as a whole is moving into the area of non-market interactions. These interactions are probably at least as important as standard market transactions in producing human happiness and possibly as important in determining economic growth as well. Most of the nonmarket interactions that are of interest to urban economists have a profoundly important spatial component. The borrowing of information, the transfer of values, and the formation of networks appear to take place primarily at short distances. The formation of cities both affects these nonmarket interactions and is affected by them. As urban economics moves forward, an understanding of our own topic will require that we center much research on the size and nature of these interactions. I also believe that a spatial orientation will be crucial for making progress on these important topics, and so urban economists should be especially well equipped to lead the way.

61. Becker (1991).

# Comments

**Vernon Henderson:** Edward Glaeser argues persuasively that a significant portion of future urban research will be focused on the role of nonmarket interactions. I have taught my students for the past twenty-five years that urban economics distinguishes itself from the rest of economics by its focus on the causes and consequences of close spatial proximity, with key aspects of the phenomenon involving externalities. That the future holds more of the same is reassuring.

Traditional approaches in the urban literature tend to view cities as necessary evils. The conventional wisdom is that spatial proximity is needed in order to exploit scale externalities, such as localized information spillovers, in production, but that this proximity breeds almost exclusively negative externalities on the consumption side. The list includes congestion, pollution, noise and health externalities, crime, discrimination, and other antisocial behavior. A considerable portion of the urban literature has examined the dimensions and policy prescriptions to deal with these negative nonmarket interactions.

What is refreshing about Glaeser's perspective is the focus on the positive aspects of close proximity. Apart from information spillovers in production, his paper examines human-capital spillovers, peer-group effects, social capital, and altruism as they relate to spatial proximity, density, and urban scale. Second, he looks beyond traditional issues of how urban economics might quantify the magnitude of damages or gains from aggregate scale externalities or human-capital spillovers.

Following, for example, the theoretical models of Masahisa Fujita, Robert W. Helsley and William C. Strange, and Gilles Duranton and Diego Puga, which spell out the microfoundations of scale externalities, Glaeser joins the call for urban economists to investigate microfoundations of externalities

139

empirically.[1] In the 1990s such an agenda for economists has been supported by both the National Science Foundation and the MacArthur Foundation. The work of Adam B. Jaffe, Manuel Trajtenberg, and Rebecca Henderson on patent citations initiates the practical inquiry about the nature of information flows.[2] Whom do firms learn from and how do they learn? Do they learn by trading employees back and forth in the labor market, through the gossip by buyers and sellers who come to the firm, through the local social circuit, and so on? Or, as another example, in an urban endogenous-growth model by Duncan Black and J. Vernon Henderson, local human-capital accumulation both enriches static information spillovers and leads to more innovation.[3] Can these two effects be disentangled?

This agenda is a difficult one for the obvious reasons. Nonmarket transactions are difficult to observe, unlike market ones. So we can get snapshots of a process such as citations for patents, but these represent only a small fraction of the flows of ideas. We can try to make indirect inferences. Are productivity benefits of scale closely related to spatial proximity? Do they relate to turnover in the labor market? Do they relate to frequency of socialization? There are doubtless other connections that could be drawn. But all these are items that are difficult to measure and they raise difficult identification issues in econometrics. As Glaeser points out, in identifying the beneficial and harmful effects of different types of peer groups, we need to control for the endogeneity of the groupings. And moreover, we have so far only investigated productivity gains for manufacturing, when in fact it is tradable services that are drawn to the largest metropolitan areas. We understand little about externalities among service activities.

Glaeser turns to a variety of phenomena economists rarely study that are of great interest. He looks at happiness indexes, socialization, and political preferences as they are affected by external opportunities to socialize. The reasons why we would expect city size and density—spatial proximity—to be related to, say, socialization are well articulated. Table 2 contains results on city size and aspects of socialization, with the required demographic controls, yielding weak associations. But in tables 2–5 there seems to be a general indication that aspects of socialization may decline, or at least not increase to the extent expected, as city size and density rise. It seems odd that socialization should not be substantially affected as the opportunities to socialize increase.

1. Fujita and Ogawa (1982); Helsley and Strange (1990); Duranton and Puga (1999).
2. Jaffe, Trajtenberg, and Henderson (1993).
3. Black and Henderson (1999).

However, a key determinant of the extent of socialization may be missing in the empirical work: the length of residence in the community. Larger cities may have more life-cycle turnover. Center cities and apartments are characterized as residences of highly mobile people, such as young professionals without children. By virtue of short tenure, these individuals have had less chance to develop social networks and have less incentive to invest in building nontransportable social capital. Controlling for these aspects, it may be found that being in cities enhances socialization, in contrast to what tables 2 and 3 seem to suggest.

Using tables 3 through 5, Glaeser attempts to determine whether socialization, voting behavior, prejudice, and fear of crime are related to city size and nature of dwelling-unit type (single-family homes versus apartments). These tables contain simple pair relationships—city size and average socialization, for example. It is unclear why Glaeser did not try simple regressions or probits for all the relations, as in table 2. These would be much more compelling.

*Forecasts for urban work.* Urban economics is taking on increasing visibility in developing countries and in development economics. About 85 percent of the world's urban population will be in developing countries twenty years from now (and the world will be 60 to 65 percent urban) according to the World Development Report 1999/2000.[4] The extent of urbanization differs by region and hence the issues differ correspondingly. Latin American countries typically are fully urbanized. The focus in these is on institutional and political reform at the local level, to manage populations growing in size and income. As income has increased, countries have increasingly decentralized public-expenditure responsibilities in response to both local and regional demands and increasing difficulty in meeting public-sector needs from a centralized system. With local public-sector growth, two issues become critical: how to design local governmental structures (a) to get the right incentives for good local governance and (b) to buffer the the national government from financial instability. For example, what should be the length and ceiling number of mayoral terms? Under what institutional arrangements is privatization of public service delivery an improvement over public provision?

In sub-Saharan Africa over the past thirty years, there has been rapid urbanization accompanied by little economic growth. This presents a puzzle: How is this possible, given the close connection between urbanization and GDP per capita? To what extent is it that the rural migrate to urban areas because

4. World Bank (1999).

conditions in rural areas have deteriorated due to civil wars and declining infra-structure provision and services that make agricultural production unprofitable? To what extent are public-sector incomes fueled by revenues from the sale of primary products drawing extended families into the city? But as people have moved to the cities, why has there not been industrialization and growth? Is it that the small population sizes of African countries and lack of transport infrastructure for intercountry trade make specialization difficult, so the intra-industry scale benefits of urban-area specialization cannot be exploited?

In South and East Asia there has been rapid urbanization and income growth, but this has taken place despite the limits of outdated institutions that were designed for rural or colonial societies and that have inadequate techni-cal know-how in the local public sector. Many Asian countries have very high degrees of urban primacy, which hinder widespread economic growth and fos-ter poor living conditions both in primate and nonprimate cities. A key issue is how to develop hinterland cities. What is the role of interregional transport investments and decentralization of government responsibilities and alloca-tions, in an orderly decentralization process, such as South Korea has experienced over the past two decades?

Within cities, inadequate institutions affect the operation of housing mar-kets. Poorer neighborhoods (*bustees, kampongs*) where there may have been generations of family residence have insecure title and tenure. Often these neighborhoods are in key downtown areas. As industrial jobs have moved to peri-urban areas, John Kain's spatial mismatch problem arises.[5] Residents can-not sell their houses to new land uses and move to the suburbs where jobs are. And developers cannot buy up land in these neighborhoods and provide much-needed mixed-use modern commercial development. Both traditional residents and local economic development suffer. One might ask why the government does not reform land markets and grant titles to families who have had pos-sessory rights over land for many years, let alone for several generations.

**Robert P. Inman:** Edward Glaeser's provocative paper offers just what the field of urban economics needs as we start a new century of research on cities. If there has been a theme to the past century of urban research, it has been the power of markets to allocate resources efficiently in competitive spatial economies. Henry George, Alfred Marshall, Harold Hotelling, and Charles Tiebout have each provided us with important insights as to how markets work to ensure economic efficiency in urban economies. Yet for all the benefits of

5. Kain (1968).

competition in spatial economies—and surely they are enormous; witness the value of real estate in New York, London, Paris, Miami, San Francisco, San Jose—it is not hard to see inefficiencies as well. Dirty air, crime, trash-strewn lots and crack houses, disruptive students undermining the education of more serious classmates, congested roadways, and homelessness are common to most cities. Each is an example of an externality not efficiently priced through the marketplace. Glaeser's paper asks us to turn our attention to the activities that occur outside the marketplace and to the nonmarket mechanisms that set their levels and distributions. He argues that urban economists have a comparative advantage in such research—at least among economists—because spatial proximity is so crucial to understanding so many of these nonmarket interactions. As Glaeser points out, productive people work near other productive people, community-directed residents associate with other community-directed residents, and happy people live near other happy people.

To understand nonmarket interactions in urban settings, Glaeser stretches our thinking with provocative facts that standard competitive urban models will not easily explain. Much of what is important in these nonmarket settings involves bargaining, sorting, and multiple ("tipping") equilibria. Glaeser emphasizes the importance of social capital—measured by joining groups, having friends, trusting others—and finds that such capital appears greater in smaller cities. He speculates that smaller cities permit more familiar interactions, more knowledge about the true motives of others, and thus stronger informal networks. Stronger networks ought to better internalize the various externalities associated with urban living. He notes that city architecture, as it affects the formation of networks, is likely to be important as well. Stairways lead to more familiarity than elevators, and front porches, sidewalks, and open space to greater interactions still. Social capital is lowest among residents of high-rise apartments, higher in multifamily dwellings, and highest in neighborhoods of single-family homes. (Although I do wonder about the residents along Philadelphia's exclusive Main Line; one would also want to control for city density in such analyses.) Finally, Glaeser suggests that not only does familiarity breed trust but it may also breed empathy for the poor. This may in part explain why large cities spend more per taxpayer on poor families than do small cities; Glaeser stresses crime control as another plausible motive, too. A more direct test would compare charitable giving for poverty relief across city sizes.

To be sure, Glaeser means his paper to be a first look at, not a last word about, the importance of nonmarket interactions in cities, but it leaves a strong impression. First, agglomeration economies are important, and for the most part the land market allocates those advantages efficiently. One important consequence, however, is large cities. Second, the resulting urban density creates a variety of external (nonmarket) interactions among residents. Third, nonmarket institutions in the guise of social capital—or networks—have arisen to manage these nonmarket interactions. Fourth, these nonmarket institutions work best when residents trust one another. Fifth, successful networks based upon trust are most likely to be found in smaller cities.

It is hard not to be intellectually stimulated by these conclusions. In my own case, that means thinking anew about the role of city government as another nonmarket institution, in addition to Glaeser's private networks, that might resolve this tension between the economic advantages of large cities and their nonmarket, often negative social consequences. Given Glaeser's analysis, what structure of government might work best in our large cities?

First, the city government should encourage, not undermine, the economic advantages of production and consumption agglomeration. This means providing the required public infrastructure for firms to function efficiently: roads to move goods and customers, public transit to move employees, pipes and tunnels to move water and waste, and communication networks to move ideas and facilitate dealmaking. Accomodating all relevant agglomeration economies will typically require geographically large infrastructure networks. Since the marginal costs of using such networks are likely to be sufficiently below average cost, government provision or regulation will be required. The financing of infrastructure's fixed costs can be done by average-cost pricing, general taxation, or (ideally) land taxes. The reach of infrastructure taxation should encompass the geographical domain of the agglomeration economies. Large governments each covering a metropolitan area and providing infrastructure and using broad-based taxation will be required here.

Second, city government must provide a social network for internalizing the negative externalities of agglomeration and urban density. It can do so directly by actually providing the governance structure for the network: a board of directors, election rules, and the assignment of responsibilities and taxing powers. Or it can charter, and perhaps regulate, freestanding private networks that meet criteria for democratic governance. Direct provision of networks is city government as we now know it, while the "charter and regulate" strategy generalizes today's efforts to privatize public education. In either case, Glaeser's empirical analysis recommends small networks. While Glaeser studies only private networks, his conclusion that smaller is better has a firm basis in what we also know about public networks. The extensive literature on the efficient provision of public services shows that governments can finance and produce police and fire protection, K–12 education, recreation, libraries, health care, charity, and santitation with networks of 10,000 to 20,000 people, the equivalent of a good-sized city neighborhood. These neighborhood governments should be assigned resident-based taxation (on property or income) and user fees to pay for services, most efficiently collected as part of a piggybacked tax structure administered by the metropolitan government. There may be some spillovers across neighborhoods—police and fire services and poverty transfers and services are the most obvious examples—but those externalities can be handled with cross-neighborhood agreements enforced and financed by the metropolitan-level government. To protect the use of voluntary agreements as the basis for metropolitan governance, supermajority approval for metropolitan spending and taxation seems appropriate.

The institutional structure for this efficient city looks a good deal different from the tax and governance structures now in place in most U.S. cities. Indeed, most U.S. cities now seem to offer the worst of both worlds, as they are neither large enough to efficiently finance and provide infrastructure nor small enough to efficiently deal with the social externalities of urban density. Urban economic historians can probably explain why today's city boundaries lie where they do—in 1854, modern Philadelphia, for example, was formed as a merger of small neighborhoods to provide infrastructure services—but the interesting question for today's urban scholars is *Will these boundaries change?* The forces now holding city boundaries in place are largely redistributive. The suburbs do not want to be taxed to support regional infrastructures now provided by the city. City public employees do not want to lose their monopoly control over service provision to city residents. And city politicians servicing the majority of poorer neighborhoods do not want to lose access to the tax base of the city's rich minority.

This redistributive but inefficient equilibrium cannot survive in a world of mobile capital, labor, and customers. Redistributive cities and regions with inadequate infrastructures will lose firms, talented labor, and market sales to their more efficient competitors. Already these competitive pressures are being felt, and alternative public governance structures are beginning to emerge, albeit slowly, in response. Recent metropolitan-area-wide initiatives are almost exclusively for new infrastructure provision and financing (for example, regional transit systems in Atlanta, Boston, Dallas, Philadelphia, San Francisco, and Washington, D.C.; regional water and waste management in

Chicago, Denver, Hartford, and Seattle). Feeling competitive pressure for mobile residents from suburban ("neighborhood") governments, many large U.S. cities are now sanctioning business improvement districts (BIDs), charter schools with parent-controlled boards, and neighborhood councils as alternative, neighborhood-based governmental structures for local service provision. "America's mayors"—Rendell, Giuliani, Goldsmith—understand these pressures and have been applauded for their ability to introduce fiscal and institutional reforms.

The likely losers in this competitive process are today's urban poor. As Glaeser points out, the redistributive budget of large U.S. cities is declining steadily, and there is no reason to expect a reversal of this trend. In my own work examining the politics of fiscal policy in Philadelphia, I found that the large increase in black and Hispanic representation on the city council in the 1980s led not to an increase in city-financed income, housing, or health care transfers to the very poor but to increased services in the previously ignored minority working-class neighborhoods: police patrols, trash pickup, recreation facilities, and expanded library hours. Minority legislators do what white legislators do: they service their median constituent. And they have been reelected; John Street, for example, a black council member first elected in 1980, is Philadelphia's newly elected mayor. The shrinking city poverty budget is likely to shrink still further as competition forces cities to adopt the more efficient neighborhood form of governance. If the poverty gap is to be filled, it will have to come from voluntary agreements at the metropolitan, state, or national levels of government.

# References

Ades, Alberto F., and Edward L. Glaeser. 1995. "Trade and Circuses: Explaining Urban Giants." *Quarterly Journal of Economics* 110 (February): 195–258.

Audretsch, David B., and Maryann P. Feldman. 1996. "R & D Spillovers and the Geography of Innovation and Production." *American Economic Review* 86 (June): 630–40.

Barro, Robert J. 1991. "Economic Growth in a Cross Section of Countries." *Quarterly Journal of Economics* 106 (May): 407–43.

Becker, Gary. 1991. "A Note on Restaurant Pricing and Other Examples of Social Influences on Price." *Journal of Political Economy* 99 (October):1109–16.

Black, D., and J. Vernon Henderson. 1999. "A Theory of Urban Growth." *Journal of Political Economy* 107: 252–84.

Case, Anne C., and Lawrence F. Katz. 1991. "The Company You Keep: The Effect of Family and Neighborhood on Disadvantaged Youth." Working Paper 3705. Cambridge, Mass.: National Bureau of Economic Research.

Coleman, James Samuel, and others. 1966. *Equality of Educational Opportunity.* U.S. Department of Health, Education, and Welfare, Office of Education. Government Printing Office.

Dumais, Guy, Glenn Ellison, and Edward Glaeser. 1997. "Geographic Concentration as a Dynamic Process." Working Paper 6270. Cambridge, Mass.: National Bureau of Economic Research.

Duranton, Gilles, and Diego Puga. 1999. "Nursery Cities." Paper presented at 1999 Regional Science Association Meetings. London School of Economics.

Evans, William N., Wallace E. Oates, and Robert M. Schwab. 1992. "Measuring Peer Group Effects: A Study of Teenage Behavior." *Journal of Political Economy* 100 (October): 966–91.

Fujita, Masahisa, and M. Ogawa. 1982. "Multiple Equilibria and Structural Transition of Non-Monocentric Urban Configurations." *Regional Science and Urban Economics* 17: 161–96.

Gaspar, Jess, and Edward L. Glaeser. 1998. "Information Technology and the Future of Cities." *Journal of Urban Economics* 43 (January): 136–56.

Glaeser, Edward L. 1999. "Learning in Cities." *Journal of Urban Economics* 46 (September): 254–77.

Glaeser, Edward L., Matthew Kahn, and J. Rappaport. 1999. "Why Do the Poor Live in Cities?" Mimeographed.

Glaeser, Edward L., and others. 1992. "Growth in Cities." *Journal of Political Economy* 100 (December): 1126–52.

Glaeser, Edward L., and David C. Mare. Forthcoming. "Cities and Skills." *Journal of Labor Economics.*

Glaeser, Edward L., and Bruce A. Sacerdote. 1999. "The Social Consequences of Housing Structure." Mimeographed.

Glaeser, Edward L., Bruce A. Sacerdote, and José A. Scheinkman. 1996. "Crime and Social Interactions." *Quarterly Journal of Economics* 111(2): 508–48.

Glaeser, Edward L., José A. Scheinkman, and Andrei Shleifer. 1995. "Economic Growth in a Cross-Section of Cities." *Journal of Monetary Economics* 36 (December): 117–43.

Helsley, Robert W., and William C. Strange. 1990. "Matching and Agglomeration Economies in a System of Cities." *Regional Science and Urban Economics* 20 (September): 189–212.

Henderson, J. Vernon, April Kuncoro, and Matt Turner. 1995. "Industrial Development in Cities." *Journal of Political Economy* 103 (October): 1067–90.

Jacobs, Jane. 1961. *The Death and Life of Great American Cities*. Vintage

———. 1969. *The Economy of Cities*. Random House.

Jaffe, Adam B., Manuel Trajtenberg, and Rebecca Henderson. 1993. "Geographic Localization of Knowledge Spillovers as Evidenced by Patent Citations." *Quarterly Journal of Economics* 108 (August): 577–98.

Kain, John F. 1968. "Housing Segregation, Negro Employment, and Metropolitan Decentralization." *Quarterly Journal of Economics* 82 (May): 175–97.

Katz, Lawrence, Jeffrey Kling, and Jeffrey Liebman. 1999. "Moving to Opportunity in Boston: Early Results from a Housing Mobility Program." Mimeographed.

Knack, Stephen, and Philip Keefer. 1997. "Does Social Capital Have an Economy Payoff? A Cross-Country Investigation." *Quarterly Journal of Economics* 112 (November): 1251–88.

Kolko, Jed. 1999. "Can I Get Some Service Here? Information Technology, Service Industries, and the Future of Cities." Mimeographed. Harvard University.

Krugman, Paul. 1991. "Increasing Returns and Economic Geography." *Journal of Political Economy* 99 (June): 483–99.

La Porta, Rafael, and others. 1997. "Trust in Large Organizations." *American Economic Review, Papers and Proceedings* 87 (May): 333–38.

———. 1999. "The Quality of Government." *Journal of Law, Economics and Organization* 15 (April): 222–79.

Lucas, Robert. 1988. "On the Mechanics of Economic Development." *Journal of Monetary Economics* 22 (July): 3–42.

Luttmer, Erzo. 1998. "Understanding Income Redistribution: The Role of Interpersonal Preferences, Information, and Mechanism Design." Ph.D. dissertation. Harvard University.

Manski, Charles F. 1993. "Identification of Endogenous Social Effects: The Reflection Problem." *Review of Economic Studies* 60 (July): 531–42.

Marshall, Alfred. 1890. *Principles of Economics*. London: Macmillan.

O'Regan, Katherine M., and John M. Quigley. 1996. "Teenage Employment and the Spatial Isolation of Minority and Poverty Households." *Journal of Human Resources* 31 (Summer): 692–702.

Putnam, Robert D. 1993. *Making Democracy Work: Civic Traditions in Modern Italy.* Princeton University Press.

———. 1999. "The Marshall Lecture." Mimeographed.

Rauch, James E. 1994. "Productivity Gains from Geographic Concentration of Human Capital: Evidence from the Cities." *Journal of Urban Economics* 34 (November): 380–400.

Romer, Paul. 1986. "Increasing Returns and Long Run Growth." *Journal of Political Economy* 94 (October): 1002–37.

Rotemberg, Julio, and Garth Saloner. 1990. "Competition and Human Capital Accumulation: A Theory of Interregional Specialization and Trade." Working Paper 3228. Cambridge, Mass.: National Bureau of Economic Research.

Saxenian, Annalee. 1994. *Regional Advantage: Culture and Competition in Silicon Valley and Rte. 128.* Harvard University Press.

Simon, Curtis C., and Clark Nardinelli. 1996. "The Talk of the Town: Human Capital, Information and the Growth of English Cities, 1861–1961." *Explorations in Economic History* 33 (July): 384–413.

Solow, Robert M. 1956. "A Contribution to the Theory of Economic Growth." *Quarterly Journal of Economics* 70 (February): 65–94.

Weitzman, Martin L. 1998. "Recombinant Growth." *Quarterly Journal of Economics* 113 (May): 331–60.

Wilson, William J. 1987 *The Truly Disadvantaged: The Inner City, the Underclass, and Public Policy.* University of Chicago Press.

Wirth, Louis. 1938. "Urbanism as a Way of Life." *American Journal of Sociology* 44: 1–24.

Young, Alwyn. 1995. "The Tyranny of Numbers: Confronting the Statistical Realities of the East Asian Growth Experience." *Quarterly Journal of Economics* 110 (August): 641–80.

JEFFREY GROGGER
*University of California, Los Angeles*

DEREK NEAL
*University of Wisconsin*

# Further Evidence on the Effects of Catholic Secondary Schooling

EDUCATION REFORM is a perennial topic of debate for both policymakers and social scientists. While most education research and related reform proposals deal with strategies for evaluating and improving current systems of financing and delivering public education, some research and a growing number of public and private initiatives focus on privately provided education and its value as an alternative to public schooling.

In recent years, Cleveland and Milwaukee have adopted voucher plans that target economically disadvantaged children, and Florida recently adopted a voucher plan that targets children attending public schools that do not meet certain performance criteria. Further, private efforts to fund scholarships, especially for economically disadvantaged students in cities, have increased dramatically in recent years. Currently, at least sixty-five programs provide privately funded scholarships for students attending private schools. In 1999, more than 57,000 students received such scholarships. Of these students, at least 45,000 received scholarships provided by a relatively new nationwide program called the Children's Scholarship Fund. This program targets low-income students in cities. The program began by providing scholarships to students in the District of Columbia, New York, Los Angeles, Chicago, and Jersey City, and is now expanding to include other cities. These scholarships may be used at either private or parochial schools.[1]

Derek Neal thanks the Andrew W. Mellon and Alfred P. Sloan foundations for support. We thank Kate Antonovics, Phil Cross, Maria Ferreyra, and Rosemary Hyson for excellent research assistance; Joe Altonji and Chris Taber for helpful conversations;. our commentators Eric Hanushek and Robert Schwab, as well as other conference participants, for their perspectives; and William Gale and Janet Rothenberg Pack for their insights.

1. The Center for Education Reform provides data on these scholarship programs. The relevant URL is http://www.edreform.com/research/pspchart.htm (February 15, 2000).

151

Of the remaining programs, one of the largest is New York City's Student-Sponsor Partnership Program. This program provides scholarships for economically disadvantaged students who attend inner-city Catholic schools. A 1990 case study by the Rand Corporation found favorable results for these students at three Catholic high schools.[2] In these schools, roughly 85 percent of scholarship students and 85 percent of tuition-paying students took the Scholastic Aptitude Test (SAT), and the average scores were quite similar for the two groups. In contrast, the gap between the scores of the scholarship students and the average scores of students from regular and magnet public schools in similar neighborhoods was large. Although a much smaller fraction of public-school students took the test, the scores for regular public and magnet school students were, on average, lower by about 160 and 90 points respectively.

More recently, studies by William Evans and Robert Schwab and by Derek Neal report that students attending Catholic secondary schools are more likely to graduate than similar students in public schools.[3] Neal's study highlights attainment gains for urban students in Catholic schools, and he reports particularly large gains for urban minorities.[4] Both of these studies, however, use data from cohorts of students who are now at least thirty-five years old. Few studies of the relative effectiveness of Catholic, public, and other private secondary schools employ data from more recent cohorts of high-school graduates.

This paper uses data from the high-school class of 1992 to estimate the effects of Catholic secondary schooling on math achievement, high-school completion rates, and college-attendance decisions. It focuses on the effects of Catholic schooling for several reasons. These schools are the largest and most homogeneous group of schools within the private sector. In addition, the question of whether or not Catholic schools may participate in publicly funded voucher programs is at the center of important current legal and political battles. Although existing legislative debates and court cases in Wisconsin, Ohio, Florida, and elsewhere focus on the issue of whether or not any religious school may receive voucher money, the vast majority of students currently attending religious schools are attending Catholic schools. Further, the current wave of

2. See Hill, Foster, and Gendler (1990), especially pp. 31–33.
3. Evans and Schwab (1995); Neal (1997). Sander and Krautmann (1995) and Coleman and Hoffer (1987) provide similar results.
4. Because the data from the National Longitudinal Survey of Youth (NLSY) do not provide precise information about type of residence during high school, Neal divides his sample according to county population size. He designates counties with more than 250,000 people as urban counties.

voucher initiatives is in large part an attempt to provide more educational choices for economically disadvantaged students in cities. Historically, Catholic schooling has been primarily an urban phenomenon, and in our empirical work we pay particular attention to potential gains from this schooling for urban students.

Results from the National Education Longitudinal Study (NELS) data for 1988–94 are in large measure consistent with results presented in previous studies that employed the National Longitudinal Survey of Youth (NLSY), 1979, and the High School and Beyond (HSB) Survey of the sophomore class of 1980. The data imply that urban students generally, and urban minorities in particular, enjoy attainment gains from Catholic schooling. With respect to high-school graduation rates and college-attendance rates, we find that urban minorities in Catholic schools fare much better than similar students in public schools. Although the results suggest that Catholic schooling improves high-school graduation rates among urban whites, there is no strong evidence that it raises college-attendance rates in this group. There is at best mixed evidence that Catholic schooling enhances attainment among suburban students. We also find evidence that it enhances achievement for urban students. However, estimates of achievement gains from Catholic schooling are somewhat sensitive to choices concerning model specification and the imputation of missing scores.

As we describe the details of the analyses, we provide several cautionary tales for those who seek to estimate treatment effects using the NELS data. Numerous sample-selection problems arise because of the rather involved sampling scheme employed in the NELS. Although some researchers ignore these problems, we demonstrate that the structure of the NELS sample design does affect the results in significant ways. Further, we argue that several aspects of the sample design severely limit the ability to estimate key parameters of interest.

The balance of the paper begins with a description of the NELS data and a discussion of sample design issues. Then we turn to univariate analyses of high-school graduation, college attendance, and math achievement. The following section addresses selection into Catholic schools on unobserved traits. The results are far from definitive, but we find no evidence that the univariate results are driven by selection of unobserved student traits.

The penultimate section of the paper describes the existing supply of Catholic secondary schools and changes in Catholic-school availability over the past twenty-five years. Among all types of communities, the supply of

Catholic high schools shrank notably between 1974 and 1994, and since 1994 has remained roughly constant. Between 1974 and 1994, the most striking reductions in the availability of Catholic secondary schools occurred in large cities. The supply of Catholic schools has stabilized in part because of a recent increase in new school openings. Relative to the existing supply of schools, these new schools tend to be located in small towns.

### Data

The National Education Longitudinal Study (1988–94) began in 1988 with a cross-sectional survey of eighth graders. The study design involved drawing a sample of schools and then sampling students from these schools. Selected students participated in follow-up interviews in 1990, 1992, and 1994. The study provides detailed family background information, information about students' academic records and test scores and information about respondent activities before, during, and after high school. In 1994, the respondents in the third follow-up answered numerous questions about their final high-school graduation status and their college-attendance patterns. Between the 1988 base-year survey and the third follow-up in 1994, however, the National Center for Education Statistics (NCES) dropped a significant number of students from the sample.

In the analyses below, we use high-school graduation data and college-attendance data from the third follow-up and test-score data from the base year and second follow-up surveys. We use the 1990 survey to determine whether a student chose to attend a Catholic or public high school and rely primarily on the base-year survey and first follow-up data to measure family background characteristics.

Here, several features of the NELS sample design are crucial for the analyses. First, in both the first follow-up in 1990 and the third follow-up in 1994, the NELS sample design did not retain the entire sample or even a random subsample of students who participated in the previous wave. In both waves, the probability that a particular student participates is in part determined by whether or not that student dropped out of school at some point in the past.[5]

---

5. The sample design also involved stratification according to each student's record of responsiveness to past questionnaires. Eighty percent of those labeled "poor responders" were eliminated from the F3 sample. After these deletions, all known dropouts in the remaining sample were retained with probability one. We do not know the dropout status of the 596 students in the "poor responders" category. See National Center for Education Statistics, *NELS: 1988–1994, Methodology Report,* NCES 96–174 (March 1996), section 1.5.

Second, in both 1990 and 1992, the survey administrators were unable to give achievement tests to a significant number of dropouts. According to NCES, "In the second follow-up, 88 percent of the dropouts provided questionnaire data but only 42 percent completed a cognitive test. This low rate of test completion is attributable to the high percentage of questionnaires that were administered by telephone."[6]

Third, in the base year, the original sample design involved two stages. Analysts chose a sample of schools and then chose samples of students from within these schools. The first-stage sample of schools was not a random sample. The survey design dictated a specific number of schools from various sampling strata. These strata are defined according to the school's location, sector, and racial composition. Locations are divided among urban, suburban, and rural categories. Public, Catholic, and other private schools make up the school sectors. In the first follow-up, the sample design designated students for retention in the sample in part according to the number of base-year students who chose their high school. The design retained with certainty any students in a high school that contained at least ten students from the base-year sample. The selection probabilities for others students are inversely proportional to the sizes of base-year student clusters in their high school.

We will return to these issues throughout the analyses.[7] The first item is of prime concern in the analyses of educational attainment. We cannot determine whether or not a given student actually graduated from high school or attended college unless the student participates in the third follow-up in 1994 (F3). However, students who experience periods of dropout are included in this third follow-up at different rates from other students. Since prior-dropout status is a strong indicator of future educational attainment, this feature of the sample design should affect the distributions of the error terms in the models of high-school graduation and college attendance. Clearly, maximum likelihood estimators of the determinants of educational attainment that employ the unweighted data from F3 are inconsistent. Below, we rely on the sampling weights to produce consistent estimators, but for purposes of comparison with related work, we also provide estimates generated without weights.

6. See National Center for Education Statistics, *NELS 1988: Second Follow-Up: Student Component Data File User's Manual*, NCES 94–374 (September 1994), section 3.4.1. The same problem arises with respect to the tenth-grade scores in the F1.

7. In related papers, Figlio and Stone (1999) and Goldhaber (1996) do not employ sample weights. However, their results are not directly comparable to ours. Both employ tenth-grade rather than twelfth-grade test scores. Further, Figlio and Stone's attainment analyses are based on twelfth-grade attendance rather than actual high-school graduation.

In a later section of this paper, we consider bivariate models of educational attainment and Catholic-school attendance. For these analyses, the NELS sample design raises additional complications. As before, the selective retention of dropouts affects the error terms in the attainment equations, but in addition, the presence of a Catholic-school attendance equation raises a choice-based sampling problem. The base-year (BY) sample design selected a target number of public schools, Catholic schools, and other private schools within various sampling strata, and the first follow-up (F1) design sought to locate clusters of students from these base-year schools. Thus, the F1 sample does not contain a representative sample of high-school students with respect to school type. The number of students in Catholic high schools is in large measure determined by the BY sampling scheme and the extent to which Catholic high schools have established relationships with Catholic elementary schools or belong to larger K–12 campuses.

Finally, the low rate of test completion in the second follow-up among those who experience dropout episodes creates a select sample of test-takers. Since dropout rates in public and Catholic schools are quite different, this form of sample selection may affect test-score comparisons among public and Catholic-school students who are similar.

## Univariate Models

There is a large body of literature on the effects of Catholic schooling. While much of the literature deals with the effects on achievement-test scores, the most consistent set of results comes from analyses of educational attainment. Previous work with both the High School and Beyond Survey and the National Longitudinal Survey of Youth indicates that Catholic schooling does enhance educational attainment for urban students. Further, these attainment gains appear to be larger among minorities in urban places.[8]

In the attainment analyses below, we are concerned with the following thought experiment. Assume that parents choose high schools for their children. A given child then starts high school and gathers information about the costs and benefits of educational attainment at her school. The costs of finishing high school involve effort, forgone earnings, and any psychic costs of attendance. The benefits involve human capital and any nonpecuniary gains

---

8. See Evans and Schwab (1996) for the most detailed analyses of attainment in the HSB. See Neal (1997) for results from the NLSY.

associated with attendance or graduation. The costs and benefits will be determined in part by student characteristics. Students who enter high school with strong academic backgrounds or who come from especially nurturing (or demanding) families may find the costs of attendance lower and the benefits of continuing through graduation greater, but if two students with identical talents from identical family backgrounds enter different schools, differences between the two in the net gains from graduation and further schooling will be determined by differences between the two schools. Below, we present results from probit models of educational attainment that contain an extensive set of controls for family background, prior academic record, and previous social problems in school.

The empirical models follow the form that is most common in the literature on private school effects:

$$y_i = x_i\beta + C_i\gamma + \epsilon_i$$
$$I_i = 1 \text{ if } y_i \geq 0, \ I_i = 0 \text{ if } y_i \leq 0,$$

where $i$ indexes individuals, $y_i$ is the latent value of graduating from high school or attending college, and $x_i$ is a set of student characteristics. The indicator variable $C_i$ equals 1 if the student attends a Catholic high school and 0 otherwise. The error term, $\epsilon_i$, is normally distributed and captures unmeasured determinants of the gains from educational attainment. The variable, $I_i$, is an attainment indicator. In the high-school graduation models, it equals 1 if individual $i$ graduated and 0 otherwise. In the college-attendance models, the indicator equals 1 for all those who attend college and 0 for everyone else.

We note two restrictions implied by this empirical model. First, because the Catholic-school effect does not vary across individuals, the gain from attending Catholic school is constant across individuals. This is a strong restriction, and it is certainly not appropriate for analyses of the full sample of students. Thus we divide the sample into subsamples based on the race of students and the location of their schools. We estimate gains from Catholic schooling for four different groups: urban minorities, suburban minorities, urban whites, and suburban whites. These are natural groupings because public-school quality may vary between cities and suburbs. Even within these four subsamples, heterogeneity in the gains from Catholic schooling may be an important consideration. Later we discuss how one might interpret the empirical results under various hypotheses concerning differences in individual gains from Catholic schooling.

In addition, although the controls for student characteristics are extensive, it is possible that unmeasured student traits captured by $G_i$ not only influence educational attainment but also are correlated with Catholic-school attendance. If this is true, the results misstate the effects of Catholic schooling on attainment. In a later section, we address selection into these schools based on unmeasured student traits.

### High-School Graduation Rates

Tables 1A and 1B provide results from the NELS that are similar in many ways to those reported in other studies. These tables present results from probit models of high-school graduation. Table 1A presents results from analyses that ignore sample weights. Table 1B incorporates the sampling weights from F3. The dependent variable records whether or not a respondent received an actual diploma by the spring of 1994. Students who did not skip grades and were not held back after the study began in 1988 would have expected to graduate in the spring of 1992. We do not treat General Equivalency Diploma (GED) recipients as graduates.

For each cell in the tables, there are three entries. The first two are the coefficient estimate and standard error. The third is the average change in the probability of high-school graduation implied by the estimated coefficient. For dummy variables, this is the average change in predicted graduation probabilities associated with changing the dummy variable from 0 to 1. For continuous variables, the average change is associated with a one-standard-deviation increase in the variable in question.

The tables present results for four samples of students and for three different model specifications. The first sample involves urban minorities. This sample includes black and Hispanic students who attended eighth grade in 1988 in a school located within the central city of a metropolitan area.[9] Suburban minorities attend schools in metropolitan areas but outside central cities. The white samples are defined in like manner. We do not include rural stu-

---

9. We rely on the 1988 variable G8URBAN for two reasons. First, this variable provides information about the student's location prior to choosing a high school. Second, the location variables in the F1 and F2 waves, G10URBAN and G12URBN3 do not provide information about school locations but rather about school districts as a whole. Since some suburban schools are located within school districts associated with a central city or urban county, these variables may provide misleading information about school locations. This is especially true for Catholic schools because districts are defined by archdiocese boundaries.

dents in any of the analyses because the NELS provides almost no records of Catholic-secondary-school students in rural areas.[10] The goal is to restrict attention to samples that include public schools that are actually alternatives for Catholic-school students and vice versa.

The three specifications are as follows. Specification A includes family background variables and demographic characteristics that are common in the previous literature on Catholic-school effects. The specification includes controls for race, parental occupation, parental education, family structure, family income, region of residence, county population, and the presence of reading materials in the home. Specifications B and C include additional variables that are unique to the NELS. Because the NELS collects data from students before they enter high school, we are able to measure several aspects of their elementary-school experience. Specification B includes all the variables in specification A plus controls for grade point average and test scores in eighth grade. Specification C includes numerous indicators of discipline, attendance, and schoolwork problems during eighth grade plus detailed indicators of family religious background in eighth grade.[11]

Several features of these results foreshadow similar results in the analyses of college attendance and math achievement below. To begin, the additional controls in specifications B and C do reduce the estimated effects of Catholic schooling. Catholic-school students have better academic records, higher achievement, and fewer discipline problems in their eighth-grade records. These differences explain part of the attainment differences between Catholic- and public-high-school students from similar family backgrounds.

However, in both the weighted and unweighted analyses, the estimated attainment gains associated with Catholic schooling are quite significant for urban students, especially urban minorities. The graduation rates reported at the bottom of table 1B indicate that among urban minorities, students in Catholic secondary schools graduate at a 0.98 rate. The corresponding figure in public schools is 0.73. The results in column C for urban minorities indicate that Catholic schooling is associated with an 18 percentage point increase in expected graduation rates. Thus among urban minorities, the most extensive set of controls accounts for far less than half of the overall 25 percentage

10. The rural minority sample in F3 does not contain any students from Catholic high schools. The corresponding rural white sample contains only eight students from Catholic high schools.

11. While our most complete specification includes four dummy variables for religious affiliation (Catholic, Baptist, Other Protestant, and no report), related studies seldom use religion as a control in attainment equations. In bivariate models, affiliation with the Catholic Church is often used as an instrument for Catholic-school attendance. We do not follow this approach.

**Table 1A. Probit Model of High School Graduation, Unweighted[a]**

| Variable | Urban minorities | | | Suburban minorities | | | Urban white | | | Suburban white | | |
|---|---|---|---|---|---|---|---|---|---|---|---|---|
| | A | B | C | A | B | C | A | B | C | A | B | C |
| Catholic school | 1.07 | 0.93 | 0.82 | 0.61 | 0.44 | 0.26 | 0.87 | 0.85 | 0.74 | 0.99 | 0.83 | 0.83 |
| | (0.31) | (0.32) | (0.33) | (0.28) | (0.29) | (0.28) | (0.18) | (0.19) | (0.19) | (0.29) | (0.30) | (0.32) |
| | 0.20 | 0.17 | 0.15 | 0.11 | 0.08 | 0.05 | 0.11 | 0.10 | 0.08 | 0.10 | 0.09 | 0.08 |
| Eighth-grade GPA | ... | 0.53 | 0.43 | ... | 0.61 | 0.47 | ... | 0.57 | 0.50 | ... | 0.49 | 0.41 |
| | | (0.07) | (0.08) | | (0.08) | (0.09) | | (0.08) | (0.09) | | (0.05) | (0.05) |
| | | 0.09 | 0.07 | | 0.08 | 0.06 | | 0.05 | 0.05 | | 0.05 | 0.04 |
| Eighth-grade test score | ... | 0.04 | 0.04 | ... | 0.02 | 0.02 | ... | 0.02 | 0.02 | ... | 0.02 | 0.02 |
| | | (0.01) | (0.01) | | (0.01) | (0.01) | | (0.01) | (0.01) | | (0.00) | (0.00) |
| | | 0.10 | 0.10 | | 0.05 | 0.03 | | 0.04 | 0.04 | | 0.04 | 0.03 |
| Black | 0.10 | 0.20 | 0.24 | 0.01 | 0.06 | 0.13 | ... | ... | ... | ... | ... | ... |
| | (0.10) | (0.10) | (0.14) | (0.12) | (0.12) | (0.15) | | | | | | |
| | 0.03 | 0.05 | 0.06 | 0.00 | 0.01 | 0.03 | | | | | | |
| Public school graduation rate | | 0.75 | | | 0.80 | | | 0.84 | | | 0.88 | |
| Catholic school graduation rate | | 0.98 | | | 0.95 | | | 0.98 | | | 0.99 | |
| Public N | | 1,130 | | | 1,009 | | | 1,080 | | | 3,454 | |
| Catholic N | | 83 | | | 81 | | | 355 | | | 267 | |

Source: For this and all subsequent tables, National Education Longitudinal Study, 1988–94, and authors' calculations.

a. The dependent variable measures receipt of a high school diploma by the spring of 1994. The first number in each cell is the estimated coefficient from the probit model. The numbers in parentheses are standard errors. The final entry in each cell is the average change in the probability of high school graduation implied by the estimated coefficient. For dummy variables, the change represents a move from 0 to 1. For the continuous variables, the change involves a one-standard-deviation increase in the relevant explanatory variable. Specification A includes two indicator variables for county population level, dummies for the professional status and educational attainment of each parent, a two-parent family indicator, region dummies, family income, and two indicators for the type of reading materials in the home. Specification B adds a composite measure of eighth-grade achievement in math and reading and eighth-grade GPA. Specification C adds twelve indicator variables for problems with fighting, attendance, schoolwork, or class conduct, and four religious-affiliation dummies. The complete set of estimated coefficients is available upon request from the authors.

**Table 1B. Probit Model of High School Graduation, Weighted**[a]

| Variable | Urban minorities | | | Suburban minorities | | | Urban white | | | Suburban white | | |
|---|---|---|---|---|---|---|---|---|---|---|---|---|
| | A | B | C | A | B | C | A | B | C | A | B | C |
| Catholic school | 1.31 | 1.29 | 1.02 | 0.59 | 0.44 | 0.27 | 0.79 | 0.79 | 0.63 | 0.61 | 0.44 | 0.47 |
| | (0.35) | (0.40) | (0.35) | (0.30) | (0.35) | (0.33) | (0.26) | (0.26) | (0.27) | (0.31) | (0.35) | (0.37) |
| | 0.24 | 0.22 | 0.18 | 0.12 | 0.08 | 0.05 | 0.10 | 0.09 | 0.07 | 0.08 | 0.06 | 0.06 |
| Eighth-grade GPA | ... | 0.72 | 0.57 | ... | 0.48 | 0.36 | ... | 0.64 | 0.56 | ... | 0.59 | 0.49 |
| | | (0.10) | (0.10) | | (0.11) | (0.10) | | (0.11) | (0.11) | | (0.07) | (0.07) |
| | | 0.12 | 0.09 | | 0.08 | 0.05 | | 0.06 | 0.05 | | 0.06 | 0.05 |
| Eighth-grade test score | ... | 0.02 | 0.02 | ... | 0.03 | 0.03 | ... | 0.02 | 0.02 | ... | 0.02 | 0.02 |
| | | (0.01) | (0.01) | | (0.01) | (0.01) | | (0.01) | (0.01) | | (0.01) | (0.01) |
| | | 0.06 | 0.07 | | 0.08 | 0.07 | | 0.03 | 0.03 | | 0.04 | 0.03 |
| Black | 0.08 | 0.11 | 0.25 | -0.15 | -0.01 | 0.02 | ... | ... | ... | ... | ... | ... |
| | (0.14) | (0.15) | (0.17) | (0.15) | (0.15) | (0.18) | | | | | | |
| | 0.02 | 0.03 | 0.06 | -0.04 | 0.00 | 0.00 | | | | | | |
| Public school graduation rate | | 0.73 | | | 0.77 | | | 0.85 | | | 0.86 | |
| Catholic school graduation rate | | 0.98 | | | 0.96 | | | 0.97 | | | 0.98 | |
| Public N | | 1,130 | | | 1,009 | | | 1,080 | | | 3,454 | |
| Catholic N | | 83 | | | 81 | | | 355 | | | 267 | |

a. Weight is F3QWT. For specifications and other details, see notes to table 1A.

point gap in graduation rates. This result stands in sharp contrast to the results for suburban minorities. Here the estimated Catholic-school effect in column C is much smaller and statistically insignificant, even though the raw gap between public-school and Catholic-school graduation rates is 0.19.

The raw differences between public- and Catholic-school graduation rates are smaller in the white sample. However, among urban whites, the effect of Catholic schooling remains noteworthy. On average, expected graduation rates are 7 percentage points higher for Catholic-school students than for their similar counterparts in public schools. Among suburban whites, the estimated effect of Catholic schooling is slightly smaller in magnitude but imprecisely estimated. Note that for both suburban whites and suburban minorities, we fail to find a statistically significant effect of Catholic schooling on graduation rates.

Readers may note that the differences between the unweighted and weighted results in tables 1A and 1B are quite modest. Nonetheless, these differences foreshadow a pattern that is much more prominent in the college-attendance and math-achievement results below. In almost every model, the estimates of the gains from Catholic schooling among urban minorities are larger in analyses that employ the sample weights. Further, the use of sample weights tends to magnify the difference between the estimated gains from Catholic schooling for minorities and the estimated gains for other groups.

## College Attendance

We noted earlier that the decision to finish high school involves a cost-benefit calculation. One of the potential benefits from attending a better school is the accumulation of more human capital from a given investment of time in school. If we view high school as a place where students learn how to learn, then students who attend good schools will expect higher returns from future human-capital investments because they will be more efficient learners.

Tables 2A and 2B contain results from models of college-attendance decisions that employ the same explanatory variables used in the analysis of high-school graduation rates. The results in table 2A show that the association between Catholic schooling and college attendance is quite strong among both urban and suburban minorities. The estimated coefficients imply roughly a 17 percentage point increase in college-attendance rates for minorities who attend Catholic schools. For urban whites, Catholic schooling yields an expected increase in college attendance of only 5 percent. The estimated effect is statistically insignificant for suburban whites.

Note the weighted results in table 2B. The implied Catholic-school effect among urban minorities is much larger. While the controls in specification C do account for a significant portion of the difference between college-attendance rates for Catholic- and public-school students, the estimated coefficient implies that a gap of 27 percentage points remains. The introduction of weights also increases the estimated Catholic-school effect for suburban minorities, but here the increase is smaller. In the weighted analyses, the estimated effects of Catholic schooling on college attendance are not statistically significant for either urban or suburban whites. The estimated Catholic-school effect, however, from the weighted analysis of urban whites is almost identical in magnitude to the estimated effect in the corresponding model without weights.

Taken together, the attainment analyses indicate that the more extensive controls for elementary-school performance provided by the NELS account for most if not all of the attainment differences between suburban whites in Catholic schools and their public-school counterparts. The results for suburban minorities and urban whites are rather mixed. Suburban minorities who attend Catholic schools may enjoy college-attendance gains, but we find no discernable increase in high-school graduation rates. Urban whites who attend these schools appear to enjoy notable gains in graduation rates and college-attendance rates, but the estimate of the college-attendance effect is somewhat imprecise.

In contrast, the results imply that urban minorities who attend Catholic schools experience significant gains in both graduation rates and college attendance. These results are consistent with those from studies that employ data on students who attended high school in the 1970s and early 1980s. In work with earlier data, both by Derek Neal and by William Evans and Robert Schwab, significant attainment gains are evident for urban students attending Catholic schools. Neal reports particularly large gains for urban minorities who attend these schools.[12]

*Test Scores*

The magnitude of these estimated attainment gains for urban minorities in Catholic schools warrants further evidence concerning these gains and potential explanations for their magnitude. Tables 3A and 3B present results from

12. Neal (1997); Evans and Schwab (1996). We find similar results in samples restricted to high-school graduates. Our college-attendance results cast doubt on the possibility that Catholic high schools have higher graduation rates because they are simply selling diplomas.

**Table 2A. Probit Model of College Attendance, Unweighted[a]**

| Variable | Urban minorities | | | Suburban minorities | | | Urban white | | | Suburban white | | |
|---|---|---|---|---|---|---|---|---|---|---|---|---|
| | A | B | C | A | B | C | A | B | C | A | B | C |
| Catholic School | 0.70 | 0.57 | 0.51 | 0.69 | 0.65 | 0.55 | 0.46 | 0.39 | 0.21 | 0.33 | 0.18 | 0.16 |
| | (0.17) | (0.18) | (0.19) | (0.17) | (0.18) | (0.18) | (0.10) | (0.10) | (0.11) | (0.10) | (0.10) | (0.11) |
| | 0.25 | 0.18 | 0.16 | 0.24 | 0.21 | 0.17 | 0.14 | 0.10 | 0.05 | 0.10 | 0.05 | 0.05 |
| Eighth-grade GPA | ... | 0.58 | 0.55 | ... | 0.41 | 0.31 | ... | 0.61 | 0.57 | ... | 0.52 | 0.46 |
| | | (0.07) | (0.08) | | (0.07) | (0.07) | | (0.07) | (0.07) | | (0.04) | (0.04) |
| | | 0.13 | 0.12 | | 0.10 | 0.07 | | 0.12 | 0.11 | | 0.11 | 0.09 |
| Eighth-grade test score | ... | 0.03 | 0.03 | ... | 0.03 | 0.03 | ... | 0.03 | 0.03 | ... | 0.03 | 0.03 |
| | | (0.01) | (0.01) | | (0.01) | (0.01) | | (0.01) | (0.01) | | (0.00) | (0.00) |
| | | 0.14 | 0.13 | | 0.13 | 0.12 | | 0.10 | 0.10 | | 0.12 | 0.11 |
| Black | 0.18 | 0.30 | 0.52 | -0.11 | 0.01 | 0.04 | ... | ... | ... | ... | ... | ... |
| | (0.09) | (0.09) | (0.13) | (0.10) | (0.10) | (0.13) | | | | | | |
| | 0.06 | 0.09 | 0.15 | -0.04 | 0.00 | 0.01 | | | | | | |
| Public school college attendance | | 0.38 | | | 0.39 | | | 0.52 | | | 0.54 | |
| Catholic school college attendance | | 0.77 | | | 0.74 | | | 0.77 | | | 0.78 | |
| Public N | | 1,130 | | | 1,009 | | | 1,080 | | | 3,454 | |
| Catholic N | | 83 | | | 81 | | | 355 | | | 267 | |

a. The dependent variable is college attendance. For specifications and other details, see notes to table 1A.

**Table 2B. Probit Model of College Attendance, Weighted[a]**

| Variable | Urban minorities | | | Suburban minorities | | | Urban white | | | Suburban white | | |
|---|---|---|---|---|---|---|---|---|---|---|---|---|
| | A | B | C | A | B | C | A | B | C | A | B | C |
| Catholic school | 1.00 | 0.92 | 0.86 | 0.89 | 0.81 | 0.69 | 0.39 | 0.34 | 0.22 | 0.28 | 0.13 | 0.09 |
| | (0.23) | (0.25) | (0.24) | (0.22) | (0.24) | (0.24) | (0.16) | (0.16) | (0.15) | (0.14) | (0.14) | (0.15) |
| | 0.35 | 0.30 | 0.27 | 0.30 | 0.25 | 0.20 | 0.12 | 0.09 | 0.06 | 0.09 | 0.03 | 0.02 |
| Eighth-grade GPA | ... | 0.54 | 0.51 | ... | 0.39 | 0.27 | ... | 0.53 | 0.59 | ... | 0.54 | 0.46 |
| | | (0.10) | (0.10) | | (0.08) | (0.09) | | (0.11) | (0.10) | | (0.05) | (0.05) |
| | | 0.13 | 0.11 | | 0.09 | 0.06 | | 0.11 | 0.12 | | 0.11 | 0.09 |
| Eighth-grade test score | ... | 0.03 | 0.03 | ... | 0.04 | 0.04 | ... | 0.03 | 0.04 | ... | 0.03 | 0.03 |
| | | (0.01) | (0.01) | | (0.01) | (0.01) | | (0.01) | (0.01) | | (0.00) | (0.00) |
| | | 0.12 | 0.12 | | 0.14 | 0.13 | | 0.11 | 0.12 | | 0.11 | 0.10 |
| Black | 0.22 | 0.30 | 0.45 | -0.04 | 0.12 | 0.12 | ... | ... | ... | ... | ... | ... |
| | (0.12) | (0.13) | (0.17) | (0.14) | (0.14) | (0.16) | | | | | | |
| | 0.07 | 0.09 | 0.13 | -0.01 | 0.03 | 0.03 | | | | | | |
| Public school college attendance | | 0.35 | | | 0.37 | | | 0.51 | | | 0.55 | |
| Catholic school college attendance | | 0.82 | | | 0.80 | | | 0.72 | | | 0.79 | |
| Public N | | 1,130 | | | 1,009 | | | 1,080 | | | 3,454 | |
| Catholic N | | 83 | | | 81 | | | 355 | | | 267 | |

a. Weight = F3QWT. The dependent variable is college attendance. For specifications and other details, see notes to table 1A.

ordinary least squares (OLS) regressions of twelfth-grade math-test scores on controls for family background and elementary-school records of achievement and conduct. Specification A includes controls only for race, gender, county population level, and the measures of eighth-grade math achievement and grades. Specification B mirrors specification C in the attainment analyses. Tables 3A and 3B provide weak evidence that Catholic schools enhance achievement. According to table 3B, urban minorities in Catholic schools score 2.12 points higher than similar students with identical eighth-grade academic records. This difference represents less than one-fifth of a standard deviation in the public-school test-score distribution, and it is not statistically significant by conventional standards. The estimated effects for both urban and suburban whites are similar in magnitude but more precisely estimated, while there is little evidence of math-achievement gains for suburban minorities in Catholic schools.

These results, however, may be affected by the NELS sample design. Thousands of students who participated in the F2 survey did not actually take the twelfth-grade battery of tests, and a disproportionate share of these students were dropouts at some point.[13] Dropout episodes are much more common in the public-school samples. This type of sample selection therefore may affect the estimates of math-achievement gains associated with Catholic schooling.

To begin exploration of these issues, we estimate median regressions on the samples used in tables 3A and 3B. Tables 3C and 3D present the results. In most samples, the estimated effects of Catholic schooling on median test scores are quite similar in magnitude to the estimated effects on mean test scores. But there is one striking exception. For urban minorities, the effects of Catholic schooling on median test scores are large, especially in the weighted models. Model B in table 3D indicates that Catholic schooling raises median scores among urban minorities by 5.9 points. This effect is more than two and a half times larger than the estimated effect of Catholic schooling on mean scores in the same sample.

These results concerning median test scores are interesting in their own right, but in addition they provide a starting point for addressing the importance of missing twelfth-grade test scores. Since median regressions are robust to outliers, we assign scores of 0 to all students who (1) were eligible to take the twelfth-grade tests but did not and (2) have dropped out of high school at least once. Then we estimate median regressions on the expanded sample.

---

13. There are 3,613 students who completed an F2 survey but did not take the F2 math test. Thirty percent of these students are currently dropouts or have dropped out in the past.

These regressions recover the effects of Catholic schooling on median test scores under the assumption that all dropouts would have scored below the median score in a sample of students who are identical apart from their dropout status.

Tables 4A and 4B present the results. For all groups other than urban minorities, we observe increases in the estimated effects of Catholic schooling on median test scores. While the estimated gains for suburban minorities in Catholic schools remain statistically insignificant, the estimated gains for whites in these schools are noteworthy, with urban students enjoying slightly larger gains. Table 4B reports a median gain of 2.82 for urban whites in these schools.

Once again the results for urban minorities stand out. The imputation strategy involves assigning 0 test scores to more than 200 urban minorities in public schools and to only three urban minorities in Catholic schools. Nonetheless, in model B the estimated effect of Catholic schooling on median test scores is smaller for the urban-minority sample that includes the imputed test scores. This result may reflect the fact that, by adding dropouts to the sample, we include additional public-school students from disadvantaged backgrounds.[14] Nonetheless, the estimated gain in median scores for urban minorities remains noteworthy. Table 4B reports a 5.12 point gain in median scores among urban minorities in Catholic schools. This gain represents more than a 0.4-standard-deviation increase among urban minorities in public schools.

To summarize the results from the univariate models, we find evidence that Catholic schooling enhances attainment for urban students in general, and for urban minorities in particular. The results indicate modest achievement gains for urban whites who attend Catholic schools. The achievement results for urban minorities are sensitive to decisions concerning model specification, but there is some evidence that Catholic schooling raises achievement among urban minorities. For both white and minority students in the suburbs, we find less consistent evidence of gains from Catholic schooling, although minority students in suburban Catholic schools seem to enjoy gains in college attendance, and white students appear to enjoy modest achievement gains. Overall, the results are consistent with the view that gains from Catholic schooling are concentrated among urban students, and among urban minorities in particular.

---

14. These results for urban minorities are not driven by the three imputations in the Catholic-school sample. Even if we eliminate these three students so that all the imputed scores belong to public-school students, the implied gains from Catholic schooling are still smaller in the expanded sample.

**Table 3A. OLS Regression Results for Twelfth-Grade Math Score, Unweighted[a]**

| Variable | Urban minorities | | Suburban minorities | | Urban white | | Suburban white | |
|---|---|---|---|---|---|---|---|---|
| | A | B | A | B | A | B | A | B |
| Catholic school | 3.37 | 2.10 | 1.05 | 0.09 | 2.02 | 1.90 | 2.20 | 1.68 |
| | (0.99) | (1.06) | (0.91) | (0.99) | (0.47) | (0.56) | (0.51) | (0.54) |
| Eighth-grade GPA | 2.75 | 2.26 | 3.30 | 2.70 | 3.92 | 3.12 | 3.88 | 3.22 |
| | (0.46) | (0.50) | (0.45) | (0.46) | (0.37) | (0.41) | (0.24) | (0.26) |
| Eighth-grade math score | 0.98 | 0.93 | 0.95 | 0.91 | 0.83 | 0.80 | 0.84 | 0.79 |
| | (0.03) | (0.03) | (0.03) | (0.03) | (0.02) | (0.02) | (0.01) | (0.01) |
| Black | -2.28 | -2.19 | -0.49 | -0.48 | ... | ... | ... | ... |
| | (0.52) | (0.73) | (0.60) | (0.83) | | | | |
| $R^2$ | 0.65 | 0.68 | 0.66 | 0.68 | 0.70 | 0.71 | 0.69 | 0.71 |
| Public mean | 39.87 | | 41.53 | | 51.02 | | 50.36 | |
| (Standard deviation) | (12.88) | | (13.40) | | (14.00) | | (13.98) | |
| Catholic mean | 48.36 | | 45.83 | | 54.98 | | 56.26 | |
| (Standard deviation) | (11.65) | | (14.11) | | (12.43) | | (10.90) | |
| Public N | 893 | | 763 | | 1,065 | | 3,288 | |
| Catholic N | 74 | | 80 | | 334 | | 208 | |

a. The dependent variable is the second follow-up math score standardized using Item Response Theory. Model A includes the reported variables, along with a female dummy and two indicators for county population size. Model B involves the same controls as model C in table 1A, except a math score rather than a composite test score measures eighth-grade achievement. Numbers in parentheses, unless otherwise indicated, are standard errors.

Table 3B. OLS Regression Results for Twelfth-Grade Math Score, Weighted[a]

| Variable | Urban minorities | | Suburban minorities | | Urban white | | Suburban white | |
|---|---|---|---|---|---|---|---|---|
| | A | B | A | B | A | B | A | B |
| Catholic school | 3.15 | 2.12 | 1.07 | 0.33 | 2.07 | 1.87 | 2.28 | 1.95 |
| | (1.40) | (1.51) | (1.05) | (1.17) | (0.59) | (0.63) | (0.68) | (0.65) |
| Eighth-grade GPA | 3.37 | 3.30 | 3.25 | 2.65 | 3.46 | 2.31 | 3.89 | 3.14 |
| | (1.07) | (0.72) | (0.59) | (0.51) | (0.44) | (0.49) | (0.29) | (0.31) |
| Eighth-grade math score | 0.93 | 0.89 | 1.00 | 0.96 | 0.83 | 0.80 | 0.84 | 0.79 |
| | (0.08) | (0.06) | (0.04) | (0.04) | (0.03) | (0.03) | (0.02) | (0.02) |
| Black | -1.56 | -1.61 | -0.89 | -0.32 | ... | ... | ... | ... |
| | (0.93) | (0.91) | (0.92) | (0.93) | | | | |
| $R^2$ | 0.59 | 0.67 | 0.68 | 0.71 | 0.71 | 0.73 | 0.70 | 0.72 |
| Public mean | 38.83 | | 40.70 | | 49.83 | | 49.90 | |
| (Standard deviation) | (12.31) | | (13.71) | | (14.13) | | (13.96) | |
| Catholic mean | 49.16 | | 45.18 | | 53.47 | | 57.32 | |
| (Standard deviation) | (11.90) | | (14.13) | | (11.92) | | (11.07) | |
| Public N | 893 | | 763 | | 1,065 | | 3,288 | |
| Catholic N | 74 | | 80 | | 334 | | 208 | |

a. Weight = F2QWT. The dependent variable is the second follow-up math score standardized using Item Response Theory. For specifications and other details, see notes to table 3A.

**Table 3C. Median Regression Results for Twelfth-Grade Math Score, Unweighted[a]**

| Variable | Urban minorities A | Urban minorities B | Suburban minorities A | Suburban minorities B | Urban white A | Urban white B | Suburban white A | Suburban white B |
|---|---|---|---|---|---|---|---|---|
| Catholic school | 5.17 | 3.66 | 0.89 | 0.22 | 1.34 | 1.59 | 2.41 | 2.02 |
|  | (2.32) | (2.43) | (2.97) | (3.24) | (1.20) | (1.42) | (1.58) | (1.65) |
| Eighth-grade GPA | 2.79 | 2.33 | 3.72 | 3.17 | 3.53 | 2.27 | 3.92 | 3.34 |
|  | (1.02) | (1.15) | (1.32) | (1.44) | (0.85) | (1.00) | (0.62) | (0.68) |
| Eighth-grade math score | 1.02 | 0.98 | 0.96 | 0.94 | 0.84 | 0.85 | 0.85 | 0.80 |
|  | (0.07) | (0.08) | (0.09) | (0.10) | (0.05) | (0.06) | (0.04) | (0.04) |
| Black | -1.72 | -2.54 | -0.58 | -0.54 | ... | ... | ... | ... |
|  | (1.26) | (1.82) | (1.82) | (2.56) |  |  |  |  |
| $R^2$ | 0.44 | 0.46 | 0.46 | 0.49 | 0.48 | 0.50 | 0.48 | 0.50 |
| Public median | 38.40 |  | 40.86 |  | 52.05 |  | 51.14 |  |
| Catholic median | 49.42 |  | 46.54 |  | 56.26 |  | 56.28 |  |
| Public N | 893 |  | 763 |  | 1,065 |  | 3,288 |  |
| Catholic N | 74 |  | 80 |  | 334 |  | 208 |  |

a. The dependent variable is the second follow-up math score standardized using Item Response Theory. Model A includes the reported variables, along with a female dummy and two indicators for county population size. Model B involves the same controls as model C in table 1A, except a math score rather than a composite test score measures eighth-grade achievement. The standard errors, reported in parentheses, are Koenker-Bassett (1982) standard errors that employ the nuisance-parameter estimator suggested by Buchinsky (1998).

**Table 3D. Median Regression Results for Twelfth-Grade Math Score, Weighted[a]**

| Variable | Urban minorities | | Suburban minorities | | Urban white | | Suburban white | |
|---|---|---|---|---|---|---|---|---|
| | A | B | A | B | A | B | A | B |
| Catholic school | 5.05 | 5.90 | 0.22 | -0.23 | 1.72 | 1.84 | 2.78 | 1.85 |
| | (2.34) | (2.47) | (3.09) | (3.37) | (1.32) | (1.55) | (1.56) | (1.65) |
| Eighth-grade GPA | 2.56 | 2.94 | 2.96 | 3.46 | 2.74 | 1.80 | 3.42 | 3.27 |
| | (0.98) | (1.19) | (1.32) | (1.47) | (0.76) | (0.99) | (0.61) | (0.68) |
| Eighth-grade math score | 1.04 | 0.97 | 1.05 | 0.98 | 0.84 | 0.84 | 0.87 | 0.79 |
| | (0.07) | (0.08) | (0.09) | (0.10) | (0.05) | (0.06) | (0.04) | (0.04) |
| Black | -0.68 | -1.88 | -1.16 | -0.10 | ... | ... | ... | ... |
| | (1.28) | (1.82) | (1.77) | (2.60) | | | | |
| $R^2$ | 0.39 | 0.48 | 0.49 | 0.52 | 0.51 | 0.54 | 0.49 | 0.51 |
| Public median | 37.64 | | 37.94 | | 49.95 | | 50.83 | |
| Catholic median | 49.26 | | 45.76 | | 54.24 | | 57.31 | |
| Public N | 893 | | 763 | | 1,065 | | 3,288 | |
| Catholic N | 74 | | 80 | | 334 | | 208 | |

a. Weight = F2QWT. The dependent variable is the second follow-up math score standardized using Item Response Theory. For specifications and other details, see notes for table 3A.

**Table 4A. Median Regression Results for Twelfth-Grade Math Score, Expanded Sample, Unweighted[a]**

| Variable | Urban minorities | | Suburban minorities | | Urban white | | Suburban white | |
|---|---|---|---|---|---|---|---|---|
| | A | B | A | B | A | B | A | B |
| Catholic school | 5.47 | 3.26 | 1.67 | 1.33 | 2.13 | 2.00 | 2.85 | 2.14 |
| | (2.74) | (2.85) | (3.52) | (3.79) | (1.47) | (1.72) | (1.61) | (1.67) |
| Eighth-grade GPA | 4.33 | 3.57 | 4.76 | 4.15 | 4.52 | 3.07 | 4.43 | 3.63 |
| | (1.08) | (1.20) | (1.44) | (1.58) | (0.98) | (1.15) | (0.60) | (0.66) |
| Eighth-grade math score | 1.10 | 1.02 | 1.00 | 0.95 | 0.88 | 0.86 | 0.89 | 0.82 |
| | (0.08) | (0.09) | (0.10) | (0.11) | (0.06) | (0.07) | (0.04) | (0.04) |
| Black | -2.52 | -2.52 | -0.17 | 0.87 | ... | ... | ... | ... |
| | (1.38) | (1.96) | (2.03) | (2.88) | | | | |
| $R^2$ | 0.32 | 0.35 | 0.34 | 0.37 | 0.41 | 0.43 | 0.41 | 0.44 |
| Public median | 34.36 | | 35.60 | | 49.49 | | 49.44 | |
| Catholic median | 49.10 | | 45.76 | | 56.00 | | 56.18 | |
| Public N | 1,113 | | 927 | | 1,189 | | 3,565 | |
| Catholic N | 77 | | 83 | | 337 | | 210 | |

a. The dependent variable is the second follow-up math score standardized using Item Response Theory. If a student selected for the second follow-up failed to take the test and is identified as a current or past dropout, we impute a score of 0. For specifications and other details, see notes to table 3A.

**Table 4B. Median Regression Results for Twelfth-Grade Math Score, Expanded Sample, Weighted[a]**

| Variable | Urban minorities | | Suburban minorities | | Urban white | | Suburban white | |
|---|---|---|---|---|---|---|---|---|
| | A | B | A | B | A | B | A | B |
| Catholic school | 6.66 | 5.12 | 1.94 | 0.84 | 2.40 | 2.82 | 3.22 | 2.43 |
| | (2.32) | (2.43) | (3.51) | (3.81) | (1.39) | (1.62) | (1.48) | (1.55) |
| Eighth-grade GPA | 3.94 | 4.05 | 4.46 | 4.14 | 3.65 | 1.61 | 3.88 | 3.58 |
| | (0.89) | (1.06) | (1.42) | (1.59) | (0.77) | (0.98) | (0.55) | (0.61) |
| Eighth-grade math score | 1.11 | 0.95 | 1.04 | 1.02 | 0.89 | 0.89 | 0.92 | 0.82 |
| | (0.07) | (0.08) | (0.10) | (0.11) | (0.05) | (0.06) | (0.03) | (0.04) |
| Black | -1.33 | -1.55 | -0.85 | 0.45 | ... | ... | ... | ... |
| | (1.21) | (1.68) | (1.88) | (2.84) | | | | |
| $R^2$ | 0.29 | 0.36 | 0.38 | 0.45 | 0.42 | 0.47 | 0.41 | 0.44 |
| Public median | 33.95 | | 33.31 | | 48.30 | | 48.65 | |
| Catholic median | 49.26 | | 44.66 | | 53.96 | | 57.15 | |
| Public N | 1,051 | | 891 | | 1,159 | | 3,526 | |
| Catholic N | 77 | | 83 | | 336 | | 210 | |

a. Weight = F2QWT. The dependent variable is the second follow-up math score standardized using Item Response Theory. If a student selected for the second follow-up failed to take the test and is identified as a current or past dropout, we impute a score of 0. The sample sizes differ slightly from those in table 4A because the NELS assigns sampling weights of zero for students who failed to complete both the cognitive test and the student questionnaire. For specifications and other details, see notes to table 3A.

## The Role of Unmeasured Traits

While the analyses above include numerous controls for previous academic performance and family background, we do not claim that these controls measure all students traits that affect attainment or achievement. Further, it seems reasonable to suspect that Catholic-school students may be different from their public-school counterparts with respect to some unmeasured traits that affect attainment and achievement. If Joe and Bob are identical with respect to all of the control variables, but Joe attends a public school and Bob attends a Catholic school, obvious questions arise concerning the unmeasured characteristics of these students and their families that led them to make different school-attendance decisions. What are these characteristics, and do they have a direct impact on achievement and attendance?

A common argument in the literature on private-school effects contends that any unmeasured traits that explain selection into private schools should have direct impacts on student performance, because families spend additional resources to send their children to private schools. These expenditures signal differences in either tastes or incomes that lead private-school families to make an additional investment in education. It seems reasonable to suspect that these private-school families make other additional investments in their children that are not measured but are related to attainment and achievement. Given this line of argument, one expects that univariate analyses will always be biased toward finding positive effects of private schooling regardless of the available controls for measured student characteristics.

It is not the case, however, that all univariate analyses yield results that imply gains in attainment and achievement in private schools. For example, the univariate analyses of white suburban students provide no evidence that Catholic schooling enhances educational attainment. Further, in tables 5A and 5B, we find similar results when we examine outcomes for students in non-Catholic private schools. These tables present univariate analyses that include not only public- and Catholic-school students, but also students from private schools that are accredited by the National Association of Independent Schools (NAIS).[15] The specifications include the same controls used in the most complete specifications. The attainment specifications are the same as model C in table 1B, and the achievement specification is the same as model B in table 4B. We esti-

15. While private schools are heterogeneous on many dimensions, the NAIS sample does provide a set of non-Catholic, private schools that share a common set of accreditation standards.

mate these models only on white samples because the NELS data contain just a handful of minority students who attend non-Catholic private schools.[16]

The descriptive statistics in tables 5A and 5B show that, with the exception of the weighted graduation rates for suburban whites, there are no significant differences in graduation rates among NAIS and Catholic schools. Both NAIS students and Catholic-school students graduate from high school more frequently than do public-school students. College-attendance rates are roughly 10 percentage points higher in NAIS schools than in Catholic schools, which are in turn 20 to 25 percentage points higher than attendance rates in public schools. Despite the high attainment levels in NAIS schools, however, neither table provides any evidence that NAIS schools perform better than public schools. In fact, the only statistically significant effect of NAIS schooling is a negative one. The high-school graduation rate of suburban whites in NAIS schools is higher than the corresponding rate in public schools but lower than expected given the NAIS students' characteristics. Appendix A shows that NAIS students come from quite privileged backgrounds and that they enter high school with strong academic records. The results in table 5A and 5B indicate that the NELS measures of family background and academic performance prior to high school fully account for the higher levels of attainment observed for NAIS students. Further, the tables show that these measures also account for differences in achievement between NAIS students and their public-school counterparts. In contrast, Catholic schooling is associated with higher math achievement among urban and suburban whites, given the same controls for student characteristics. These estimated achievement effects are noteworthy because Catholic-school students do not score nearly as well on the twelfth-grade exam as their NAIS counterparts.

The NAIS results illustrate that the NELS data provide important controls for student aptitude and family background. Among white students, these controls account for the large attainment and achievement gaps observed between public- and NAIS-school students. Further, the results dispel the notion that univariate models necessarily yield positive treatment effects for private schools. Nonetheless, these results do not speak directly to the potential correlation between unmeasured student traits and Catholic-school attendance. Thus the next section develops an explicit bivariate model of Catholic-school attendance and student outcomes.

16. In fact, if we restrict our attention to students who participated in the third follow-up, the NELS provides only twenty-two urban minority students and nineteen suburban minority students attending NAIS schools in tenth grade.

**Table 5A. Attainment and Achievement Analyses Involving NAIS Schools, Unweighted[a]**

| Variable | High school graduation | | College attendance | | Twelfth-grade math median test score | |
|---|---|---|---|---|---|---|
| | Urban white | Suburban white | Urban white | Suburban white | Urban white | Suburban white |
| Catholic school | 0.72 | 0.83 | 0.23 | 0.16 | 2.10 | 2.35 |
| | (0.19) | (0.32) | (0.11) | (0.11) | (1.53) | (1.59) |
| | 0.07 | 0.08 | 0.06 | 0.04 | ... | ... |
| NAIS school | -0.10 | -0.27 | 0.42 | 0.11 | 1.16 | 0.72 |
| | (0.25) | (0.27) | (0.17) | (0.20) | (1.68) | (1.73) |
| | -0.01 | -0.04 | 0.10 | 0.03 | ... | ... |
| Graduation and attendance rate: Public schools | 0.84 | 0.88 | 0.52 | 0.54 | ... | ... |
| Graduation and attendance rate: Catholic schools | 0.98 | 0.99 | 0.77 | 0.78 | ... | ... |
| Graduation and attendance rate: NAIS schools | 0.97 | 0.97 | 0.93 | 0.91 | ... | ... |
| Public median | ... | ... | ... | ... | 49.49 | 49.44 |
| Catholic median | ... | ... | ... | ... | 56.00 | 56.18 |
| NAIS median | ... | ... | ... | ... | 66.33 | 64.42 |
| Public N | 1,080 | 3,454 | 1,080 | 3,454 | 1,189 | 3,565 |
| Catholic N | 355 | 267 | 355 | 267 | 337 | 210 |
| NAIS N | 235 | 131 | 235 | 131 | 424 | 207 |

a. The model specifications are the same as those for table 1A, model C, and table 4A, model B.

**Table 5B. Attainment and Achievement Analyses Involving NAIS Schools, Weighted[a]**

| Variable | High-school graduation | | College attendance | | Twelfth-grade math median test score | |
|---|---|---|---|---|---|---|
| | Urban white | Suburban white | Urban white | Suburban white | Urban white | Suburban white |
| Catholic school | 0.63 | 0.46 | 0.23 | 0.09 | 2.79 | 2.63 |
| | (0.26) | (0.37) | (0.15) | (0.15) | (1.62) | (1.60) |
| | 0.07 | 0.06 | 0.06 | 0.02 | | |
| NAIS school | −0.24 | −0.92 | 0.16 | −0.20 | 0.54 | −2.41 |
| | (0.33) | (0.39) | (0.22) | (0.26) | (3.38) | (3.27) |
| | −0.04 | −0.18 | 0.04 | −0.06 | | |
| Graduation and attendance rate: Public schools | 0.85 | 0.86 | 0.51 | 0.55 | ... | ... |
| Graduation and attendance rate: Catholic schools | 0.97 | 0.98 | 0.72 | 0.79 | ... | ... |
| Graduation and attendance rate: NAIS schools | 0.98 | 0.90 | 0.86 | 0.86 | ... | ... |
| Public median | ... | ... | ... | ... | 48.30 | 48.65 |
| Catholic median | ... | ... | ... | ... | 53.96 | 57.15 |
| NAIS median | ... | ... | ... | ... | 66.55 | 65.67 |
| Public N | 1,080 | 3,454 | 1,080 | 3,454 | 1,159 | 3,526 |
| Catholic N | 355 | 267 | 355 | 267 | 336 | 210 |
| NAIS N | 235 | 131 | 235 | 131 | 424 | 206 |

a. Weights = F3QWT, F2QWT. For specifications, see table 5A.

Before turning to the bivariate analyses, we note that the NAIS results raise questions concerning the motivations of parents who send their children to these schools. Why would these parents pay significant tuition to send their children to schools that do not enhance achievement or attainment? We conjecture that there may be human-capital or social-capital gains from private schooling that are realized later in life. These gains may arise from social networks developed in school or from access to better colleges after high school.

Finally, while the empirical model treats the gain from a particular type of private schooling as a constant within the geographic subsamples, we are not assuming that all schools within a given sector are of equal quality. It seems reasonable to assume that those students who attend the most elite private schools would have attended elite public schools if they had been forced to chose a public school. Wealthy families have financial resources that make it easier to live in school districts or attendance zones with the best public schools. These same families may also use their resources to help their children gain access to the best magnet schools.

*Bivariate Models*

Tables 6A and 6B present results from bivariate models of high-school graduation and college attendance. These models contain two equations. The first captures the determinants of the value of attending a Catholic school. The second is the attainment equation. In table 6A the attainment equation captures the determinants of the value of graduating from high school. In table 6B the attainment equation captures benefits of college attendance. We assume that the error terms from the equations are drawn from a bivariate normal distribution. Even if both equations contain the same measures of student characteristics, the model is still identified by assumptions concerning the functional forms of the equations and the joint normality of the errors.

In an effort to improve this model, however, we create variables that are intended to help explain students' choices among Catholic and public schools but are not related to student outcomes given their choice of school. Following earlier work, we constructed the number of Catholic schools per square mile in each county.[17] This density index serves as a measure of the transportation costs involved in attending a Catholic school. We also compute the fraction of each county's population that reports adherence to the Catholic

17. Neal (1997).

religion.[18] We use this adherent index as a measure of local support for schol-arship funds and other subsidies to Catholic schools. By constructing measures that capture geographic differences in the cost of attending these schools, we hoped to create indexes that would help explain Catholic attendance decisions yet still be orthogonal to unmeasured traits that influence individual achieve-ment and attainment. The aforementioned work by Neal has provided a simple model of school choice that illustrates how costs of private schooling may affect attendance decisions but have no direct effect on student outcomes. Nonetheless, because the indexes vary geographically, they may be correlated with unmeasured student traits that vary across localities. We used standard likelihood-ratio tests to evaluate the hypothesis that the adherent and density indexes affect school choice but do not affect student outcomes. Even though the analyses include controls for geographic region, we found that the adher-ent and density indexes cannot be excluded from the attainment models for minorities. Therefore, we estimate bivariate probit models for the minority samples that are identified only by the assumptions concerning the functional form of the model and the joint normality of the errors.

The results for urban minorities are as follows. The estimated covariance between the error terms in the attainment equations and the Catholic-school attendance equations implies negative selection into Catholic schools, and therefore the estimated effects of Catholic schooling on high-school gradua-tion and college attendance are even larger than those reported in the univariate models. However, the estimated treatment effect in the college-attendance equation is imprecisely estimated, and we fail to reject the null hypothesis that the errors in the college attendance and Catholic-school attendance equations are uncorrelated.

For suburban minorities, both models provide weak evidence of positive selection into Catholic schools. The estimated effect of Catholic schooling on college attendance is much smaller than the corresponding estimate from the univariate model, but it is imprecisely estimated. Once again, we cannot reject the null hypothesis that the error terms are uncorrelated.

Among whites, we exclude the density index from the attainment equation as well as an interaction term between the index and Catholic religious affil-

18. The school data come from *Catholic Schools in America* (Washington: National Catholic Education Association, 1989). The data on Catholic adherents come from *The Survey of Churches and Church Membership* (SCCM, 1990), We eliminated several counties and inde-pendent cities in Virginia because the SCCM data code counties containing independent cities differently from the census bureau.

**Table 6A. Bivariate Probit Model of High-School Graduation and Catholic-School Attendance[a]**

| Variable | Urban minorities | | Suburban minorities | | Urban white | | Suburban white | |
|---|---|---|---|---|---|---|---|---|
| | High school graduate | Catholic school | High school graduate | Catholic school | High school graduate | Catholic school | High school graduate | Catholic school |
| Catholic school | 2.76 | ... | 0.13 | ... | 1.55 | ... | 0.07 | ... |
| | (0.40) | | (1.19) | | (0.29) | | (0.47) | |
| Density index[b] | −3.83 | 4.95 | 6.25 | 20.11 | ... | 7.71 | ... | 22.97 |
| | (1.11) | (0.96) | (4.68) | (3.18) | | (2.21) | | (4.77) |
| Adherent index[c] | −1.09 | 0.14 | −0.05 | 2.11 | −0.41 | 0.28 | 0.48 | 2.47 |
| | (0.56) | (1.07) | (0.55) | (1.06) | (0.56) | (0.52) | (0.36) | (0.36) |
| Catholic | 0.01 | 2.02 | 0.03 | 1.79 | −0.26 | 1.46 | 0.03 | 1.53 |
| | (0.33) | (0.55) | (0.38) | (0.45) | (0.31) | (0.35) | (0.21) | (0.31) |
| Catholic*density | 2.04 | −2.20 | −3.05 | −8.27 | ... | −0.40 | ... | −0.11 |
| | (1.62) | (1.63) | (4.15) | (3.33) | | (2.53) | | (5.61) |
| Catholic*adherent | 1.15 | −1.34 | 0.07 | −1.48 | 0.06 | 0.47 | 0.52 | −0.90 |
| | (0.76) | (1.23) | (0.78) | (1.17) | (0.92) | (0.66) | (0.56) | (0.51) |
| ρ | −1.00 | | 0.15 | | −0.59 | | 0.15 | |
| Wald test for ρ = 0 p value | 5.81 | | 0.07 | | 7.94 | | 0.76 | |
| ρ = ρ | 0.02 | | 0.79 | | 0.00 | | 0.38 | |
| N | 1,213 | | 1,090 | | 1,435 | | 3,721 | |

a. Weight = F3QWT. Due to problems with model convergence, these models do not contain eighth-grade behavior-problem indicators. Numbers in parentheses, unless otherwise specified, are standard errors.

b. The density index is Catholic schools per square mile.

c. The adherent index is the fraction of the county population that reports affiliation with the Catholic Church.

**Table 6B. Bivariate Probit Model of College Attendance and Catholic-School Attendance[a]**

| Variable | Urban minorities | | Suburban minorities | | Urban white | | Suburban white | |
|---|---|---|---|---|---|---|---|---|
| | College attendance | Catholic school | College attendance | Catholic school | College attendance | Catholic school | College attendance | Catholic school |
| Catholic school | 2.20 | ... | 0.30 | ... | 0.36 | ... | 0.21 | ... |
| | (7.32) | | (1.70) | | (0.54) | | (0.31) | |
| Density index | -3.22 | 4.70 | 3.42 | 20.19 | ... | 7.93 | ... | 23.53 |
| | (3.98) | (1.82) | (5.39) | (3.16) | | (2.17) | | (4.78) |
| Adherent index | 0.05 | 0.47 | 0.26 | 2.17 | 0.18 | 0.38 | 0.83 | 2.41 |
| | (0.68) | (0.91) | (0.48) | (0.99) | (0.48) | (0.51) | (0.37) | (0.39) |
| Catholic | -0.26 | 2.21 | 0.25 | 1.88 | -0.05 | 1.49 | 0.24 | 1.53 |
| | (1.08) | (1.73) | (0.32) | (0.56) | (0.27) | (0.36) | (0.15) | (0.31) |
| Catholic*density | 3.19 | -1.75 | 0.11 | -8.55 | ... | -0.29 | ... | -0.91 |
| | (2.30) | (1.67) | (3.30) | (3.62) | | (2.55) | | (5.78) |
| Catholic*adherent | 0.44 | -1.68 | 0.09 | -1.59 | 1.34 | 0.45 | -0.44 | -0.85 |
| | (1.80) | (1.90) | (0.58) | (1.06) | (0.82) | (0.67) | (0.39) | (0.51) |
| ρ | -0.72 | | 0.25 | | -0.09 | | -0.08 | |
| Wald test for ρ = 0 p-value | 0.01 | | 0.08 | | 0.09 | | 0.24 | |
| ρ = ρ | 0.93 | | 0.78 | | 0.76 | | 0.63 | |
| N | 1,213 | | 1,090 | | 1,435 | | 3,721 | |

a. See notes to table 6A.

iation.[19] We do not exclude terms involving the adherent index, because Neal's aforementioned work with the NLSY data found that Catholic-adherent indexes are correlated with unmeasured traits that influence attainment. The results also indicate that, all else constant, college-attendance rates among suburban whites vary positively with the fraction of Catholics in the local population. Among whites, the most noteworthy result comes from the high-school graduation model for urban students. Here we can reject the univariate model in favor of the bivariate model, and there is evidence of negative selection into Catholic schools. Relative to their public-school counterparts, urban whites who attend these schools appear to possess unmeasured traits that inhibit attainment.[20] These results strengthen the case that Catholic schooling does raise graduation rates for urban whites as well as for urban minorities.

The univariate results indicate large gains in attainment for urban minorities attending Catholic schools, and the bivariate results provide no evidence that these gains are driven by selection into these schools on unmeasured student traits. However, bivariate models do not perform well. Among urban minorities, these models provide little information concerning selection into Catholic schools on unmeasured traits. Estimates of the covariances between the error terms in these models are quite imprecise. The bivariate models perform a little better among urban whites, and they provide some additional support for the view that Catholic schooling enhances graduation rates among urban whites.

Among suburban students, univariate results suggest that Catholic schooling may enhance college attendance among minorities, but bivariate results provide some support for the hypothesis that this result may be driven by positive selection into suburban Catholic schools. Neither univariate nor bivariate

19. Likelihood-ratio tests indicate that, among both suburban and urban whites, we cannot reject these exclusion restrictions in either the graduation or college-attendance models.

20. Evidence of negative selection is common in this literature. Coleman and Hoffer (1987), Evans and Schwab (1995), and Neal (1997) all report evidence of negative selection into Catholic schools. A common hypothesis concerning this result is that some parents send their children to Catholic schools seeking a remedy for existing problems with discipline and motivation. We note that this conjecture is shared by one of our commentators, Robert Schwab, and conference participant Edwin Mills. Coleman and Hoffer (1987) also discuss this possibility. Joseph Altonji, Todd Elder, and Christopher Taber (1999) address selection on unmeasured traits in a different way. Their paper focuses on the sample of students who attended Catholic schools in eighth grade. They argue that selection on unobserved traits may be less of a concern in their analyses because, among students who attend Catholic school in eighth grade, there are small differences between the observed characteristics of public- and Catholic-high-school students. They report significant attainment gains associated with Catholic schooling, but find little evidence that Catholic schooling enhances achievement.

analyses provide any evidence that Catholic schooling enhances attainment among suburban whites.

### Heterogeneity within Groups

Because the bivariate models perform poorly, we must rely heavily on the univariate results in drawing overall conclusions. Before turning to the data on the geographic distribution of Catholic schools, we explore one more issue concerning the interpretation of the univariate results. Recall that the univariate models take the following form:

$$y_i = x_i \beta + C_i \gamma + \epsilon_i \; .$$

As an example, consider the test-score regressions, where $y_i$ is the twelfth-grade math score, $x_i$ is a vector of individual characteristics, and $\epsilon_i$ captures unmeasured individual traits that affect achievement. Thus far we have been primarily concerned with the hypothesis that students in Catholic schools, $C_i = 1$, are somehow more able or more motivated than their equivalent counterparts in public schools. This represents a concern about differences in general talents among Catholic-school students and similar students in public schools. However, even if Catholic-school students do possess the same general levels of talent as similar students in public schools, it is still possible that students in Catholic schools are somehow better suited to Catholic schooling than their counterparts in public schools. Even though the samples are homogeneous with respect to minority status and community type, it is possible that individuals within these samples still differ in how well they match with Catholic schooling. Catholic schools are highly structured environments guided by a specific set of values and beliefs. Thus unmeasured differences in personality type and beliefs may affect how much individual students stand to gain from Catholic schooling.

Suppose we relax the assumption that $\gamma$ is a common gain from Catholic schooling and entertain the possibility that students in the samples do differ in the gains they receive from this schooling. Given another set of assumptions about the error term in the model, we can still provide a straightforward interpretation of the empirical results. Begin by assuming that the error term in the empirical model takes the form:

$$\epsilon_i = C_i \theta_i + \nu_i .$$

As before, $\in_i$ captures all unmeasured determinants of either test scores or the value of educational attainment. But now these determinants consist of two components. The first, $C_i \theta_i$, captures factors that relate specifically to Catholic schooling. The indicator $C_i$ equals 1 if the student attends Catholic school. The match value, $\theta_i$, captures how well student $i$ is suited to Catholic schooling. Obviously, if a student attends public school, $C_i = 0$, and this component plays no role. The second component, $v_i$, captures general individual traits such as motivation and ability.

Given this analytical framework, we can offer the following interpretation of the parameter $\gamma$ and the error component $\theta_i$. Define $\gamma$ as the average gain from Catholic schooling among those who do in fact attend Catholic school, $C_i = 1$, and among these students define $\theta_i$ as an individual deviation from $\gamma$. In addition, make two assumptions concerning the error-term components. First, as always, general unobserved traits, $v_i$, must be uncorrelated with both Catholic-school attendance, $C_i$, and observed student characteristics, $x_i$. But in addition, assume that, among those attending Catholic schools, the unobserved individual matches with Catholic schooling, $\theta_i$, are not correlated with individual characteristics, $x_i$.[21] This approach recognizes that individuals may differ in their gains from Catholic schooling; given this approach, one may interpret the estimated Catholic-school effects as estimates of *average* gains enjoyed by those who actually attend Catholic schools.[22] This alternative interpretation of the results highlights the possibility that any future expansions of Catholic schooling in response to increased funding through public or private

21. More formally, we define $\gamma$ as $E(\eta_i \mid C_i = 1)$, where $\eta_i$ captures how well individual $i$ matches with Catholic schooling. Futher, $\theta_i = \eta_i - \gamma$. We assume that $E(v_i \mid x_i, C_i) = 0$, and that $E(\theta_i \mid x_i, C_i = 1) = 0$ for all individuals $i$. These assumptions imply that $E(\in_i \mid x_i, C_i) = 0$ for all $i$. To apply this approach to the attainment models, we need the additional assumption that the error term $\in_i$ is an independent and identically distributed draw from a normal distribution for all individuals. Since $\in_i$ is the sum of two components for individuals in Catholic schools, this maintained assumption requires that the variance of unmeasured general skills, $v_i$, is smaller among students attending Catholic school. Here we do not explore analyses that specify separate distributions for each error component. See Heckman and Robb (1985) for a more extensive treatment of models with heterogeneous treatment effects.

22. Based on the estimated Catholic-school effects in the attainment models, we have recalculated the average effects of Catholic schooling on the probabilities of high-school graduation and college attendance using only students who attend Catholic high schools. Given the complete set of controls, this procedure yields average gains from Catholic schooling that are usually the same as or slightly smaller than the overall average gains reported in tables 1B and 2B. The only noteworthy changes involve high-school graduation rates. Among urban minorities, the average change in the probability of graduation implied by the estimated Catholic-school effect is 0.10 among those in Catholic schools compared to 0.18 overall. Among urban whites, the corresponding figures are 0.04 among those in Catholic schools versus 0.07 overall.

voucher programs may involve students who will not experience the same gains from Catholic schooling that current Catholic-school students enjoy.


## The Availability of Catholic Schools

We now turn to a description of the geographic distribution of Catholic secondary schools and the changes in this distribution in recent decades. Because the evidence suggests that the gains from Catholic schooling are concentrated in cities, especially in those cities where large numbers of minority students attend Catholic schools, we feel it is important to understand more about the locations of these schools, although we are not prepared to offer detailed explanations for the existing distribution of these schools or its evolution during the past several decades.

The National Catholic Educational Association (NCEA) publishes an annual directory of all Catholic schools entitled *Catholic Schools in America*. The earliest available directory provides data for 1974. Here we employ data from the 1974, 1979, 1984, 1989, 1994, and 1999 directories. We used the zip code associated with each school's address to map each school to a place, county, and state. Some schools are in areas that are not part of a census-defined place. For these schools, we identify only state and county, but for the purpose of several analyses below, we assume that these schools are located in communities of less than 25,000 people.

Tables 7A and 7B describe the evolution of the geographic distribution of Catholic secondary schools by city size. Three results from these tables stand out. First, across all types of cities, the supply of Catholic high schools shrank notably from 1974 to 1994 and then remained relatively constant between 1994 and 1999. The total supply of Catholic high schools shrank by more than 28 percent during the period 1974–99, but almost all of this change occurred by 1994. Some may wonder whether this reduction, in part, reflects a move toward larger schools and related efforts to merge schools operating at small enrollment levels. This seems unlikely. Across large cities, small cities, and more rural areas, the average enrollment of existing Catholic high schools has declined as the number of existing schools has diminished.[23]

---

23. Across all schools located in cities with 1990 populations greater than 500,000, initial enrollment exceeds the most recent recorded enrollment by an average of 147 students. For other city sizes, the corresponding differentials range from 31 to 95 students.

Table 7A. Supply of Catholic Secondary Schools, 1974–99, by City Size
Number of schools

| Population | 1974 | 1979 | 1984 | 1989 | 1994 | 1999 | Percentage change |
|---|---|---|---|---|---|---|---|
| More than 500,000 | 347 | 307 | 282 | 265 | 229 | 223 | –36 |
| 250,000–500,000 | 171 | 160 | 142 | 130 | 118 | 118 | –31 |
| 100,000–250,000 | 185 | 167 | 154 | 140 | 127 | 128 | –31 |
| 50,000–100,000 | 226 | 204 | 192 | 179 | 166 | 161 | –29 |
| 25,000–50,000 | 225 | 214 | 207 | 201 | 192 | 193 | –14 |
| Less than 25,000 | 565 | 517 | 486 | 444 | 406 | 407 | –28 |
| Total | 1,719 | 1,569 | 1,463 | 1,359 | 1,238 | 1,230 | –28 |

Source: The city population measure comes from the 1990 census.

Table 7B. Changes in the Supply of Catholic Secondary Schools, by City Size
Number of schools

| Population | 1974–79 | | 1979–84 | | 1984–89 | | 1989–94 | | 1994–99 | |
|---|---|---|---|---|---|---|---|---|---|---|
| | New schools | Closed schools | New schools | Closed schools | New schools | Closed schools | New schools | Closed schools | New schools | Closed schools |
| More than 500,000 | 6 | 46 | 4 | 29 | 6 | 23 | 3 | 39 | 7 | 13 |
| 250,000–500,000 | 6 | 17 | 4 | 22 | 4 | 16 | 1 | 13 | 4 | 4 |
| 100,000–250,000 | 5 | 23 | 2 | 15 | 1 | 15 | 4 | 17 | 5 | 4 |
| 50,000–100,000 | 2 | 24 | 4 | 16 | 0 | 13 | 5 | 18 | 7 | 12 |
| 25,000–50,000 | 5 | 16 | 8 | 15 | 7 | 13 | 3 | 12 | 10 | 9 |
| Less than 25,000 | 20 | 68 | 12 | 43 | 13 | 55 | 17 | 55 | 27 | 26 |

Second, Catholic schools have been and remain more prominent in cities than in rural areas. In table 7A, the category "Population < 25,000" captures all census-recognized places with fewer than 25,000 people in 1990, as well as communities that are too small to be recognized as a place. Note that in both 1974 and 1999 these places and communities contain roughly one-third of all Catholic high schools. However, in 1990 these places and communities contained roughly 54 percent of the United States population.[24]

Third, although the fraction of Catholic schools in small towns and rural areas appears to be relatively stable during the 1974–99 period, the relative supplies of Catholic schools have not remained constant across cities of different sizes. Both in relative and absolute terms, large cities experienced the greatest declines in their stocks of Catholic high schools. Cities with more than 500,000 residents in 1990 experienced a decline of 36 percent in their stocks of Catholic schools. In contrast, cities with 1990 populations between 25,000 and 50,000 saw a decline of only 14 percent.

Table 8 provides details concerning the stock of Catholic schools in all cities that had more than five Catholic schools in 1974. During the period from 1974 to 1999, many cities lost a significant fraction of their Catholic high schools. The number of schools in Chicago shrank from fifty-one to twenty-seven. Further, Boston, Detroit, Pittsburgh, San Francisco, and Washington, D.C., all lost at least half of their Catholic high schools. In unreported analyses, we created similar figures for all cities with at least 250,000 persons in 1990. Of these sixty-seven cities, only Austin, Fresno, Fort Worth, and Virginia Beach experienced an increase in the availability of Catholic secondary schools. A second school opened in both Fresno and Fort Worth, while the first Catholic high schools opened in Austin and Virginia Beach.

In table 9, we examine correlates of the changes in Catholic-school availability. Here the unit of observation is a city. We restrict our attention to cities that had at least one Catholic school in 1974, and we also eliminate cities that we could not match with population data from both the 1970 and 1990 summary counts for census places. Further, we do not include cities from Virginia, due to difficulties with Virginia data on Catholic adherents.[25] The dependent variable is the change in the number of Catholic secondary schools between 1974 and 1999. Column A includes only a set of dummies for city size. The

---

24. The numbers in table 7A do not provide the exact total of Catholic high schools in the United States. We eliminated four schools in Alaska from our analyses because of changes in geocode definitions over time.

25. We lose thirteen cities in Virginia. However, this restriction does not affect the results in any noteworthy way.

**Table 8. Availability of Catholic Secondary Schools, 1974–99[a]**

| City | 1974 | 1979 | 1984 | 1989 | 1994 | 1999 |
|---|---|---|---|---|---|---|
| New York | 84 | 71 | 68 | 66 | 61 | 60 |
| Chicago | 51 | 45 | 36 | 32 | 29 | 27 |
| Los Angeles | 24 | 24 | 23 | 22 | 20 | 18 |
| Philadelphia | 24 | 22 | 21 | 20 | 16 | 14 |
| New Orleans | 20 | 20 | 19 | 17 | 14 | 14 |
| Boston | 19 | 15 | 13 | 13 | 8 | 7 |
| Detroit | 17 | 15 | 11 | 10 | 7 | 8 |
| Washington | 15 | 12 | 12 | 10 | 6 | 7 |
| Pittsburgh | 14 | 12 | 8 | 6 | 5 | 6 |
| San Francisco | 14 | 13 | 12 | 10 | 7 | 7 |
| Buffalo | 13 | 11 | 10 | 7 | 7 | 7 |
| San Antonio | 12 | 10 | 10 | 10 | 9 | 8 |
| St. Louis | 12 | 8 | 9 | 7 | 7 | 7 |
| Omaha | 11 | 10 | 9 | 9 | 6 | 6 |
| Cincinnati | 10 | 10 | 9 | 9 | 9 | 9 |
| Baltimore | 10 | 10 | 10 | 9 | 9 | 8 |
| Milwaukee | 9 | 8 | 7 | 6 | 5 | 6 |
| Louisville | 9 | 7 | 8 | 9 | 8 | 8 |
| Cleveland | 9 | 8 | 7 | 7 | 5 | 5 |
| Indianapolis | 9 | 6 | 6 | 6 | 6 | 6 |
| Columbus | 8 | 7 | 7 | 6 | 5 | 5 |
| Kansas City | 8 | 8 | 5 | 5 | 5 | 4 |
| Houston | 7 | 8 | 8 | 8 | 7 | 7 |
| Toledo | 7 | 7 | 6 | 5 | 5 | 5 |
| Honolulu | 6 | 6 | 6 | 6 | 5 | 5 |
| Miami | 6 | 5 | 3 | 3 | 3 | 3 |

a. Sample includes all the cities that had more than five Catholic secondary schools in 1974. The numbers for 1979 differ in some cases from those reported in Neal (1997). Neal used the city listed in each school's mailing address to calculate city-specific totals. This procedure led to false counts for two reasons. First, some schools in suburbs use a central-city name in their mailing address. Second, some schools located in unincorporated communities within cities list the community name in their mailing address—for example, East Boston, Massachusetts, actually lies within the Boston city limits.

omitted category includes small towns with populations less than 25,000 in 1990. The results indicate that cities with more than 500,000 residents lost about five schools more, on average, than small towns. Column B highlights the relationship between population changes and changes in the supply of Catholic high schools. We use the difference in the number of children under age fourteen between 1970 and 1990 to measure changes in the youth population for cities, and include separate measures for black, Hispanic, and white youth.[26] Two interesting results emerge from this regression. First, the measures of youth-population change account for a large portion of the school closings in large cities. Holding changes in youth population constant, cities

26. The "white" category includes all nonblack and non-Hispanic youth.

**Table 9. Change in the Supply of Catholic Secondary Schools (OLS)[a]**

| Variable | A | B | C |
|---|---|---|---|
| Population | | | |
| More than 500,000 | –5.24 | –1.13 | –1.18 |
| | (0.31) | (0.24) | (0.25) |
| 250,000–500,000 | –1.09 | –0.30 | –0.33 |
| | (0.24) | (0.16) | (0.17) |
| 100,000–250,000 | –0.24 | –0.08 | –0.10 |
| | (0.17) | (0.11) | (0.11) |
| 50,000–100,000 | –0.12 | 0.02 | 0.01 |
| | (0.14) | (0.09) | (0.09) |
| 25,000–50,000 | 0.14 | 0.21 | 0.21 |
| | (0.14) | (0.09) | (0.09) |
| Change in youth (units of 10,000) | | | |
| White | ... | 0.42 | 0.42 |
| | | (0.02) | (0.02) |
| Black | ... | 0.74 | 0.74 |
| | | (0.06) | (0.05) |
| Hispanic | ... | 0.23 | 0.23 |
| | | (0.04) | (0.04) |
| Region | | | |
| Northeast | ... | ... | –0.001 |
| | | | (0.13) |
| North-central | ... | ... | 0.26 |
| | | | (0.12) |
| South | ... | ... | 0.34 |
| | | | (0.11) |
| Change in Catholic adherents | ... | ... | 0.004 |
| (Units of 10,000; counties: 1980–90) | | | (0.0017) |
| N | 764 | 764 | 764 |
| $R^2$ | 0.30 | 0.71 | 0.72 |

a. We include cities with at least one Catholic high school in 1974 and population data for 1970 and 1990. We also dropped cities in Virginia because the SCCM data on Catholic adherents provide nonstandard county codes for Virginia. Numbers in parentheses are standard errors.

in the largest population category experience a net loss of between 0.83 and 1.34 schools relative to cities of other sizes. Second, the racial composition of changes in youth populations matters for changes in school availability. In table 9, population changes are measured in units of 10,000 persons. Therefore, the coefficient of 0.42 in column B implies that a decline of about 24,000 in the white-youth population is associated with the loss of one Catholic high school. However, the corresponding effect for black youth implies that changes in the supply of Catholic high schools are more highly correlated with changes in the population of black youth. Here the estimated coefficient associates a one-unit change in school availability with a change of approximately 13,500 in the black youth population.

Column C adds region dummies and controls for changes in the number of Catholic adherents in the county associated with the city in question. We measure the change in adherents between 1980 and 1990 because data are not available for 1970. Further, we measure the change at the county level because the Survey of Churches and Church Membership does not provide data for units smaller than counties. The introduction of these variables does not greatly affect the other coefficient estimates. However, the region dummies are interesting in their own right. The omitted region is the West. Cities in the North Central and Southern regions exhibit a small edge in maintaining Catholic-school availability. The coefficient for change in Catholic adherents is quite small in magnitude. A change in Catholic adherents of 2.5 million is associated with only a one-school change in supply. We conjecture that this coefficient understates the actual correlation between changes in Catholic adherents and changes in school availability. The measure of adherent change is quite noisy for two reasons. First, it only captures changes over the period 1980–90. Second, it measures changes at the county rather than at the city level. Thus far we have not found data on Catholic adherents that will allow us to construct more accurate measures.

In sum, the NCEA data on Catholic-school availability show a marked decline in Catholic secondary schools through 1994 and little change since then. While the supply of these schools has diminished generally, the supply has declined most dramatically in large cities, the places in which they have their greatest value added. Changes in youth populations account for much but not all of the additional school losses in large cities.

Several questions become apparent in light of the NCEA data. Is the recent growth of both publicly and privately funded voucher programs in part a response to the loss of Catholic-school or other private-school options over the past three decades? Does the reduction in school closings after 1994 reflect support or expected support from publicly or privately funded voucher programs that have been proposed, started, or expanded in recent years? Answers to these questions lie beyond the scope of this paper, but the 1994–99 data should not be ignored. For some reason, a decline in the number of Catholic secondary schools that had continued for at least two decades came to a halt during the last five years. Understanding the reason for this turnaround may be an important step toward understanding how the supply of Catholic and other private schools will change in response to future changes in education policy.

## Conclusion

Analyses of the NELS data provide results that are fairly consistent with previous results reported by Neal and by Evans and Schwab.[27] Catholic secondary schooling is associated with attainment gains for urban students generally and for urban minorities in particular. Suburban whites in Catholic schools do not enjoy significant attainment gains. There is some evidence that Catholic schooling enhances college attendance among suburban minorities but little evidence that Catholic schooling raises high-school graduation rates among these students. With respect to gains in math achievement, the effect of Catholic schooling on median scores is large among urban minorities, although the OLS results imply smaller gains in mean scores. Among whites, Catholic schooling is generally associated with modest achievement gains. There is little evidence, however, that Catholic schooling enhances math achievement among suburban minorities.

Overall, the univariate results suggest that urban minorities gain the most from Catholic schooling, and the bivariate analyses provide no evidence that the univariate results for urban minorities are driven by positive selection into Catholic schools on unmeasured student traits. Nonetheless, we rely primarily, and in many instances exclusively, on assumptions concerning functional forms and error distributions to identify the bivariate models, and we do not offer these results as definitive proof that the univariate results for urban minorities are not affected by selection into Catholic schools on unmeasured student traits.

We noted above the possibility that students in NAIS schools experience small gains in attainment and achievement because their next best option is an elite public school. Similar reasoning may yield some insight into the differences between the estimated gains from Catholic schooling among urban minorities and the estimated gains from such schooling among other groups. Catholic schooling should yield larger benefits among urban minorities if public schools differ greatly in quality and urban minorities face a particularly poor menu of schools within the public sector.[28]

---

27. Neal (1997); Evans and Schwab (1995).

28. Neal (1997) provides some evidence that this is the case. Within the public-school sector, predicted graduation rates for whites and minorities are similar, except in large cities. Urban minorities in large cities graduate at lower rates than expected relative to urban whites, given the similarity between the graduation rates of minorities and white students elsewhere.

Many advocates of publicly funded vouchers hold this view, arguing that voucher programs are especially needed in cities because urban public schools are performing quite poorly, especially in minority communities. Further, most privately funded scholarship programs target disadvantaged students in cities.[29] Such students are often black or Hispanic, and the NELS results suggest that these students may gain the most from access to Catholic schools.

We do not completely understand the determinants of Catholic-school availability in the absence of vouchers, and we do not know what might happen to Catholic-school supply or quality if large-scale voucher plans are adopted. But the track record of success among urban minorities in Catholic secondary schools, combined with the diminished supply of these schools in cities, indicates that much may be at stake in future court decisions that will determine whether or not Catholic schools are allowed to participate in voucher plans.

29. See ⟨http://www.edreform.com/research/pspchart.htm⟩.

**Appendix A. Summary Statistics[a]**

| Variable | Catholic school | | | | Public school | | | | NAIS school | |
|---|---|---|---|---|---|---|---|---|---|---|
| | Urban minority | Suburban minority | Urban white | Suburban white | Urban minority | Suburban minority | Urban white | Suburban white | Urban white | Suburban white |
| Female | 0.54 | 0.49 | 0.47 | 0.38 | 0.53 | 0.48 | 0.49 | 0.49 | 0.47 | 0.36 |
| Black | 0.46 | 0.46 | ... | ... | 0.60 | 0.51 | ... | ... | ... | ... |
| Two-parent family | 0.56 | 0.68 | 0.83 | 0.82 | 0.45 | 0.53 | 0.65 | 0.68 | 0.84 | 0.78 |
| Catholic | 0.54 | 0.56 | 0.80 | 0.80 | 0.32 | 0.33 | 0.30 | 0.27 | 0.17 | 0.46 |
| Eighth-grade GPA[b] | 3.02 | 2.90 | 3.16 | 3.30 | 2.68 | 2.72 | 2.89 | 2.92 | 3.32 | 3.39 |
| | (0.51) | (0.61) | (0.63) | (0.52) | (0.72) | (0.73) | (0.85) | (0.75) | (0.58) | (0.39) |
| 1988 math score[b] | 34.16 | 32.27 | 39.31 | 42.42 | 27.95 | 29.91 | 37.61 | 37.39 | 52.25 | 47.63 |
| | (9.63) | (10.54) | (10.45) | (10.52) | (8.85) | (9.98) | (12.23) | (11.96) | (8.66) | (12.39) |
| Math gain, 1992–88 | 14.53 | 11.33 | 13.98 | 14.80 | 10.31 | 10.02 | 11.64 | 11.80 | 12.10 | 13.71 |
| | (8.83) | (7.63) | (7.17) | (7.56) | (8.25) | (8.05) | (7.45) | (7.74) | (7.76) | (5.27) |
| Family income | 37,900 | 40,852 | 63,493 | 68,606 | 22,574 | 30,695 | 45,358 | 48,622 | 137,005 | 209,015 |
| | (27,822) | (23,720) | (50,614) | (53,957) | (18,519) | (31,312) | (37,429) | (37,242) | (79,788) | (109,519) |
| N | 77 | 83 | 336 | 210 | 1051 | 891 | 1,159 | 3,526 | 424 | 206 |

a. Weight = F2QWT. We make no imputations. Numbers in parentheses are standard errors.
b. The GPA and test-score statistics are based on samples that contain no missing observations.

# Comments

**Eric A. Hanushek:** Understanding the performance of alternative school organizations has become increasingly important. The necessity of school reform has been accepted by a wider and wider segment of the population. And, while the majority still emphasizes finding ways to improve the existing public schools, an increasing sentiment favors introducing alternatives and more parental choice—either charter schools or expanded private schools. Unfortunately, experience with such alternatives remains limited, at least in the United States, so predicting the outcomes of some of these reform ideas rests on inferences and extrapolations from "close substitutes." Jeffrey Grogger and Derek Neal turn to performance in Catholic schools to provide insights. While the approach is not new, their paper provides more evidence on the potential gains from introducing competitive schools.

Catholic schools offer an interesting but complex laboratory for considering competitive alternatives to public schools. Catholic schools, which educate about 5 percent of K–12 students, have evolved over a long time. Thus, in contrast to recent experiences with charter schools or with public or private voucher experiments, they provide observations of outcomes that reflect long-term development of alternatives. The size of the Catholic sector also means that these schools are found across the nation, offering a broad comparison group to the public schools. They are particularly important in urban settings, where Catholic schools offer viable alternatives to urban public schools—schools that remain the object of intense policy concern.

On the other hand, as many previous researchers have noted, inferences about the impacts of these schools are difficult, in large part because of the difficult selection issues. Students in Catholic schools are different from those in public schools. When faced with free public schools, they choose to pay extra to attend the Catholic-school alternative. This fact by itself suggests the

194

potential for problems in extrapolating the experiences of Catholic-school students to others who currently are not attending private alternatives.

The long history of work in this area, reviewed in an earlier paper by Neal, has concentrated on understanding the reasons for choosing Catholic schools and then using that information to modify the estimates of performance differences in the two sectors.[1] This approach is of course difficult to implement in a convincing manner. First, it is difficult to find factors that influence selection but do not influence student performance, making identification of parameters of the selection process difficult. Second, there is a strong suspicion that selection follows from unobserved and unmeasured factors, such as the importance parents attach to school quality. Selection on the basis of unobservable factors makes the task even more difficult.

Grogger and Neal, building particularly on Neal's previous work, extend this analysis to data from the National Education Longitudinal Study (NELS). The NELS data set has both advantages and disadvantages for this analysis. It is more recent than the data sets previously used, allowing insights into more current situations. It also draws a large sample with many private-school observations. But it employs a sampling design that complicates the analysis, because it involves choice-based sampling on important outcomes (dropout behavior).

The analysis has a series of innovative features. Specifically, looking at median scores to provide robust estimation of models in the face of missing test data is very interesting. Additionally, the investigation of the supply of Catholic schools is novel and provides entirely new information about the scope and changes of Catholic education. Finally, while contained in previous work by Neal, the attention to the appropriate public-school comparison group is noteworthy.

*The results.* The central result of their work is the finding that Catholic schools on average appear to provide more learning than the relevant public counterparts. The effectiveness of Catholic schools is concentrated in urban settings, where the public-school performance is of greatest concern and where school choices, at least by the poor, are probably most limited. The differential effectiveness of Catholic schools is much less apparent in suburban areas.

The estimates are derived from rather standard achievement models that have been estimated directly and corrected for selection through estimation of auxiliary Catholic-school attendance equations. Unfortunately, identifica-

1. See Neal (1997).

tion in the selection models comes entirely from the different functional form for the probit selection equation and the linear achievement equation. There is little reason to believe that these are the correct functional forms for either, making the identification based on differential curvature questionable.

They also provide some sensitivity analysis by comparing their results to the private nonsectarian sector (National Association of Independent Schools, or NAIS schools). This analysis suggests that Catholic schools are indeed the highest-performing sector. Correcting for differentials in family background, NAIS schools perform no differently than public schools and worse than Catholic schools. This result is quite surprising, because it appears to violate simple price theory. Public schools are free; Catholic schools charge tuition, although it tends to be rather low; and NAIS schools often charge substantial tuition, making them noticeably more expensive than the alternatives. Yet some percentage of parents systematically chooses NAIS schools despite high cost and mediocre performance. Is this real? Or does it suggest some problem with the analysis?

*Interpretation and policy.* The puzzle remains: when it comes to policy purposes, what do these results mean? Taken literally, the differential performance of Catholic schools that exceeds that of public *and* nonsectarian private leads to a suspicion that what accounts for the difference is not just a competitive alternative but something about Catholic schools per se. This finding leaves the policy implications in serious doubt. Does the religious instruction of Catholic schools matter? Is it something special about the background of parents of Catholic-school children? Is there something about the match of kids to a more discipline-oriented (Catholic) school versus a less discipline-oriented (public) school? The policy implications of the Catholic-school differential are a bit unclear. In any event, it is infeasible to think of an active school-reform policy that promotes the use of Catholic or other religious schools. Vouchers might increase the demand for Catholic schools, but then the source of any performance differential becomes crucial in the determination of achievement outcomes.

From my perspective, there is another important issue. It is interesting that the average performance of Catholic urban schools exceeds that of public urban schools, but that finding by itself falls somewhat short of what we really want to know. Other analyses of educational production functions for the public sector (such as my own work in 1997) have emphasized the heterogeneity of public schools. Based on this observation, the obvious policy vis-à-vis public schools, which is reflected in the reform proposals of today, is that attention should be given to adjusting the tails of the distribution, particularly to failing schools. It is reasonable to believe that the Catholic schools exhibit a similar distribution of success and failure. Do the Catholic schools achieve their higher mean by lopping off the bottom of the distribution? By shifting the entire distribution? By compressing the distribution at both ends? The relative shape of the distribution of Catholic-school performance has important implications for the interpretation of the results and for any translation into policy terms.

Grogger and Neal cannot really address this issue of heterogeneity of Catholic schools but must be content with estimation of central tendencies. It would nonetheless be very useful to take this analysis to the larger issues surrounding variations in performance within and across school sectors.

*Conclusions.* This paper follows on a series of others that hint at real gains to be had from opening up public schools to more competition. In particular, it reinforces the idea that private alternatives are likely to be very important for urban students who potentially face more severe mobility constraints. Urban students, who tend to be more economically disadvantaged, often do not have the mobility options that allow them to shop among various public-school systems, forcing them to deal with the options that are directly available. Pinpointing the exact magnitude of any such potential gains from expanded options remains difficult nonetheless. One still cannot be too confident about the separation of school factors from other forces on selection. Grogger and Neal have helped, however, by providing more evidence about the potential impact of selection and of Catholic schools.

**Robert M. Schwab:** This paper is a fine contribution to the literature on the relative effectiveness of Catholic schools. Jeffrey Grogger and Derek Neal argue convincingly that minority students in urban areas who attend Catholic schools are more likely to finish high school, are more likely attend to college, and are likely to have higher standardized test scores than their public-school counterparts. They find little evidence that these results simply reflect selection bias or that Catholic schools offer significant benefits to suburban students (regardless of race). Their interpretation of these results is persuasive. If the received wisdom that suburban public schools are significantly better than central-city public schools is correct, then we should not be surprised to find the pattern that emerges in this paper.

Grogger and Neal focus on heterogeneity. They might want to consider taking their examination of heterogeneity one step further. Their sample is divided into several subsamples; within each subsample, the full impact of

Catholic schools is captured by a dummy variable. There is some interesting evidence that suggests this might not be the best way to think about Catholic schools. For example, Anthony S. Bryk, Valerie E. Lee, and Peter B. Holland show that Catholic schools have the greatest impact on students from low-income families.[1] That is, it seems that observables (such as family income) have a much smaller effect on outcomes in Catholic schools than in public schools. In order to capture this sort of heterogeneity, Grogger and Neal would need to allow all of the coefficients in their achievement and attainment equations to differ between public and Catholic schools. Admittedly, given the sample size in NELS, this might not be possible if Grogger and Neal want to estimate separate models for cities and suburbs by race. Some of the subsamples are already small (there are, for example, only eighty-three urban minority Catholic school students in NELS), and so we should be somewhat concerned about sample size, despite their dummy-variable specification.

There is also significant heterogeneity among Catholic schools. Virtually all of the research on Catholic schools (including my joint work with William Evans) treats the local parish school as the equivalent of a highly selective Catholic high school with a national reputation.[2] This sort of research might prove to be difficult (selection issues, for example, are daunting), but could in the end prove to be valuable.

I would argue that this paper should mark the end of a particular line of research on private schools and the beginning of several new lines. If people are not persuaded at this point that Catholic-school students (particularly urban minority students) enjoy better education outcomes, it seems to me unlikely that this type of research ever will convince them. The econometric work in the Grogger and Neal paper is careful, thorough, and creative; they have probably extracted as much from NELS as is possible. Their results are consistent with earlier work based on other large national data sets, including NLSY and High School and Beyond. The question then becomes: where do we go from here?

To a large extent, the research on Catholic schools is interesting and important because of what it can and cannot tell us about the potential consequences of school choice and vouchers. Vouchers and choice are part of what many regard as the key policy debate in education. The Catholic-school results are often offered as "proof" that the private sector should play a larger role in edu-

1. Bryk, Lee, and Holland (1993).
2. See Evans and Schwab (1995).

cation, and the Grogger and Neal paper almost certainly will become part of the debate.

I would argue that if we want to make progress on the choice-and-vouchers issue, future research should go in three directions. First, if Catholic schools are in fact more effective than public schools, we need to know much more about *why* they are more effective. In particular, we need to know whether the Catholic-school results could be replicated by private nonreligious schools and whether new Catholic-school students would receive the same benefits as current students. Some aspects of a Catholic-school education can be replicated. Bryk, Lee, and Holland, for example, conclude that the more equitable distribution of achievement in Catholic schools is in part a direct result of the way Catholic schools are organized: far more Catholic-school students are placed in academic tracks; nearly all students in Catholic schools are required to take a rigorous set of academic courses; and Catholic schools are more likely to insist on strict discipline in the classroom. On the other hand, these schools also stress the importance of a shared sense of community and mission. Private nonreligious schools (and public schools for that matter) can require more students to take algebra instead of shop and consumer math, but it would obviously be more difficult for them to replicate other aspects of a Catholic-school education. The Grogger and Neal results on private nonreligious schools are intriguing; they find that these schools are in fact no more effective than public schools. Grogger and Neal argue that these results are difficult to interpret, in part because of selection issues that are hard to handle and in part because the alternative to an elite private school is often an elite public school. As a consequence, I would conclude that this is an issue that deserves a good deal of additional attention.

Second, it is quite possible that an entirely different research approach will be required to shed significant new light on the choice-and-vouchers issue. Studies of Catholic schools based on large national data sets may not be the best evidence that the private sector could succeed where the public sector (by some people's accounting) has failed. Perhaps better evidence will come from careful evaluations of ongoing private scholarship programs. As Grogger and Neal explain, there are roughly sixty-five programs that provide scholarships to 57,000 students, many of whom are from economically disadvantaged families. Perhaps in the end nothing short of a large-scale demonstration project—comparable to the experiments with negative income taxes and housing allowances—will settle this debate.

Third, future research should focus on sensible designs of voucher programs. One way to interpret the Grogger and Neal paper is to conclude that while central-city schools might be "broken," suburban schools are not. Thus, given the Grogger and Neal results, it might be sensible to focus vouchers on low-income urban families rather than design an entirely new education system for the entire country.

# References

Altonji, Joseph G., Todd Elder, and Christopher Taber. 1999. "Selection on Observed and Unobserved Variables: Assessing the Effectiveness of Catholic Schools." Mimeographed. Northwestern University.

Bryk, Anthony S., Valerie E. Lee, and Peter B. Holland. 1993. *Catholic Schools and the Common Good*. Harvard University Press.

Buchinsky, Moshe. 1998. "Recent Advances in Quantile Regression Methods." *Journal of Human Resources* 33: 88–123.

Coleman, James, and Thomas Hoffer. 1987. *Public and Private High Schools: The Impact of Communities*. Basic Books.

Evans, William, and Robert Schwab. 1995. "Finishing High School and Starting College: Do Catholic Schools Make a Difference?" *Quarterly Journal of Economics* 110 (November): 941–74.

Figlio, David N., and Joe A. Stone. 1999. "School Choice and Student Performance: Are Private Schools Really Better?" *Research in Labor Economics* 18: 115–140.

Goldhaber, Dan D. 1996. "Public and Private High Schools: Is School Choice an Answer to the Productivity Problem?" *Economics of Education Review* 15 (April): 93–109.

Hanushek, Eric A. 1997. "Assessing the Effects of School Resources on Student Performance: An Update." *Educational Evaluation and Policy Analysis* 19(2): 141–64.

Heckman, James J., and Richard Robb. 1985. "Evaluating the Impact of Treatment on Outcomes." In *Longitudinal Analysis of Labor Market Data*, edited by James J. Heckman and Burton Singer. Cambridge University Press.

Hill, Paul T., Gail E. Foster, and Tamar Gendler. 1990. *High Schools with Character*. Rand R-3944-RC. Santa Monica, Calif.: RAND.

Koenker, Roger, and Gilbert Bassett Jr. 1982. "Robust Tests for Heteroscedasticity Based on Regression Quantiles." *Econometrica* 50 (January): 43–61.

Neal, Derek. 1997. "The Effect of Catholic Secondary Schooling on Educational Attainment." *Journal of Labor Economics* 15 (January, Part 1): 98–123.

Sander, William, and Anthony Krautmann. 1995. "Catholic Schools, Dropout Rates, and Educational Achievement." *Economic Inquiry* 33 (April): 217–33.

INGRID GOULD ELLEN
*Wagner School of Public Service, New York University*

# Is Segregation Bad for Your Health?
# The Case of Low Birth Weight

THIS PAPER EXPLORES the relationship between racial segregation and racial disparities in the prevalence of low birth weight. The paper has two parallel motivations. First, the disparities between black and white mothers in birth outcomes are large and persistent. In 1996, 13 percent of infants born in the United States to black mothers weighed less than 2,500 grams (5.5 pounds, or low birth weight), compared with just 6.3 percent of all infants born to white mothers. And the consequences may be grave. Low birth weight is a major cause of infant mortality and is associated with greater childhood illness and such developmental disorders as cerebral palsy, deafness, blindness, epilepsy, chronic lung disease, learning disabilities, and attention deficit disorder.[1] Given the strong connection between race and residence in this country, it seems plausible that residential location may shape these differentials.

Second, while there is a growing literature on the costs of racial segregation, it has largely focused on economic outcomes such as education and employment. This paper aims to develop a fuller understanding of the costs of racial segregation by considering birth outcomes as well as such behaviors as tobacco and alcohol use among pregnant mothers. As Glaeser emphasizes (in his paper in this volume), information, ideas, and values are often transmitted through face-to-face interaction, and thus their transmission may be

The author is grateful to Amy Ellen Schwartz, Mark Schlesinger, Karl Kronebusch, Kathy O'Regan, George Galster, Tod Mijanovich, Jeffrey Milyo, and Dalton Conley for their insights; to participants at the first annual meeting of the Brookings-Wharton Conference on Urban Affairs; and especially to David Cutler, William Dickens, Janet Rothenberg Pack, and William Gale for providing excellent comments. This work was undertaken while the author was a Robert Wood Johnson Health Policy Scholar at Yale University.
1. Paneth (1995).

blocked by segregation. This includes information related to job openings and may include information and norms related to behavior and care during pregnancy.

Adopting in large part the methodology of David Cutler and Edward L. Glaeser, the paper thus examines how levels of racial segregation affect the birth outcomes of black mothers.[2] It examines influences on both black and nonblack mothers in an attempt to identify the differential effect of segregation on black mothers.

## Theory and Past Literature

This section summarizes what is known about the costs of segregation from prior research, discusses several alternative pathways through which segregation may influence outcomes, and reviews previous literature on the causes of low birth weight. Given this understanding, the section then explores how segregation might contribute to the lower birth weights of infants born to black mothers.

### Costs of Racial Segregation

There is a growing body of work demonstrating a negative correlation between the degree of racial segregation in a metropolitan area and the economic success of its African American population.[3] Parallel to this work is a growing literature suggesting a link between racial segregation and the health of African Americans. In more segregated neighborhoods and metropolitan areas, African Americans have been found to suffer higher rates of homicide, suicide, infant mortality, and overall age-adjusted mortality.[4]

While these correlations are striking both in magnitude and significance, determining the direction of causality is naturally more difficult. It may be that greater disparities in economic status lead to greater residential segregation and not the reverse. And the link between segregation and health outcomes

---

2. Cutler and Glaeser (1997).

3. Galster (1987); Galster (1991); O'Regan and Quigley (1996); Cutler and Glaeser (1997).

4. Yankauer (1950); Polednak (1991); Potter (1991); LaVeist (1992); Krivo and Peterson (1993); LaVeist (1993); Shihadeh and Flynn (1996); LeClere, Rogers, and Peters (1997); Polednak (1997); Almgren and others (1998); Guest, Almgren, and Hussey (1998); Burr, Hartman, and Matteson (1999); Collins and Williams (1999).

may simply reveal that blacks who are more economically disadvantaged tend both to be at greater risk of poor health outcomes and to live in more segregated areas.

Despite this ambiguity, researchers considering health outcomes and segregation have paid scant attention to the issue of causality. They tend to rely strictly on aggregate, cross-sectional correlations, and thus it is difficult to interpret their results. The researchers concentrating on employment and education have focused a great deal more on causality and have made substantial strides.[5] Cutler and Glaeser make the most thorough attempt to discern causality.[6]

First, they study cross–metropolitan area differences in segregation. Many prior studies examining the effects of segregation have focused on a particular city or metropolitan area and compared the outcomes of blacks living in neighborhoods of varying racial compositions.[7] This approach may overstate the effects of segregation, however, since the more successful blacks may migrate to the more integrated neighborhoods. This approach may also lead one to understate the effects of segregation, since the degree of segregation in a metropolitan area may influence all minorities living there, even those living in largely white communities.[8]

When measuring segregation at the metropolitan level, such mobility concerns are naturally reduced. Moreover, Cutler and Glaeser focus on youth, for whom mobility should be less of a problem, and also examine the effects of segregation in the city of residence five years earlier.[9] Finally, to ensure that their measure of segregation is exogenous, Cutler and Glaeser use two different sets of variables to instrument for segregation across cities. In all cases, and with two different data sets, their results point to the same conclusion: segregation leads to poor outcomes for minorities and not the reverse.

## *Through What Channels Does Segregation Influence Outcomes?*

Although the empirical evidence indicates that racial segregation reduces the educational attainment, wages, and likelihood of marriage among blacks, there is little evidence about which of several mechanisms is central. Past researchers have speculated about the ways in which segregation may under-

5. Galster (1987); O'Regan and Quigley (1996); Cutler and Glaeser (1997).
6. Cutler and Glaeser (1997).
7. Yankauer (1950); Holzer (1991); Borjas (1995); Krivo and Peterson (1996); LeClere, Rogers, and Peters (1997); Almgren and others (1998); Guest, Almgren, and Hussey (1998).
8. Ellwood (1986); Cutler and Glaeser (1997).
9. Cutler and Glaeser (1997).

mine the economic achievement of minorities. As John Kain first noted, segregation may result in a "spatial mismatch" between where blacks live and where the vast majority of appropriate job opportunities exist.[10] Katherine O'Regan and John Quigley instead stress the social isolation produced by segregation: the harm of segregation is that it creates a barrier that prevents information about job opportunities from flowing from white and more affluent populations to black and more economically deprived populations.[11]

Douglas S. Massey and Nancy Denton, meanwhile, argue that because of higher poverty rates among blacks, racial segregation means that blacks live in neighborhoods with higher poverty.[12] And as a growing literature suggests, neighborhoods with higher poverty may have powerful negative effects on the social and economic outcomes of residents, due perhaps to peer effects or social networks.[13] Others have emphasized the role of differential public services, while still others have emphasized the role that residential segregation may play in fueling, or at least maintaining, racial prejudice.[14]

Segregation might also benefit minorities. For example, it may provide greater political power, as well as improved services, to minority communities as a result. Racial segregation may also mean that black mothers live in communities where they enjoy stronger social networks and support.[15]

### Birth Outcomes

The causes of low birth weight are surprisingly poorly understood.[16] Some medical risk factors are known—most important are the age and weight of the mother, and certain preexisting medical conditions. These are unlikely to be

10. Kain (1968).
11. O'Regan and Quigley (1996).
12. Massey and Denton (1993). Jargowsky (1997) finds that a one-standard-deviation increase in the level of segregation increases the average neighborhood poverty rate experienced by blacks by about one-fifth of a standard deviation.
13. For review, see Ellen and Turner (1997).
14. Galster (1991); Yinger (1995). One possible cause of differential services is discrimination on the part of public or private actors. Another possibility is that raised by Cutler, Elmendorf, and Zeckhauser (1993), who hypothesize that individuals may favor redistribution only to those living in their immediate area. If this is true, then separation of the races may result in less desire among whites to direct spending toward blacks.
15. Stack (1974).
16. Low birth weight is caused either by preterm delivery or by intrauterine growth retardation. Although it would be interesting to study preterm delivery and fetal growth retardation separately, data on gestational age are not very reliable, so the focus here is on birth weight. In general, the best evidence suggests that most of the racial disparity in the risk of low birth weight is driven by differences in preterm delivery. See Paneth (1995).

greatly shaped by the urban environment.[17] However, there are other known risk factors that are likely to be much more vulnerable to environmental threats. I group these into four categories of observed variables: socioeconomic status; behavior during pregnancy; stress; and exposure to various toxins.

In terms of socioeconomic status, numerous studies have shown that women with less education are far more likely to give birth to low-weight infants.[18] There is less consensus as to why this is the case. Less-educated women have lower incomes and are therefore less able to afford good pregnancy care. Alternatively, less-educated women may have inferior information about pregnancy care. Finally, the day-to-day stress of being poor may play a role as well. As will be discussed further below, there is some evidence that such stress leads to inferior birth outcomes.

Marital status is also strongly correlated with poor birth outcomes, perhaps because it too is a proxy for income. But marital status may also reflect social isolation. Prospective studies, which control for baseline health status, consistently show worse health outcomes for people with fewer social relationships.[19] Finally, marriage may be correlated with more desired, or at least more expected, pregnancies.

The second set of factors linked to poor birth outcomes are those relating to health-related behavior during pregnancy. These include tobacco use, alcohol use, drug use, nutrition, and the utilization of prenatal care. With varying degrees of certainty, all of these behaviors have been linked to poor birth outcomes.

The third factor related to poor birth outcomes is stress. Although the impact of stress on physical health is still poorly understood, there is growing evidence that psychological stress may place a toll over time on the body's immune system.[20] And there is at least some evidence that stress may specifically increase the risk of low birth weight and preterm delivery, and may do so independently of any influences on health-related behaviors.[21] Finally, there is some evidence that certain environmental conditions may contribute to poor

17. Although the age of the mother is potentially influenced by social conditions, the effects of age on birth weight appear to be nonlinear, and age only seems to matter once a mother gets beyond thirty or thirty-five years old. It seems less plausible that social norms will influence whether a mother chooses to have a baby after age thirty-five.

18. Rowley and others (1993).

19. House, Landis, and Umberson (1988).

20. Geronimus (1992).

21. McAnarney and Stevens (1990); Rowley and others (1993); Hoffman and Hatch (1996).

birth outcomes, perhaps because of oxygen flows to the fetus or exposure to particular toxins, such as lead.[22]

Is it plausible that the effects of residential segregation might operate through any of these channels? As mentioned already, there appears to be ample evidence that segregation leads to inferior social and economic outcomes on the part of minorities. Thus to the extent that segregation contributes to higher rates of out-of-wedlock birth and lower rates of educational attainment among black women, it may contribute in turn to elevated rates of low birth weight.

Second, it seems likely that the level of segregation could influence the health-related behaviors of pregnant mothers. In metropolitan areas that are more segregated, African Americans tend to live in neighborhoods with higher poverty rates, and the cost of undertaking or avoiding certain behaviors may be effectively higher in these areas. Resources such as health clinics and grocery stores may, for example, be less available. The quality of doctors serving minority and white communities may also vary. Similarly, the cultural gaps between blacks and whites may simply be larger in more segregated areas, which may hinder effective communication between black women and their typically white doctors. In such an environment, pregnant minority women may be less eager to visit their doctors. Moreover, minority neighborhoods in more segregated metropolitan areas may have higher crime rates and inferior access to transportation, which make it more difficult to reach such resources. One recent ethnographic study of heart patients in Harlem Hospital, for instance, suggests that worries about street-level safety may lead some mothers to avoid, or at least postpone, seeking medical care that is not immediately pressing.[23] Information networks about pregnancy care may also be more racially divided in more segregated cities. As mentioned above, some researchers argue that segregation creates a barrier that prevents information about job opportunities from flowing from white and more affluent populations to minority and more economically deprived populations. Perhaps segregation similarly constrains the flow of information about pregnancy.[24]

22. O'Campo and others (1997); Wang and others (1997); Chay and Greenstone (1999).
23. Blustein and others (1998).
24. Another possibility is that violent crime rates are generally higher in poorer areas. And it may be that people are more likely to undertake risky behavior in more-dangerous neighborhoods. If expected life spans are reduced, residents may have less to lose from less proximate health threats such as smoking, alcohol use, and delayed prenatal care. See Dow, Philipson, and Sala-i-Martin (1997); Ganz (1997).

Third, the day-to-day stresses experienced by black women in more segregated cities may be relatively higher due to crime, unemployment, or overall levels of racial tension. To cope with such stresses, pregnant women may turn to smoking and other behaviors that are temporarily comforting despite being unhealthy in the long term. Such stress may also in fact place a direct toll on the immune system.[25]

Finally, in more segregated metropolitan areas, blacks may be constrained to inferior physical environments and cut off from higher-quality public goods. This may occur because some combination of housing market discrimination, white household behavior, and income differences constrains blacks to communities that not only have a greater share of blacks but also possess older housing, more noxious factories, fewer safe places for outdoor recreation, and so forth.[26]

Although it is not possible to test all of these hypotheses, the results below do shed some light on the relationship between segregation and birth outcomes and provide some suggestive evidence about which of these various mechanisms are more plausible than others.

## Data and Methods

The paper relies on the 1990 national linked birth and death files, which contain information about every infant born in the United States in 1990 and its mother. This data set includes background information about the mother (including race, age, education, and alcohol and tobacco use) and allows one to examine the individual determinants of birth weight and infant mortality. With the cooperation of the National Center on Health Statistics, this paper uses a unique version of the files that reveals the mother's metropolitan area of residence at the time of birth and thus enables measures of segregation and other metropolitan area characteristics to be linked to the file.

The sample is restricted to singleton births and to mothers living in metropolitan areas with at least 100,000 residents and at least 5,000 black residents. In total, the sample contains approximately 3 million births taking place in

25. Hoffman and Hatch (1996).
26. It is conceivable that black residents tend to choose different packages of public services. Few studies have explored this question, but Galster (1979) analyzes preferences for housing and finds few differences across racial groups.

**Table 1. Summary Statistics of the Sample**
Percent unless otherwise indicated

| Variable | Black mothers | Nonblack mothers |
|---|---|---|
| *Infants* | | |
| Low birth weight | 12.0 | 4.7 |
| Infant mortality rate | 1.5 | 0.6 |
| *Mothers* | | |
| Mean age | 24.6 | 27.1 |
| First birth | 38.0 | 42.8 |
| With anemia | 3.3 | 1.4 |
| With hypertension | 2.5 | 2.4 |
| With diabetes | 1.8 | 2.2 |
| Not completing high school[a] | 28.0 | 18.5 |
| College graduates | 7.4 | 23.1 |
| Married | 33.4 | 79.4 |
| Using tobacco | 16.5 | 17.9 |
| Using alcohol | 4.0 | 3.4 |
| Receiving inadequate prenatal care[b] | 30.1 | 14.7 |
| N | 563,539 | 2,479,624 |

Source: National Center on Health Statistics, 1990 Linked Birth and Death files. Sample is restricted to those women living in metropolitan areas with at least 100,000 total residents and 5,000 black residents. Low birth weight refers to an infant that weighs less than 2,500 grams (5.5 pounds).

a. Educational outcomes defined only for those at least 19 years of age.

b. Measured by the Adequacy of Prenatal Care Utilization (APNCU) Index; see footnote 34 for explanation.

261 metropolitan areas around the country.[27] Table 1 offers a brief summary. Approximately 18.5 percent of the infants are born to black mothers.[28] As shown, black mothers are more than two and one-half times more likely to give birth to low-weight infants. Their infants are also two and one-half times more likely to die within the first year. Some of this differential is due to economic status—black mothers are less educated and less likely to be married than their nonblack counterparts. And some of this difference may be due to differential utilization of prenatal care. But even after controlling for all of

27. Of these 261 metropolitan areas, nine are in fact counties in New England. In the case of mothers residing in New England, the NCHS data set identified the county of mother's residence rather than the metropolitan area. In certain cases, these counties spanned several metropolitan areas. In these cases, the share of the county population living in various metropolitan areas was calculated. A weighted mean of the characteristics of all of these metropolitan areas is then used. The mean is weighted by the number of county residents living in each metropolitan area.

28. It is important to point out that this paper considers births to black mothers, not black infants. Identification of the race of infants has been shown to be inaccurate, and the aim of this paper is to explore how mothers of different races are influenced by racial segregation.

these factors, black mothers remain about 2.1 times more likely to give birth to a low-birth-weight infant than nonblacks.[29]

Most of the analysis centers on logistic regressions of the probability of low birth weight.[30] The core equation is the following:

$$\log\left[\frac{P_i}{(1-P_i)}\right] = X'\beta + Z'\gamma + \gamma_1 segregation + \gamma_2 segregation * black,$$

where $P$ is the probability that mother $i$ has a low-birth-weight infant, $X$ represents the matrix of individual level variables, and $Z$ represents the matrix of metropolitan area–level variables. The coefficient $\gamma_1$ measures the effect of segregation on nonblacks, and the coefficient $\gamma_2$ measures the differential effect of segregation for blacks relative to nonblacks. Standard errors are adjusted for heteroskedasticity and clustering within a metropolitan area.[31]

To help to understand the effect of segregation and to identify which of the possible causal explanations above appears more valid, the individual variables are divided into four different categories. The first includes the race and ethnicity of the mother. The second group measures medical risk. These variables include the mother's age and medical conditions (hypertension, anemia, and diabetes), and a set of pregnancy variables representing birth order and interval.[32] The latter includes a variable indicating a first birth, since mothers giving birth for the first time are at higher risk; a variable indicating four or more previous births, since pregnancy risk increases after a large number of births; and a variable indicating a short interval (less than fourteen months) since the previous birth, because pregnancy outcomes tend to be worse when

29. Regression results are not shown. Other studies that use smaller samples including information about parental income find that the racial differential persists and remains approximately the same. See Hummer (1993).

30. I experimented with several different measures of birth outcomes, including infant mortality and actual birth weight. The core results were the same. The focus of this analysis is on birth weight because it is a better measure of a birth outcome per se. And the probability of low birth weight is analyzed since there is no reason to believe that differences in birth weight above this threshold are medically significant. Finally, the core results are also the same when a probit model is used.

31. The correction involves Huber standard errors that assume clustering at the level of the metropolitan area. See Rogers (1993).

32. Age of the mother is measured by two dummy variables (under 16 and at least 35). In one specification, age was represented by five age dummies (under 20; 20–24; 30–34; 35–39; and 40+), and the coefficients on the metropolitan variables were the same.

intervals between births are very short.[33] While all of these medical risk variables are potentially influenced by segregation, the link is weaker than those for health-related behavior and socioeconomic status.

The third set measures the mother's social status. These variables include the mother's education and marital status at the time of the birth. The final set of variables represents behaviors during pregnancy, including variables indicating the adequacy of prenatal care,[34] and tobacco and alcohol use during pregnancy.

The key metropolitan-area characteristic is the degree to which blacks are residentially segregated in the metropolitan area. I use two measures of housing segregation: the dissimilarity index and the relative centralization index. While often used interchangeably, these indexes examine different aspects of segregation and thus may help to clarify the ways in which racial segregation affects minority birth outcomes.

The dissimilarity index, or D, is the most commonly used measure of segregation. Derived from the Lorenz curve, D may be understood as an indicator of how far the population distribution is from a situation in which every neighborhood (or census tract) contains the same proportion of the minority group at hand—say, blacks. Varying between 0 and 1, the index may be interpreted as the share of blacks (or nonblacks) that would have to move to a different neighborhood for the city to be completely integrated.[35] The dissimilarity index reflects neighborhood-level separation and may be seen as capturing

33. This may be because a mother's body needs a chance to recover from the previous birth. Mothers giving birth after short intervals also may not discover that they are pregnant for a longer period of time and may therefore undertake more risky behavior.

34. The Adequacy of Prenatal Care Utilization (APNCU) Index is used, which categorizes the care received as "inadequate," "intermediate," "adequate," or "adequate plus." See Kotelchuck (1994). These categories separate women getting different levels of care according to guidelines established by the American College of Obstetricians and Gynecologists. These guidelines consider both the number and the timing of visits. Women receive "adequate plus" care primarily because of pregnancy complications and maternal health risks. It is therefore important to separate out these women so that prenatal care does not appear to be detrimental to birth outcomes.

35. This definition holds only if we assume that no majority group members move out of their neighborhoods to make room for the minorities. Given the durability of housing, it is more reasonable to consider the number of black and white households that would have to switch homes in order for a city to be totally integrated. Thus a more accurate (though much less common) interpretation is that D represents the ratio between the number of households that must move for the area to be completely integrated and the maximum number that would have to move, assuming that the population of every tract remains constant. See Winship (1977).

the degree to which blacks and whites are isolated from one another socially and the extent to which they face different social and economic environments.

The formula for the index is

$$\text{Dissimilarity Index} = \frac{\sum t_i \mid p_i - P \mid}{2TP(1-P)},$$

where $p_i$ represents the proportion of blacks in neighborhood $i$, $P$ the proportion of blacks in the overall metropolitan area, $t_i$ the population in neighborhood $i$, and $T$ the population of the overall metropolitan area.

The index of relative centralization measures the extent to which a group is spatially concentrated near the center of an urban area, and thus perhaps exposed to inferior physical environments—older housing, deteriorating infrastructures, and industrial hazards. To the extent that it suggests that minorities are located in a central city as opposed to a suburban jurisdiction, this index may also capture differing levels of public services.

The relative centralization index varies between 1 and −1, with positive values indicating a tendency for blacks to live in inner-city environments. More technically, the centralization index may be interpreted as indicating the proportion of blacks that would have to move to match the degree of centralization of nonblacks.[36] The formula is as follows:

$$\textit{Relative Centralization Index} = (\sum Black_{i-1} * Nonblack_i)$$
$$- (\sum Black_i * Nonblack_{i-1}),$$

where $Black_i$ and $Nonblack_i$ are the respective cumulative proportions of blacks and nonblacks in tract $i$, and the $n$ census tracts in the metropolitan area are ordered by increasing distance from the central business district.[37]

Regional dummy variables and additional contextual variables are also included in all regressions to control for other characteristics of metropolitan areas that may influence birth outcomes: population size, the proportion of blacks, and median household income. The log of population size and the log

36. Negative values are interpreted in the same way, but in this case blacks are less centralized than nonblacks, and they would have to move to become as centralized as nonblacks.

37. An alternative measure is the isolation index, which measures the extent to which blacks tend to live in largely black communities. Specifically, it represents the probability for a black resident of a given metropolitan area that a randomly picked resident of his or her census tract is also black. The regressions here were also estimated using the isolation index, but the results were highly similar to those using the dissimilarity index. Thus only the results for the dissimilarity index and the relative centralization index are shown. (The correlation between the dissimilarity index and the isolation index is 0.79.)

**Table 2. Descriptive Statistics and Simple Correlation Matrix: Metropolitan-Area-Level Variables**

| Variable | Dissimilarity index | Relative centralization | Log (MSA population) | Proportion black | Log (median income) |
|---|---|---|---|---|---|
| Number of metro areas | 252 | 220 | 252 | 252 | 252 |
| Mean | 0.584 | 0.358 | 12.96 | 0.123 | 10.31 |
| Standard deviation | 0.122 | 0.232 | 0.975 | 0.091 | 0.199 |
| Minimum | 0.206 | −0.274 | 11.58 | 0.009 | 9.92 |
| Maximum | 0.873 | 0.752 | 16.0 | 0.457 | 10.97 |
| *Correlations* | | | | | |
| Dissimilarity index | 1.0 | | | | |
| Relative centralization index | 0.407 | 1.0 | | | |
| Log (MSA population) | 0.312 | 0.015 | 1.0 | | |
| Proportion black | 0.062 | −0.000 | 0.007 | 1.0 | |
| Ln(median income) | 0.104 | −0.010 | 0.425 | −0.281 | 1.0 |

Source: For index of relative centralization, Harrison and Weinberg (1992). All other data, Cutler, Glaeser, and Vigdor (1999).

**Table 3. Regional Differences in Levels of Segregation**

|  | *Northeast* | *South* | *Midwest* | *West* |
|---|---|---|---|---|
| *Dissimilarity index* | | | | |
| Mean | 0.626 | 0.555 | 0.662 | 0.464 |
| Standard deviation | 0.085 | 0.115 | 0.109 | 0.102 |
| Maximum | 0.807 | 0.766 | 0.873 | 0.673 |
| Minimum | 0.354 | 0.206 | 0.355 | 0.322 |
| N | 58 | 105 | 57 | 32 |
| *Relative centralization index* | | | | |
| Mean | 0.316 | 0.315 | 0.495 | 0.297 |
| Standard deviation | 0.250 | 0.194 | 0.194 | 0.182 |
| Maximum | 0.749 | 0.651 | 0.752 | 0.599 |
| Minimum | −0.274 | −0.153 | −0.101 | −0.232 |
| N | 40 | 95 | 55 | 30 |

of median household income are used in the regression. Since these characteristics might have different effects on mothers of different races, each of these variables is interacted with a dummy variable indicating whether a mother is black. Table 2 shows the simple correlation matrix for these metropolitan-area variables. The correlation between the two segregation measures is 0.407. The dissimilarity index is positively correlated with population size in the metropolitan area (and modestly positively correlated with the proportion black and the median income). Interestingly, the index of relative centralization is not correlated with any of these variables. Table 3 shows how segregation patterns differ across regions and reveals some sharp contrasts. The metropolitan areas located in the Midwest are significantly more segregated than those in other regions, while those in the West are significantly less segregated.

## Results

Table 4 shows that 36.7 percent of low-birth-weight (LBW) babies are born to black mothers, whose babies make up only 18.5 percent of total births. Mothers of LBW infants also differ in other ways consistent with previous analyses. They are more likely, for instance, to have hypertension, to be a first-time mother, or to have at least four previous births. Class differences are perhaps most striking. LBW mothers are 40 percent more likely to be high school dropouts, 40 percent less likely to have graduated from college, and 27 percent less likely to be married. Finally, LBW mothers are also far more likely to use alcohol and tobacco during pregnancy and far more likely to receive inadequate prenatal care.

**Table 4. Comparison of Mean Characteristics of Mothers Delivering Low-Birth-Weight Infants and Mothers Delivering Normal-Weight Infants**
Percent unless otherwise noted

| Variable | Low-birth-weight infant | Normal-weight infant |
|---|---|---|
| Black | 36.7 | 17.3 |
| Hispanic | 14.4 | 16.8 |
| Asian | 3.9 | 4.2 |
| Mother's age | 25.9 | 26.7 |
| First birth | 46.1 | 41.6 |
| Four or more births | 5.5 | 3.8 |
| Short birth interval | 6.5 | 2.8 |
| With hypertension | 6.1 | 2.2 |
| With anemia | 2.5 | 1.6 |
| With diabetes | 2.0 | 2.1 |
| Not completing high school | 31.9 | 23.1 |
| College graduates | 11.8 | 19.5 |
| Married | 52.9 | 72.0 |
| Using tobacco | 30.0 | 16.8 |
| Using alcohol | 6.1 | 3.3 |
| Receiving inadequate prenatal care | 26.0 | 16.9 |

*Basic Regression Results*

Table 5 shows the estimated coefficients from some simple logistic regressions of low birth weight.[38] Two columns show the results when the dissimilarity index is used as a measure of racial segregation, and two columns present estimated coefficients from regressions using the index of relative centralization.[39] The table also shows predicted probabilities of low birth weight for black and nonblack mothers living in high- and low-segregation metropolitan areas. (In a high-segregation metropolitan area, the level of segregation is one standard deviation above the mean, while in a low-segregation metropolitan area, the level of segregation is one standard deviation below the mean.)

The probability of low birth weight for black mothers is predicted to be significantly higher in more segregated metropolitan areas. When the dissimilarity index is used, the probability of low birth weight is predicted to be 1 percentage point or 11 percent higher in high-segregation areas. When the index of relative centralization is used, the probability of low birth weight for

38. The results here and in later regressions are highly similar when a probit model is used.
39. The fact that the coefficient on the black race dummy variable becomes negative when metropolitan-area interaction terms are included does not suggest that the model has "explained" the black disadvantage. As shown in the predicted probabilities, over normal ranges, black mothers are still at a large disadvantage.

**Table 5. Estimated Coefficients and Predicted Probabilities from Preliminary Logistic Regressions of Low Birth Weight[a]**

| Variable[b] | Dissimilarity index | | Relative centralization index | |
|---|---|---|---|---|
| | No controls | MSA controls | No controls | MSA controls |
| Segregation | −0.039 | −0.076 | −0.091 | −0.086 |
| | (0.086) | (0.110) | (0.063) | (0.044) |
| Segregation*black | 0.514 | 0.438 | 0.313 | 0.313 |
| | (0.103) | (0.094) | (0.054) | (0.054) |
| Black | 0.675 | −3.39 | 0.891 | −3.45 |
| | (0.062) | (0.709) | (0.022) | (0.590) |
| Asian | | 0.279 | | 0.277 |
| | | (0.029) | | (0.289) |
| Hispanic | | 0.140 | | 0.140 |
| | | (0.025) | | (0.025) |
| Hispanic origin missing | | 0.141 | | 0.133 |
| | | (0.051) | | (0.052) |
| Northeast | | 0.029 | | 0.024 |
| | | (0.017) | | (0.156) |
| South | | −0.012 | | −0.028 |
| | | (0.021) | | (0.017) |
| West | | −0.033 | | −0.035 |
| | | (0.044) | | (0.030) |
| Log population | | −0.008 | | −0.006 |
| | | (0.012) | | (0.009) |
| Log population*black | | 0.016 | | 0.021 |
| | | (0.020) | | (0.012) |
| Proportion black | | 0.219 | | 0.196 |
| | | (0.124) | | (0.122) |
| Proportion black*black | | 0.124 | | 0.226 |
| | | (0.153) | | (0.135) |
| Log median income | | −0.404 | | −0.440 |
| | | (0.043) | | (0.045) |
| Log median income*black | | 0.374 | | 0.387 |
| | | (0.083) | | (0.064) |
| Intercept | −2.98 | 1.29 | −2.97 | 1.63 |
| | (0.052) | (0.389) | (0.326) | (0.420) |
| N | 3,043,163 | 3,043,163 | 2,847,986 | 2,847,986 |
| *Predicted probability of low birth weight (percent)* | | | | |
| Black mothers | | | | |
| Low segregation[c] | 11.0 | 11.4 | 11.4 | 11.5 |
| High segregation | 12.2* | 12.3* | 12.5* | 12.6* |
| Nonblack mothers | | | | |
| Low segregation[c] | 4.7 | 4.8 | 4.8 | 4.8 |
| High segregation | 4.7 | 4.7 | 4.6 | 4.6 |

*Predicted differences between high- and low-segregation metropolitan areas are statistically significant.

a. The analysis using the dissimilarity index covers 252 metropolitan areas. The analysis using the index of relative centralization covers 220 metropolitan areas. Standard errors are reported in parentheses and, here and throughout the paper, are adjusted for heteroskedasticity and clustering within a metropolitan area.

b. With the exception of segregation, all variables are evaluated at the sample means.

c. A low-segregation metropolitan area is one in which the level of segregation is one standard deviation below the mean. A high-segregation metropolitan area is one in which the level of segregation is one standard deviation above the mean.

black mothers is predicted to be 1.1 percentage points or 9.6 percent higher. According to these results, if segregation levels fell to zero in all metropolitan areas, the model predicts that the probability of low birth weight for black mothers would fall to 9.1 percent, meaning that black mothers in 1990 would have been 1.9 times more likely to have low-birth-weight infants than would white mothers. The actual probabilities in the sample show that black mothers were in fact 2.6 times more likely to have low-birth-weight infants in 1990 (see table 1).

As shown in the second and fourth columns in table 5, these differentials persist after controlling for the ethnicity of the mother and other metropolitan-area characteristics. They shrink somewhat in the case of the dissimilarity index, but they are unchanged when the index of relative centralization is used.

By contrast, there is little difference between the predicted birth outcomes of infants born to nonblack women in these two types of metropolitan areas. In all four regressions, the coefficient on the racial segregation variable is negative, but in only one regression does it reach statistical significance. In other words, there is at most weak evidence that racial segregation affects the birth outcomes of nonblack mothers, and if anything, segregation is related to improved birth outcomes among these mothers.

*Exploring the Pathways: Controlling for Other Individual Characteristics*

Table 6 shows results from three sets of regressions that control for other individual characteristics. The first set—the columns marked (1)—includes the individual factors considered to be relatively independent of racial segregation (age, race, and ethnicity of mother; birth order and interval; and medical conditions).[40] The individual-level coefficients (not shown) provide few surprises. A woman is more likely to give birth to a low-weight infant if she is black, Asian, or Hispanic, if she is older, or if she has hypertension or anemia. She is also at greater risk of low birth weight if it is her first birth, if she has already had at least four children, or if the interval since her last birth is less than fourteen months.

The estimated coefficients for all metropolitan-area variables are shown. When these additional variables are included, the coefficients on the black

40. The three medical conditions were in fact considered as a separate category—one that might be more influenced by environmental conditions. However, including these medical variables had virtually no effect on the racial segregation coefficients. Therefore the regression that includes age, race, ethnicity, and pregnancy variables (but not medical conditions) as independent variables is not shown.

**Table 6. Estimated Coefficients from Regression of Low Birth Weight**

| Metropolitan area variable | Dissimilarity index | | | Index of relative centralization | | |
|---|---|---|---|---|---|---|
| | (1)[a] | (2)[b] | (3)[c] | (1)[a] | (2)[b] | (3)[c] |
| Segregation | -0.072 | -0.081 | -0.079 | -0.088 | -0.097 | -0.051 |
| | (0.109) | (0.112) | (0.108) | (0.038) | (0.039) | (0.046) |
| Segregation*black | 0.364 | 0.130 | -0.013 | 0.300 | 0.235 | 0.106 |
| | (.099) | (0.083) | (0.097) | (0.055) | (0.045) | (0.063) |
| Log population | -0.013 | -0.013 | -0.000 | -0.011 | -0.012 | -0.004 |
| | (0.010) | (0.010) | (0.012) | (0.008) | (0.009) | (0.011) |
| Log population*black | 0.020 | 0.030 | 0.029 | 0.021 | 0.023 | 0.022 |
| | (0.020) | (0.019) | (0.022) | (0.013) | (0.012) | (0.019) |
| Proportion black | 0.214 | 0.303 | 0.287 | 0.189 | 0.290 | 0.241 |
| | (0.114) | (0.115) | (0.133) | (0.112) | (0.113) | (0.143) |
| Proportion black*black | 0.172 | 0.004 | 0.201 | 0.252 | 0.032 | 0.205 |
| | (0.150) | (0.139) | (0.151) | (0.127) | (0.117) | (0.151) |
| Log median income | -0.399 | -0.282 | -0.294 | -0.427 | -0.307 | -0.284 |
| | (0.037) | (0.040) | (0.059) | (0.038) | (0.042) | (0.059) |
| Log median income*black | 0.347 | 0.322 | 0.161 | 0.366 | 0.352 | 0.168 |
| | (0.083) | (0.074) | (0.077) | (0.064) | (0.059) | (0.075) |
| N | 3,043,163 | 3,043,163 | 3,043,163 | 2,847,986 | 2,847,986 | 2,847,986 |

a. Regression 1 includes demographic information about the mother such as age, ethnicity, and race. It also includes information on medical conditions—specifically, anemia, hypertension, and diabetes, all of which influence birth weight—as well as variables to indicate birth order and interval—specifically, whether this is a mother's first birth, whether she has already had at least four children, and whether the mother gave birth in the previous 14 months. Finally, regional dummies are included as well.

b. Regression 2 includes the same variables in model 1 plus measures of education and marital status. Specifically, variables are added that indicate whether or not the mother is married and whether or not she has completed high school or college.

c. Regression 3 includes the same variables in model 2 plus measures of behavior during pregnancy. Variables are added that indicate whether the mother used tobacco during pregnancy or whether she used alcohol. In addition, an index of prenatal care utilization is included that reflects the number and timing of prenatal visits. Dummy variables are included here to note if the information is missing. Both the coefficients for "missing tobacco" information and "missing prenatal care" information are positive and statistically significant. This may reflect the fact that these women in fact received inferior care, or that lower-status women (who are more likely to have low-birth-weight infants) have less complete medical records.

dummy*racial segregation interaction terms are changed very little and remain highly significant, suggesting that black mothers living in more segregated metropolitan areas are indeed more likely to give birth to low-birth-weight babies, even after controlling for birth order, age, and selected medical conditions.

In the columns marked (2), estimated coefficients are shown for a regression that also controls for the education and marital status of the mother.[41] The coefficient on the segregation*black term falls substantially when these variables are included. It falls by 64 percent compared with the first specification when the dissimilarity index is used and by 22 percent when the index of relative centralization is used. This suggests that much of the apparent effect of segregation operates through the educational attainment and marital status of the mother.

In the columns marked (3), estimated coefficients are shown for a regression that also controls for tobacco and alcohol use during pregnancy and the utilization of prenatal care. Including these variables reduces the magnitude of the coefficient still further. It falls to effectively zero in the case of the dissimilarity index and falls by 55 percent compared with the second specification when the index of relative centralization is used.[42] (It remains statistically significant at the 10 percent level of significance.)

Summarizing these various results, table 7 shows the differences in the predicted probabilities of low birth weight for black and nonblack mothers living in a high- as compared to a low-segregation metropolitan area. Again, the segregation level in a high-segregation area is one standard deviation above the mean, and segregation in a low-segregation area is one standard deviation below the mean. The table shows the absolute percentage point difference. In percentage terms, these differences are naturally far larger, since the mean probability of low birth weight for black and nonblack mothers is 12 and 4.7 percent respectively.

In contrast to the results for the segregation*black term, the coefficient on racial segregation is consistently negative, relatively small in magnitude, and in all but two cases, statistically insignificant. Thus there is little reason to believe that segregation per se is proxying for some other metropolitan-area attribute that is related to low birth weight. In the case of centralization, the

41. Again, the coefficients on the individual-level variables are as expected—mothers who are high-school dropouts are more likely to deliver low-birth-weight infants, while those who are married and college graduates are less likely to.

42. When including behaviors and not class, the effects of segregation do not disappear. The coefficient on the segregation*black variable suggests an effect very similar in magnitude to that effect predicted when class variables are included and behavior is omitted.

**Table 7. Predicted Difference in Probability of Low-Birth-Weight Babies for Black and Nonblack Mothers, High- versus Low-Segregation Areas[a]**
Percentage points

| | Black mothers | | Nonblack mothers | |
| | Dissimilarity | Index of relative | Dissimilarity | Index of relative |
| Control variables | index | centralization | index | centralization |
|---|---|---|---|---|
| Race of mother | 1.2* | 1.1* | 0.0 | −0.2 |
| + Ethnicity and MSA controls | 0.9* | 1.1* | −0.1 | −0.2 |
| + Age, medical conditions, birth order | 0.7* | 1.0* | −0.1 | −0.2* |
| + Education, marital status | 0.3 | 0.7* | −0.1 | −0.2* |
| + Tobacco, alcohol, and prenatal care | 0.0 | 0.2 | −0.1 | −0.2 |

*Statistically significant difference between high- and low-segregation areas.
a. A low-segregation metropolitan area is one in which the level of segregation is exactly one standard deviation below the mean. A high-segregation metropolitan area is one in which the level of segregation is one standard deviation above the mean.

coefficient on racial segregation is negative and statistically significant in two regressions, providing some evidence that nonblack women may benefit somewhat when blacks are relatively concentrated in the center of the city, and when nonblacks are therefore more concentrated in outlying areas.

With the exception of income, the other metropolitan characteristics included in these six regressions do not seem to have much effect on low birth weight, either for black or nonblack mothers. Income at the metropolitan-area level does have an effect, which is not surprising. Wealthier cities are generally likely to have better hospitals, better doctors, and better public services. Yet the coefficients on median income interacted with the black dummy variable suggest that these benefits are a great deal smaller for blacks.

In an additional regression (not shown), both measures of racial segregation were included. With both included, the coefficient on the dissimilarity index falls substantially and is not statistically significant in any of the three regressions. The coefficient and standard error for the index of relative centralization, meanwhile, are unchanged.

In summary, these regressions suggest that the aspect of segregation most related to birth outcomes is the degree to which black mothers are concentrated near the central city, and thus perhaps exposed to differing social services and physical environments. The importance of the centralization index may also reflect the fact that it measures the extent to which blacks are clustered not only in individual neighborhoods but also in larger geographic areas (that is, black neighborhoods next to black neighborhoods). A second key result is that most of the apparent effect of racial segregation on black mothers appears to operate either through its effects on the social status of the mother or through influences on her behavior during pregnancy.

*Instrumental Variables Estimation*

There are some potential problems with these estimates. Most fundamental, both segregation and disparities in birth outcomes might be the result of poor economic outcomes of minorities. In an attempt to address this issue, an instrumental variables approach is used. Following Cutler and Glaeser, I instrument for segregation using the natural log of the number of local governments in the metropolitan area and the share of local revenue that comes from intergovernmental sources.[43] Both of these variables measure the extent to which the government structure of a metropolitan area encourages residential sorting. With more governments and less aid, there is a greater incentive for households to segregate. In both cases, the 1962 values of these fiscal variables are used to ensure that they are unrelated to birth outcomes in 1990. These figures are available for only a subset of the metropolitan areas, so the sample size falls to 215 in this analysis.

As expected, the dissimilarity index is positively correlated with the number of governments and negatively correlated with the share of revenue that comes from intergovernmental sources. Specifically, a regression of the dissimilarity index on these two variables yields the following estimates:

$$\textit{Dissimilarity Index} = 0.501$$
$$(0.038)$$
$$+ 0.047*\textit{Log}(\textit{number of governments})$$
$$(0.006)$$
$$- 0.192*\textit{Transfer share},$$
$$(0.096)$$

with $N = 215$, $R^2 = 0.252$.

Unfortunately, these fiscal factors explain much less of the variation in the index of relative centralization ($R^2 = 0.08$), so the instrumental variables estimation is performed only in the case of the dissimilarity index. Because of the difficulty of performing instrumental variables with a logistic regression, a linear probability model is used here, and the instrumental variables results are therefore compared to ordinary-least-squares (OLS) estimates of low birth weight.[44] Consistent with Cutler and Glaeser,[45] the results are largely unchanged when instrumenting with these fiscal variables—both the coeffi-

43. Cutler and Glaeser (1997).
44. The ordinary-least-squares estimates (not shown) of the effect of segregation on black birth weight are quite similar to those in table 6, although they suggest a slightly larger effect, at least for regressions (1) and (2).
45. Cutler and Glaeser (1997).

cients and the standard errors of the segregation variables increase somewhat. Naturally, this is not a perfect correction, but this does provide some modest support for the hypothesis that greater segregation leads to worse birth outcomes for black mothers.

## How Does Segregation Affect Birth Outcomes? Further Evidence

This section explores two ways of further probing the relationship between segregation and birth outcomes. First, it examines the relationship between our two different measures of racial segregation and various intermediate outcomes. Second, it considers other measures of black-white disparity in metropolitan areas.

### Intermediate Outcomes

Table 8 examines the relationship between racial segregation and characteristics of the mother and her pregnancy (marital status, education, tobacco and alcohol use during pregnancy, and inadequate prenatal care), controlling for the same metropolitan-area characteristics used above and for selected individual variables. Two sets of regressions were estimated, one using the dissimilarity index and the other using the index of relative centralization.

The coefficient on segregation*black is negative and statistically significant in both regressions of the probability of being married. Black women giving birth, in other words, are less likely to be married in more segregated metropolitan areas. The effect is larger when the dissimilarity index is used. The educational attainment of black mothers appears strongly related to segregation, but only when the dissimilarity index is used.

Alcohol and tobacco use during pregnancy are also related to segregation, but here the effect is only apparent when the index of relative centralization is used. In brief, black mothers are more likely to drink and smoke during pregnancy when they live in metropolitan areas where blacks are more residentially concentrated in the central city. Perhaps surprisingly, all mothers are less likely to receive inadequate prenatal care in more segregated metropolitan areas. Perhaps this is because there are a greater number of doctors in these more segregated areas. But this does raise doubts about whether the effect is really due to segregation as opposed to some other omitted factor.

Causality is of course in question here, but these simple regressions do demonstrate that segregation is related to a variety of poor outcomes on the

**Table 8. Estimated Coefficients on Segregation Variables in Regressions of Various Intermediate Variables**

| Segregation index | Dependent variable | | | | | |
|---|---|---|---|---|---|---|
| | Marital status[a] | High school drop-out[a] | College graduate[a] | Tobacco use[b] | Alcohol use[b] | Inadequate prenatal care[b] |
| *Dissimilarity* | | | | | | |
| Segregation | -0.240 | 0.010 | -0.140 | 0.21 | -0.299 | -1.14 |
| | (0.247) | (0.351) | (0.308) | (0.296) | (0.815) | (0.378) |
| Segregation*black | -1.61 | 1.75 | -1.01 | 0.281 | 0.416 | 0.425 |
| | (0.308) | (0.396) | (0.236) | (0.296) | (0.665) | (0.271) |
| N | 3,047,035 | 2,478,880 | 2,478,880 | 2,057,224 | 2,102,596 | 2,216,661 |
| *Relative centralization* | | | | | | |
| Segregation | 0.047 | 0.407 | -0.137 | -0.389 | -0.577 | -0.452 |
| | (0.124) | (0.185) | (0.098) | (0.122) | (0.271) | (0.163) |
| Segregation*black | -0.645 | -0.452 | 0.003 | 0.733 | 1.01 | 0.057 |
| | (0.205) | (0.331) | (0.138) | (0.169) | (0.333) | (0.116) |
| N | 2,851,512 | 2,313,592 | 2,313,592 | 1,878,211 | 1,920,522 | 2,076,059 |

a. Regression also controls for race, ethnicity, and age of mother (five-year dummies), and other metropolitan-area controls.

b. Regression controls for these same variables plus education and marital status of mother, birth order, and whether or not the previous birth (if any) occurred within the last fourteen months.

part of black mothers that may in turn be detrimental to birth outcomes.[46] These results also show that the two measures of segregation capture very different aspects of residential separation. The neighborhood-level separation measured by the dissimilarity index may be critical to spillover effects on educational attainment and out-of-wedlock birth. But differences in physical location—and proximity to the central city—may be critical in determining the extent to which black women engage in unhealthy behaviors during pregnancy. This is somewhat of a puzzle. The concentration of blacks in large central areas may allow for geographically targeted advertising campaigns, or tobacco and alcohol may be more readily available in downtown central-city areas. Alternatively, peer effects may be stronger when minority neighborhoods are located next to other minority neighborhoods.

## Controlling for Black Exposure in Metropolitan Areas

A second approach is through constructing variables that actually measure the extent to which blacks and nonblacks are exposed to different sorts of environments. Two hypotheses in particular are explored. The first posits that black mothers fare worse in more segregated metropolitan areas because they are exposed to less-educated neighbors and therefore receive less useful information about prenatal care, appropriate behavior during pregnancy, risks, and so on. To the extent that less-educated mothers also tend to smoke during pregnancy, exposure to less-educated neighbors may also mean greater exposure to these behavioral influences as well.[47] To test this hypothesis, I use an index constructed by Cutler and Glaeser that measures the extent to which blacks disproportionately live in neighborhoods with residents having some amount of college education.[48] The formula is as follows:

---

46. Instrumental variable analysis, again using 1962 fiscal variables as instruments for segregation, supports a causal link between segregation and out-of-wedlock birth and worse educational outcomes on the part of blacks.

47. High-school dropouts are more likely to use alcohol during pregnancy than women who have completed high school and perhaps attended some college. Interestingly, college graduates are also more likely to use alcohol during pregnancy than are high-school graduates.

48. Cutler and Glaeser (1997).

$$Black\ Education\ Exposure\ Index\ = \sum \frac{Black_i}{Black}$$
$$*\frac{Educated\ persons_i}{Total\ persons_i}$$
$$-\frac{Educated\ persons}{Total\ persons}.$$

Note that this index effectively states the average black exposure to college-educated neighbors minus the overall proportion of college-educated residents in the metropolitan area. Thus the index measures the extent to which blacks differentially live in census tracts with college-educated residents.

A similar index is constructed to measure the extent to which blacks are disproportionately exposed to older housing in a metropolitan area. The formula for this index is as follows:

$$Black\ Old\ Housing\ Exposure\ Index\ = \sum \frac{Black_i}{Black}$$
$$*\frac{Old\ housing\ units_i}{Total\ housing\ units_i}$$
$$-\frac{Old\ housing\ units}{Total\ housing\ units},$$

where old housing units are those that were at least forty years old in 1990. The risks of older housing might include lead paint, dust, inadequate ventilation, inadequate heating, and older water pipes. Old housing may also serve as a proxy for conditions in older neighborhoods.

Both measures of racial segregation are highly correlated with the old-housing-exposure index. They are also negatively correlated with the education-exposure index, though less so, especially in the case of the index of relative centralization. In other words, blacks in segregated metropolitan areas do appear to be confined to inferior neighborhoods.

Table 9 shows the results of regressions of low birth weight that include the black education-exposure index, the black old-housing-exposure index, and each index interacted with a black dummy variable. Again, only the coefficients on metropolitan-area variables are shown.[49] Since the aim is to explain

---

49. The inclusion of these additional variables generates virtually no change in the individual-level coefficients.

**Table 9. Effects of Relative Black Exposure to Educated Neighbors and Old Housing Estimated Coefficients from Regression of Low Birth Weight[a]**

| Metropolitan area variable | Dissimilarity index | | Index of relative centralization | |
|---|---|---|---|---|
| | (1)[b] | (2)[c] | (1)[b] | (2)[c] |
| Segregation | 0.042 | 0.074 | −0.067 | −0.064 |
| | (0.125) | (0.127) | (0.044) | (0.044) |
| Segregation*black | 0.033 | −0.138 | 0.199 | 0.194 |
| | (0.107) | (0.102) | (0.048) | (0.047) |
| Log population | −0.015 | −0.016 | −0.011 | −0.011 |
| | (0.010) | (0.011) | (0.008) | (0.009) |
| Log population*black | 0.033 | 0.039 | 0.023 | 0.023 |
| | (0.012) | (0.013) | (0.011) | (0.011) |
| Proportion black | 0.168 | 0.217 | 0.190 | 0.251 |
| | (0.106) | (0.107) | (0.115) | (0.116) |
| Proportion black*black | 0.354 | 0.217 | 0.312 | 0.119 |
| | (0.115) | (0.113) | (0.118) | (0.118) |
| Log median income | −0.397 | −0.278 | −0.418 | −0.300 |
| | (0.045) | (0.047) | (0.045) | (0.049) |
| Log median income*black | 0.303 | 0.334 | 0.328 | 0.371 |
| | (0.063) | (0.060) | (0.061) | (0.060) |
| Education exposure | 0.104 | 0.127 | 0.087 | 0.099 |
| | (0.243) | (0.226) | (0.233) | (0.218) |
| Education exposure*black | −0.173 | 0.282 | −0.261 | 0.280 |
| | (0.291) | (0.252) | (0.277) | (0.246) |
| Old–housing exposure | −0.344 | −0.438 | −0.141 | −0.221 |
| | (0.148) | (0.150) | (0.165) | (0.175) |
| Old–housing exposure*black | 0.847 | 0.736 | 0.489 | 0.266 |
| | (0.183) | (0.170) | (0.161) | (0.154) |
| N | 2,935,885 | 2,935,885 | 2,763,311 | 2,763,311 |

a. The education-exposure index is defined for only 217 metropolitan areas, and thus the sample used in these regressions is somewhat smaller than that used in table 6. However, the changes apparent here (in comparison with table 6) are not the effect of a changed sample. The results in table 6 are largely identical when this smaller sample is utilized for both sets of regressions.

b. Regression 1 includes demographic information about the mother such as age, ethnicity, and race. It also includes information on medical conditions—specifically, anemia, hypertension, and diabetes, all of which influence birth weight—as well as variables to indicate birth order and interval, specifically whether this is a mother's first birth, whether she has already had at least four children, and whether the mother gave birth in the previous 14 months. Finally, regional dummies are included as well.

c. Regression 2 includes the same variables in Model 1 plus measures of education and marital status. Specifically, variables are added that indicate whether or not the mother is married and whether or not she has completed high school or college.

the apparent effect of segregation and thus to test if the coefficient on the black*segregation variable diminishes, the analysis here is limited to regressions (1) and (2).

In the regressions using the dissimilarity index, the inclusion of these indexes in the regressions renders the coefficient on racial segregation*black insignificant. Notably, the coefficient on the racial segregation*black variable actually becomes *negative* in the second regression. This at least hints that after controlling for these potentially negative influences of segregation (that is, greater exposure to older housing and less-educated neighbors), the presence of a greater number of black neighbors may bring some benefits to black women, such as enhanced social networks and political power.[50]

When the index of relative centralization is used instead, the coefficient on segregation*black remains statistically significant in all of the models, even after the inclusion of these exposure indexes, though the magnitude of the coefficients is generally diminished. The persistence of the effect of the relative centralization measure suggests that there are other aspects of central-city residence, beyond the existence of older housing, that may be detrimental to birth outcomes. One possibility is inferior city services.

Surprisingly, perhaps, there is little evidence that exposure to educated neighbors matters in shaping birth outcomes. In terms of older housing, black women are more likely to give birth to a low-weight infant when living in metropolitan areas in which blacks disproportionately live in older neighborhoods. Nonblacks in these metropolitan areas are meanwhile less likely to give birth to low-weight infants. In the case of the relative centralization index, the effect of older housing exposure is weaker, perhaps because the proximity to the central city is the better measure of environmental risk. Older housing may indeed simply serve as a proxy for central-city residence.

### Conclusion

This analysis yields three main conclusions. First, there does appear to be a link between racial segregation and low-birth-weight outcomes among black women, and there is some evidence here that greater segregation in fact leads to worse birth outcomes. It still may be true that segregation has positive influences as well, but on net the influence appears to be negative. By contrast, there is little evidence that segregation has an effect on the birth weight of nonblack infants.

Second, much of the apparently harmful effect of segregation may be traced to its effect on the long-term social status of the mother as well as on behaviors during pregnancy.

Third, this study suggests that the concentration of blacks in central-city environments, and to a lesser extent their concentration in neighborhoods with older housing, is more damaging than the neighborhood-level racial separa-

---

50. In a regression that includes behavioral variables as well, the coefficient remains negative and becomes marginally significant.

tion that is measured by the dissimilarity index. Generally, these results reveal important differences between distinct measures of racial segregation, differences that future researchers studying the consequences of segregation should bear in mind.

In sum, while further research should be done to define more precisely the nature of the link between segregation and poor birth outcomes, these results imply that an increase in residential integration in U.S. metropolitan areas would help to diminish our troubling and persistent racial disparities in birth outcomes. More generally, this research also suggests that this country's stubbornly high levels of racial segregation—and in particular, the high concentration of minorities in central-city areas—may have serious consequences far beyond the economic outcomes that researchers have typically explored.

# Comments

**David M. Cutler**: Ingrid Gould Ellen has written a fascinating paper on the impact of segregation on birth outcomes. Ellen shows clearly and convincingly that blacks living in more segregated cities have worse birth outcomes than do blacks living in less segregated cities. This is not true for whites. She also shows that the causality runs from segregation to outcomes and not the reverse.

The methodology that Ellen uses is similar to the one that Edward Glaeser and I employed in our study of the impact of segregation on economic outcomes for blacks.[1] Thus it is no surprise that I find it persuasive. Ellen's paper explores a new dimension of outcomes, however, and makes substantial headway. I take her finding to be true and robust: segregation is harmful to the health of black babies.

The central question raised by these results is why this is the case. The question is posed in the paper and speculated about, but it is never really resolved. Ellen shows that segregation matters because it is correlated with behavioral decisions that women make—both socioeconomic behaviors (education, marital status) and health behaviors (smoking, drinking). This finding echoes that of Ellen Meara, who has shown in a recent paper that less-educated women smoke more than more-educated women, and this explains a significant share of why low-birth-weight infants are more common among less educated women.[2]

But why does segregation matter for these behaviors? The paper is unable to answer this question with the data available. I'd like to raise a few theories and discuss how they might be tested.

*Income theory.* The first theory is that segregation affects health because higher-income women can afford better health behaviors. Less-educated women may not be able to buy necessary food, medical care, and other ser-

1. Cutler and Glaeser (1997).
2. Meara (1999).

vices, and this may adversely affect fetal development. This theory would not explain why segregation leads to increased smoking and drinking, but it could explain the effect of segregation through changes in educational attainment.

One way to test this theory is to examine the consumption patterns of women by income or education, matched with data on where they live. This has not been done, but other evidence suggests that this theory is not the complete explanation. National data show that the incidence of low birth weight among most Hispanic and Asian women is very similar to that of non-Hispanic whites, despite much lower income among these groups. In fact, the incidence is slightly lower for Mexican and Chinese mothers.[3] Thus it is clear that income by itself is not the explanatory factor.

*Peer effects.* A second theory is that segregation matters for birth outcomes because in more-segregated areas some women have worse behaviors and this is imitated by other women in a contagious way. Such peer effects may be bad (smoking, drinking) or good (vitamin intake, prenatal care).

I do not have a strong sense about whether this view is correct. Behaviors certainly do differ by racial group (although not always negatively—black women smoke less than white women). But whether this results from peer effects or from other factors that similarly influence women from different racial groups is unknown. I consider this a major research question.

*Time allocation.* The third theory is that segregation matters for health because women in more segregated areas have to spend more time on basic aspects of living and have less time for appropriate medical or nonmedical inputs to health. Depictions of life for poor mothers frequently stress the great complications of seemingly simple tasks. Taking the children to day care may involve a half hour or hour each way. Commuting to work or shopping, which are often not near the home, may involve similar amounts of time. With such a large time allocation devoted to these activities, it may be difficult for women to find time for doctors' visits or to ensure adequate rest and nutrition.

This theory would explain why centralization in particular affects health. Women who are isolated in central-city neighborhoods without much link to wealthier neighborhoods may find the time costs of good behaviors particularly high. The additional hardship of basic life may also lead women to engage in other unhealthy activities, such as smoking and drinking, as compensation for an already difficult life.

---

3. Table 11 in National Center for Health Statistics (1999).

Testing this theory requires two additional pieces of information: time diaries and neighborhood characteristics on the availability of different services. If supermarkets are less plentiful in segregated areas but fast food is more plentiful, that may explain different dietary patterns among women living in segregated environments. I do not know of any data sets that have this information, but I would place a high priority on obtaining it.

*Allostatic load.* The final theory is that segregation affects health because it is associated with greater long-term stress, which has a cumulative adverse impact on women's health. This has been termed the theory of "allostatic load."[4] Increased stress may result simply from living in a segregated neighborhood, or may be a consequence of specific time pressures or other constraints faced by women living in these areas. To date, most of the research on allostatics and health has focused on diseases that occur later in life, such as cardiovascular disease, but such theories could be applied to younger women as well. Indeed, research suggests that maternal stress during gestation predicts certain components of fetal development.[5]

Allostatic load can be measured in one of two ways. Case histories can be used to measure the degree of stress encountered in daily life and in particularly difficult circumstances. Allostatic load is often measured clinically by monitoring levels of cortisol or other hormones. Measurement of both of these factors is feasible and could be used to test this theory.

In sum, Ingrid Gould Ellen's paper makes a striking case for the importance of segregation in influencing birth outcomes. But it leaves open the mechanisms through which these effects occur. Understanding such mechanisms should be the next step in this very important line of research.

**William Dickens**: Ingrid Ellen makes a good case for her main thesis—that segregation or centralization has negative consequences for black birth outcomes. However, the paper misses several opportunities to make its case stronger and to shed light on the mechanism by which segregation or centralization affects birth outcomes.

Although the paper uses individual data on birth weight, most results are driven by differences in the independent variables between metropolitan areas. It is very hard to make a convincing case for causality on the basis of cross-section correlations at the metropolitan level. The main reason for this is that

4. McEwen (1998).
5. Hobel and others (1999).

one cannot be sure which way causation flows—did A cause B, B cause A, or did some other factor C cause both? The paper's main strength is in finding multiple contrasts across metropolitan areas that strain the credulity of alternative interpretations of the primary result. In particular, the contrast between the coefficient on segregation for whites and for blacks in a logistic regression of low birth weight on individual and metropolitan-area characteristics is compelling. If this showed that segregation was associated with bad birth outcomes for both blacks and whites, the interpretation of the result would be highly suspect. It would seem most likely that some other characteristic of the city, one not controlled for in the regression, was a common cause of birth outcomes and segregation. However, segregation is seen to have virtually no relation to birth outcomes for whites, while it has a substantial relation to birth outcomes for blacks.

This is not the case for some other variables. In table 5, for example, city size has no relation to birth outcomes for either blacks or whites. If there were many unobserved city characteristics that were affecting birth outcomes, it would be surprising that none are correlated with city size (or that their correlations with city size lead to effects on those coefficients that are exactly offsetting). In cities with higher median incomes, whites do have fewer low-birth-weight babies, but this is not the case for blacks. Were these results nonsensical, or if they mimicked the pattern for the two segregation measures, this would raise a question about the meaning of the correlation between segregation and birth outcome in the black population. But the results are not nonsensical, and they do not mimic the other patterns, so this lends credence to the method of contrasting outcomes for blacks and whites.

By this argument, the positive relation between proportion black in a metropolitan area and the likelihood of a low-birth-weight baby being born to a white is troubling. This suggests that there are some ignored metropolitan-area characteristics that are influencing the results. But the size effect is very small. A one-standard-deviation increase in proportion black increases the probability of a low-weight birth to an average white mother by no more than 0.13 percentage point. In contrast, the size effect of concentration on the probability of a low-weight birth to a black mother is more than five times as large. Even though the results for whites for this variable are statistically significant, they do not suggest a major problem with unobserved third-factor causes.

Taken together, the results strongly suggest that something about the environment in segregated cities is leading to a higher probability of low birth weight in black babies. But is segregation the *cause,* so that integration would be a cure? There are two ways that we might think about answering this question. The first would be to try to find city characteristics that lead to segregation but are not themselves likely to have been caused by some other city characteristic that could also be related to poor birth outcomes. We could then look to see if variation in segregation caused by differences in these antecedents was related to birth outcomes. If that were the case, we would have strong evidence that segregation is the cause. This is the method of instrumental variables. A second approach would be to try to identify the way in which segregation affects outcomes. If this could be done convincingly, then again we would know whether integration could be a tool for improving black birth outcomes. Further, the process might allow us to identify other ways in which we might intervene to improve outcomes. The paper tries both approaches.

Following David M. Cutler and Edward L. Glaeser, Ellen relates segregation to two possible antecedents: the number of governments in a metropolitan area and the share of local revenue that comes from intergovernmental sources.[1] Segregation is understandably higher in cities with more governments and lower in those in which a higher percentage of revenue is shared. When these variables are used as instruments for the dissimilarity index, the results are largely the same as in the OLS case. This would add considerably to the credibility of the claim that segregation causes bad birth outcomes were it not for the author's selective reporting of results. The regressions are run for the dissimilarity index but not for the centralization index. Worse, these are not the most convincing instruments. It is not inconceivable that preexisting patterns of segregation have affected the number of governments in a region and the extent of revenue sharing within it. Cutler and Glaeser had another instrument that they used in their paper—the number of rivers dividing a metropolitan area. This factor is naturally related to segregation, and it is much more believable that this variable is a cause and not a result of segregation. But Ellen does not even mention it. If some objective criterion has been used to decide in which circumstances to use which instruments, it should be motivated and reported. Without this, the reader cannot help but worry that the results that are being reported are not representative of all that could be obtained.

There is another problem with the instrumental variables analysis. It is done using OLS rather than logit. This makes it hard to compare the results of the IV analysis to the earlier work. This problem could have been avoided if the

---

1. Cutler and Glaeser (1997).

author had used a continuous measure of birth weight throughout the paper. Ellen never justifies her use of a dichotomous variable for birth weight.

Turning to the second mode of demonstrating causality, the paper misses a golden opportunity to narrow the range of suspects for causal paths. In the discussion Ellen suggests that centralization is more the cause of the problem than segregation per se. Although she presents the dissimilarity index and centralization index as measures of the same concept—segregation— it is in fact clear from their correlation (.4) that they are measuring different things. Therefore there is no reason that they could not both have been included in all regressions. We would then know whether it is segregation or centralization that is causally related to birth outcomes—or whether both are related to the outcomes.

I find the results presented in table 6 interesting and indicative of the mechanisms relating segregation to low birth weight. They further confirm the causal nature of the relation. Here the author introduces, in sequence, controls for the mother's social status and some behaviors during pregnancy. The introduction of these controls significantly reduces the impact on blacks of living in a segregated city, suggesting that either segregation or some other aspect of segregated cities is leading black women to be less educated and less likely to marry and that these factors influence their birth outcomes. Introducing controls for behaviors such as drinking and smoking during pregnancy completely eliminates the effect of segregation in at least some specifications. Again, this fits well with the story that the author is telling and adds to its plausibility.

What I find far less interesting is the material contained in tables 7 through 10. Here the author attempts to account for difference in marital status and to explore for other causal routes. The results are disappointing. It seems all too easy to read into the findings other explanations than those the author prefers. In particular, the often counterintuitive coefficients on segregation for whites suggest that many unobserved factors are at work in creating these outcomes and confounding the interpretation of the results.

## References

Almgren, Gunnar, and others. 1998. "Joblessness, Family Disruption, and Violent Death in Chicago, 1970–1990." *Social Forces* 76 (June): 1465–93.

Blustein, Jan, and others. 1998. "Treatment of Heart Disease in Harlem: An Ethnographic Study." New York University, Wagner School of Public Service.

Borjas, George. 1995. "Ethnicity, Neighborhoods, and Human Capital Externalities." *American Economic Review* 85 (June): 365–90.

Braithwaite, Ronald L., and Ngina Lythcott. 1989. "Community Empowerment as a Strategy for Health Promotion for Black and Other Minority Populations." *Journal of the American Medical Association* 261 (January 13): 282–83.

Burr, Jeffrey A., John T. Hartman, and Donald W. Matteson. 1999. "Black Suicide in U.S. Metropolitan Areas: An Examination of the Racial Inequality and Social Integration-Regulation Hypothesis." *Social Forces* 77 (March): 1050–80.

Chay, Kenneth, and Michael Greenstone. 1999. "The Impact of Air Pollution on Infant Mortality: Evidence from Geographic Variation in Pollution Shocks Induced by a Recession." University of California, Berkeley, Department of Economics.

Collins, Chiquita, and David Williams. 1999. "Segregation and Mortality: The Deadly Effects of Racism?" University of Michigan, Department of Sociology and Institute for Social Research.

Cutler, David M., Douglas W. Elmendorf, and Richard J. Zeckhauser. 1993. "Demographic Characteristics and the Public Bundle." *Public Finance* 48 (supp.): 178–98.

Cutler, David M., and Edward L. Glaeser. 1997. "Are Ghettos Good or Bad?" *Quarterly Journal of Economics* 112 (August): 827–72.

Cutler, David M., Edward L. Glaeser, and Jacob L. Vigdor. 1999. "The Rise and Decline of the American Ghetto." *Journal of Political Economy* 107: 455–506.

Dow, William H., T. Philipson, and Xavier Sala-i-Martin. 1997. "Disease Complementarities and the Evaluation of Public Health Interventions." Working Paper 5216. Cambridge, Mass.: National Bureau of Economic Research.

Ellen, Ingrid Gould, and Margery Austin Turner. 1997. "Does Neighborhood Matter? Assessing Recent Evidence." *Housing Policy Debate* 8 (4): 833–66.

Ellwood, David T. 1986. "The Spatial Mismatch Hypothesis: Are There Teenage Jobs Missing in the Ghetto?" In *The Black Youth Unemployment Crisis,* edited by Richard Freeman and Harry Holzer, 147–90. University of Chicago Press.

Galster, George C. 1979. "Interracial Variations in Housing Preferences." *Regional Science Perspectives* 9: 1–17.

———. 1987. "Residential Segregation and Interracial Economic Disparities: A Simultaneous Equations Approach." *Journal of Urban Economics* 21 (January): 22–44.

———. 1991. "Housing Discrimination and Urban Poverty of African-Americans." *Journal of Housing Research* 2 (2): 87–122.

Ganz, Michael. 1997. "Health Threats and Health Practices: Complementaries in the Production of Health." Columbia University.

Geronimus, Arlene T. 1992. "The Weathering Hypothesis and the Health of African-American Women and Infants: Evidence and Speculations." *Ethnicity and Disease* 2 (Summer): 207–21.

Guest, Avery M., Gunnar Almgren, and Jon M. Hussey. 1998. "The Ecology of Race and Socioeconomic Distress: Infant and Working-Age Mortality in Chicago." *Demography* 35 (February): 23–34.

Hobel, C. J., and others. 1999. "Maternal Plasma Corticotropin-Releasing Hormone Associated with Stress at Twenty Weeks' Gestation in Pregnancies Ending in Preterm Delivery." *American Journal of Obstetrics and Gynecology* 180 (January, part 3): S257–63.

Hoffman, Susie, and Maureen C. Hatch. 1996. "Stress, Social Support, and Pregnancy Outcome: A Reassessment Based on Recent Research." *Pediatrics and Perinatal Epidemiology* 10: 380–405.

Holzer, Harry. 1991. "The Spatial Mismatch Hypothesis: What Has the Evidence Shown?" *Urban Studies* 28 (February): 105–22.

House, James S., Karl R. Landis, and Debra Umberson. 1988. "Social Relationships and Health." *Science* 241: 540–45.

Hummer, Robert A. 1993. "Racial Differentials in Infant Mortality in the U.S.: An Examination of Social and Health Determinants." *Social Forces* 72(2): 529–54.

Jargowsky, Paul A. 1997. *Poverty and Place: Ghettos, Barrios, and the American City.* New York: Russell Sage Foundation.

Kain, John F. 1968. "Housing Segregation, Negro Unemployment, and Metropolitan Decentralization." *Quarterly Journal of Economics* 82 (May): 175–97.

Kotelchuck, Milton. 1994. "An Evaluation of the Kessner Adequacy of Prenatal Care Index and a Proposed Adequacy of Prenatal Care Utilization Index." *American Journal of Public Health* 84 (September): 1414–20.

Krivo, Lauren J., and Ruth D. Peterson. 1996. "Extremely Disadvantaged Neighborhoods and Urban Crime." *Social Forces* 75 (December): 619–50.

LaVeist, Thomas A. 1992. "The Political Empowerment and Health Status of African-Americans: Mapping a New Territory." *American Journal of Sociology* 97 (January): 1080–95.

———. 1993. "Segregation, Poverty, and Empowerment: Health Consequences for African Americans." *Milbank Quarterly* 71(1): 41–64.

LeClere, Felicia B., Richard G. Rogers, and Kimberley D. Peters. 1997. "Ethnicity and Mortality in the United States: Individual and Community Correlates." *Social Forces* 76: 169–98.

Massey, Douglas S., and Nancy Denton. 1993. *American Apartheid: Segregation and the Making of the Underclass.* Harvard University Press.

Matteson, Donald W., Jeffrey A. Burr, and James R. Marshall. 1998. "Infant Mortality: A Multilevel Analysis of Individual and Community Risk Factors." *Social Science and Medicine* 47(11): 1841–54.

McAnarney, E. R., and Simon C. Stevens. 1990. "Maternal Psychological Stress/Depression and Low Birth Weight: Is There a Relationship?" *American Journal of Diseases of Children* 144 (July): 789–92.

McEwen, Bruce S. 1998. "Protective and Damaging Effects of Stress Mediators." *New England Journal of Medicine* 338 (January 15): 171–79.

Meara, Ellen. 1999. "Why Is Socioeconomic Status Related to Health?: The Case of Low Birth Weight." Mimeographed. Harvard University.

National Center for Health Statistics. 1999. *Health, United States, 1999*. Hyattsville, Maryland.

O'Campo, Patricia, and others. 1997. "Neighborhood Risk Factors for Low Birthweight in Baltimore: A Multilevel Analysis." *American Journal of Public Health* 87 (July): 1113–18.

O'Regan, Katherine M., and John M. Quigley. 1996. "Teenage Employment and the Spatial Isolation of Minority and Poverty Households." *Journal of Human Resources* 31 (Summer): 692–702.

Paneth, Nigel S. 1995. "The Problem of Low Birth Weight." *Future of Children* 5 (Spring): 19–34.

Polednak, Anthony P. 1991. "Black-White Differences in Infant Mortality in Thirty-Eight Standard Metropolitan Statistical Areas." *American Journal of Public Health* 81 (November): 1480–82.

———. 1997. *Segregation, Poverty, and Mortality in Urban African Americans*. Oxford University Press.

Potter, Lloyd B. 1991. "Socioeconomic Determinants of White and Black Males' Life Expectancy Differentials, 1980." *Demography* 28 (May): 303–21.

Rogers, William. 1993. "Regression Standard Errors in Clustered Samples." *Stata Technical Bulletin Reprints* 3: 88–94.

Rowley, Diane L., and others. 1993. "Preterm Delivery among African-American Women: A Research Strategy." *American Journal of Preventive Medicine* 9 (6, supp.): 1–6.

Shihadeh, Edward S., and Nicole Flynn. 1996. "Segregation and Crime: The Effect of Black Social Isolation on the Rates of Black Urban Violence." *Social Forces* 74 (June): 1325–52.

Stack, Carol B. 1974. *All Our Kin: Strategies for Survival in a Black Community*. Harper and Row.

Wang, Xiaobin, and others. 1997. "Association between Air Pollution and Low Birth Weight: A Community-Based Study." *Environmental Health Perspectives* 105 (May): 514–20.

Winship, Christopher. 1977. "A Revaluation of Indexes of Residential Segregation." *Social Forces* 55: 1058–66.

Yankauer, Alfred. 1950. "The Relationship of Fetal and Infant Mortality to Residential Segregation: An Inquiry into Social Epidemiology." *American Sociological Review* 15 (October): 644–48.

Yinger, John. 1995. *Closed Doors, Opportunities Lost: The Continuing Cost of Housing Discrimination*. New York: Russell Sage Foundation.

RICHARD VOITH
*Federal Reserve Bank of Philadelphia*

# Zoning and the Tax Treatment of Housing

DECENTRALIZATION—or suburbanization—is probably the single most important fact of recent urban development. Peter Mieszkowski and Edwin Mills have convincingly argued that suburbanization has been occurring in most developed countries throughout most of the twentieth century.[1] Decentralization in the United States has been particularly rapid, and it has been associated with considerable geographic sorting by income. Lower-income households have become increasingly concentrated in American central cities, while more wealthy households have opted for suburban communities.[2] The rapid pace of U.S. decentralization is often seen as the reflection of the intrinsic tastes of the American public, and hence some argue that it should not be an issue for public policy.[3] Persistent concerns about central-city decline and suburban sprawl, however, suggest some dissatisfaction with current patterns of metropolitan development.

Observed patterns of decentralization are broadly consistent with the implications of the basic monocentric urban model developed by Edwin Mills, Richard F. Muth, and William Alonso more than thirty years ago.[4] In the basic model and the generalizations that followed, land prices adjust to compensate for differential commuting costs across residential locations. This model implies that, as rising incomes increase the demand for residential land and

Alex Anas, Jan Brueckner, Theodore Crone, William Gale, Joseph Gyourko, Douglas Holtz-Eakin, and Janet Pack provided helpful comments on an earlier draft.

1. Mieszkowski and Mills (1993).
2. Madden (2000); Voith (1999); Mills and Lubuele (1997).
3. Brueckner (1999) examines the appropriate role for public policy with respect to the decentralization process.
4. Mills (1967); Muth (1969); Alonso (1964).

239

240 Brookings-Wharton Papers on Urban Affairs: 2000

as improved transportation systems lower the cost to commute to distant locations, metropolitan areas should become more decentralized and have lower population densities. The model further suggests that higher-income households will outbid lower-income households for the most desirable locations, leading to communities that are stratified by income. If high-income households strongly prefer large residential lots, they will tend to locate in more distant suburban locations where land is relatively less expensive, while lower-income households reside in more central locations.

To the extent that decentralization is driven by the forces described in the basic urban model, the process of decentralization is efficient and there should be few public policy concerns regarding the trend toward less dense residential patterns or the geographic sorting by income. There are at least three reasons, however, to reexamine the role of public policy in the process of decentralization. First, the pace of decentralization appears to be more rapid in the United States than in other developed countries, and it has frequently been associated with severe central-city decline.[5] Severe decline in urban centers is not necessarily an implication of the monocentric model. Second, there is little evidence regarding the relative importance of preferences versus prices in the process of decentralization. Both commuting costs and house prices are significantly affected by public policies, which makes it less clear whether the observed pattern is solely a result of preferences, or whether the outcome is altered by policy-related effects on the prices of land and transportation. Third, the basic urban model does not address the actions of local jurisdictions, such as those related to zoning, that may affect patterns of development. Although more sophisticated Tiebout-type models suggest that efficient sorting by income across communities can occur without zoning, large-lot zoning, which has the effect of making some suburban communities inaccessible to lower-income households, remains common.

One national policy that can potentially affect both individuals' choices regarding residence and land consumption and communities' choices regarding zoning rules is the federal tax treatment of housing. Two aspects of the tax treatment of housing may affect patterns of metropolitan development. First, the U.S. tax code effectively reduces the price of housing, including residential land, relative to other goods.[6] This increases the demand for housing and,

5. Mieszkowski and Mills (1993).
6. The subsidy to owner-occupied housing is the nontaxation of imputed rent, coupled with the mortgage interest and property-tax deductions. The tax code changes the price of housing relative to other goods differentially across households of different income levels. This differential will result in diverging choices of high- and low-income households in our analysis.

because housing is a composite good consisting of structures and land, it also increases the demand for residential land. Because land is often a fixed factor in cities, the suburbs, with an elastic supply of land, have a productive advantage in housing. Thus the tax treatment of housing, by increasing the demand for housing, tends to favor suburban communities with elastic supplies of land. Second, the value of the tax-related housing subsidy is greater for higher-income individuals. In an earlier paper, Richard Voith and Joseph Gyourko show that in the presence of exclusionary zoning, these factors result in a concentration of higher-income people in suburban communities and a corresponding concentration of lower-income people in the city.[7]

The purpose of this paper is to provide a new framework to analyze the potential role of the federal tax treatment of housing in the patterns of metropolitan development. In contrast to the work of Voith and Gyourko,[8] which examined only the marginal responses of individuals to the tax treatment of housing given a set of institutional rules regarding zoning, this paper also seeks to examine how the tax treatment of housing may provide incentives that could affect the choice of institutional rules, such as zoning, that constrain individual choices. In particular, it analyzes how the tax treatment of housing affects the profitability of suburban residential development with and without exclusionary zoning.

This paper develops an equilibrium model of two communities: a city with fixed boundaries and a suburb that is unbounded. Individuals in these communities are assumed to have similar systematic tastes regarding housing and community amenities, but they also have an idiosyncratic preference for either the city or the suburbs. For a given individual, the relative attractiveness of the city and the suburbs depends on his or her idiosyncratic taste, the relative amenities of the city and suburbs, and the relative price. Community amenities are endogenously determined and are assumed to depend on the distribution of high- and low-income individuals. High concentrations of low-income residents in a community may adversely affect the attractiveness of the community. Within this framework, this paper examines the residential choices of high- and low-income individuals with and without zoning constraints. Given these outcomes, it evaluates the relative profitability of communities' choosing exclusionary zoning or not by comparing the aggregate land values under both regimes.

7. Voith and Gyourko (1998).
8. Voith and Gyourko (1998).

In this framework, this paper shows that housing-related tax incentives are likely to increase the relative profitability of development under exclusionary zoning, creating an incentive for the adoption of such regulation. To the extent that these incentives actually result in more exclusionary zoning, they reinforce the marginal effects on decentralization and sorting that result from the tax code's effects on individuals' choices regarding land consumption and residential location. This is an important result, because it suggests that the spatial and sorting impacts of the tax treatment of housing may be larger than its effects on individuals' choices of residential location and housing consumption alone. In fact, the tax incentives, because they may affect community choices with respect to issues such as zoning, can result in large changes in equilibrium land prices, community choices, and community characteristics. For example, if changing tax law makes exclusionary zoning unprofitable, the changes in spatial patterns of development may be larger than the changes associated only with individuals' marginal responses to the change in tax treatment of housing.

## Tax Treatment of Housing, Residential Choices, and Exclusionary Zoning

It has long been recognized that the U.S. tax code favors housing consumption and that this favored treatment has increased the level of investment and consumption of housing above that which would occur in the absence of the tax subsidy.[9] To the extent that land is an input to housing, the tax advantages of housing likely increase the desired consumption of land, potentially resulting in less dense patterns of development. In a strict monocentric framework, however, this outcome is not necessary. Dixie Blackley and James R. Follain, for example, show that although tax-related housing subsidies increase the consumption of housing services, the relationship between subsidies and the residential location choices of households within the metropolitan area is ambiguous. Housing subsidies lower the after-tax price of housing services throughout the region, but because the market price of housing services is higher near the center, proportional subsidies flatten the after-tax gradient for the price of housing services. This flattening increases the relative attractiveness of a central location (the subsidy reduces its after-tax price of housing services near the center more in absolute terms when compared with that of

9. Mills (1987); Feldstein (1982); Hendershott (1982); Poterba (1984).

more distant housing). This effect goes in the opposite direction of the incentive to buy more housing services, and hence more land, which causes decentralization. Blackley and Follain argue that it is not implausible that the net effect is that the housing subsidy favors more central locations and hence the subsidy fosters more dense development. For this to be the case, however, it must also be the case that residential consumption of land must fall, even as the after-tax implicit price of land declines.[10]

When there are high- and low-income residents, it is well known that the monocentric model will result in the segregation of the two groups. The group with the steepest bid-rent function will locate nearest to the center.[11] In the United States, it is generally assumed that preferences are such that higher-income groups locate in more distant locations and consume more land. Mieszkowsi and Mills note that there is a natural progression whereby as income grows, wealthier residents purchase new, larger houses on the perimeter and lower-income residents live in older, smaller houses nearer the center.[12] It is possible, however, for the housing subsidies to affect the equilibrium location choices of the two groups. If the demand for residential land is elastic, the tax subsidies have the effect of flattening the bid-rent functions of the rich (but not of the poor).[13] Thus it is possible, within the framework of the monocentric model, that the choice of more distant locations by wealthier residents is, in part, the result of housing subsidies rather than simply a matter of preferences.

In an essentially nonspatial framework, Voith and Gyourko show that, in the absence of other constraints on the housing market, housing tax subsidies unambiguously result in larger numbers of high- and low-income residents choosing suburban locations and less dense patterns of metropolitan development. With exclusionary zoning in the suburbs, high-income residents depart the city in higher numbers. And in the case in which community amenities are assumed to depend positively on the number of high-income individuals in the community, they show that the housing subsidies for the high-income group can lead to decentralization, income sorting, and potentially to land-value declines in the central city.[14]

10. Blackley and Follain (1983).
11. DiPasquale and Wheaton (1996).
12. Mieszkowsi and Mills (1993).
13. Jan Brueckner has pointed out in his comments that if demand for residential land is inelastic, the impact goes in the opposite direction.
14. Voith and Gyourko (1998).

The Voith and Gyourko models that generate income sorting across communities are complementary to, rather than competitors with, the sorting process that occurs in the monocentric framework. Unlike the monocentric framework, which generates a concentration of high-income households in communitites more distant from the center as a result of strong preferences for housing services and land, the Voith and Gyourko models generate the same sorting independent of preferences, but as a result of housing subsidies and residential zoning. Thus these alternative models reinforce the preference-based outcomes of the monocentric city model. In addition, the fact that the tax treatment of housing essentially finances individuals' choices of homogeneous communities is also complementary to the sorting associated with Tiebout and exclusionary zoning.

The extent to which housing subsidies may encourage lower-density communities and income sorting depends on individual and community choices. On the margin, the effect of the tax subsidy on individuals' land consumption depends, in part, on the price elasticity of demand for residential land.[15] Muth estimates the price elasticity of demand for residential land to be –0.8,[16] while Gyourko and Voith estimate this price elasticity to be about –1.6.[17] Given an average subsidy of 15 percent, the effect of the tax treatment of housing is to reduce density 12 percent (using Muth's elasticity estimate) or 24 percent (using Gyourko and Voith's estimate). This paper uses James Poterba's estimate that tax subsidies reduce the cost of housing 15 percent.[18] Poterba's estimate focused only on the impacts of taxes on the cost structure; this paper implicitly assumes that the reduction in the after-tax use of land is the same. Of course, the actual impact of the tax treatment of housing on the cost of residential land will depend on the elasticity of demand for residential land as an input to the production of housing services as well as on the elasticity of supply of residential land.

The average price elasticity of residential land does not, however, yield any insight into the process of geographic sorting by income associated with housing subsidies when there are zoning constraints in the suburbs. More important, those estimated marginal responses in the quantity of residential land con-

15. Of course, the elasticity of supply plays an important role as well. If supply is perfectly inelastic, the subsidy is fully capitalized into land prices and there is no change in residential land consumption. We believe, however, that suburban residential land is relatively elastically supplied.

16. Muth (1964, p. 230).

17. Gyourko and Voith (1999).

18. Poterba (1991).

sumed in response to changes in after-tax land prices do not capture the potential equilibrium shifts associated with the effects of housing subsidies on communities' decisions concerning exclusionary zoning. These changes are shifts in equilibrium outcomes that could potentially be larger than marginal movements along the demand schedule.[19] This paper develops a framework to evaluate the effects of the tax code on the economic incentives to adopt exclusionary zoning.

## The Model

The basic strategy to evaluate the role of the tax treatment of housing in the decision to pursue exclusionary zoning is to set up an equilibrium model of residential location choice and housing consumption for high- and low-income residents. The framework developed below is an extension and specialization of that analyzed in Voith and Gyourko. The framework presented here departs from the Voith-Gyourko model in two important ways.[20] First, this paper assumes that the suburban community is created by a developer that chooses suburban prices to maximize its profits.[21] Second, the paper evaluates a specific functional form of the model in order to quantitatively compare equilibria with and without zoning constraints.

In this economy, there are two communities. The city is a bounded community with a fixed stock of land suitable for development. The suburb is an unbounded community having a potentially infinite supply of land. There are two types of worker households—high skill (h) and low skill (l)—whose distribution across the metropolitan area depends on preferences, equilibrium prices, local amenities, and housing subsidies. The subsidy for land is charac-

19. There is a growing literature that examines endogenous zoning choices and motivations. Epple, Romer, and Filimon (1988) examine equilibrium zoning outcomes and show that communities may adopt inefficient exclusionary zoning choices when the zoning process is controlled by existing owners. Pogodzinski and Sass (1994) attempt to estimate the determinants of zoning in a Tiebout-type setting and find evidence for fiscal, externality, and exclusionary motives for zoning. Bogart (1993), however, cautions that it is hard to identify empirically the underlying motivations for zoning. The analysis in this paper focuses on how the tax code changes the underlying financial incentives to zone but the analysis is not intended to supplant other motivations for zoning.

20. Voith and Gyourko (1998).

21. While the model formally examines a profit-maximizing developer, the suburban community decisionmaker can also be viewed as a property-value-maximizing local government that chooses the zoning regime to maximize total land value.

terized as the fraction of the price of housing services paid by the government. If $r_j$ is the market price of land in community $j$, the effective price individuals pay for land is $\tau^i r_j$ where $\tau^i$ is one minus the subsidy, and $I = h$ or $l$, denoting high- or low-income household. For simplicity, this work assumes that the standard deduction and progressivity of the tax code combine so that the subsidy is available only to high-skill workers.[22] Thus $0 < \tau^h < 1$, with $\tau^l = 1$.

Individual households (indexed by $k$) maximize utility by choosing residential location and the optimal quantities of housing ($g$) and the numeraire good ($x$) given rents ($r$), the housing subsidy ($1 - \tau^i$), local amenities ($A$), and wages ($w^h$ earned by high-skill workers and $w^l$ earned by low-skill workers). Individuals of a given type have identical preferences regarding $x$, $h$, and $A$, so their systematic preferences over the composite good and land, given amenities, can be expressed by the indirect utility function: $V^i(\tau r_j, w^i; A_j)$. Individual households also have idiosyncratic preferences, $\in^{ik}$, regarding city or suburban locations. Thus total utility is given by $V^i + \in^{ik}$. Normalizing $\in^{ik}$ to represent preference for a suburban location, we can define the marginal consumer with idiosyncratic preference $\in^{I*}$, who is indifferent between city and suburb as $V^i(\tau r_s, w^i; A_s) - V^i(\tau r_c, w^i; A_c) = \in^{i*}$.

*Community Choice*

There are $N^h$ high-income consumers and $N^l$ low-income consumers choosing their residential community and level of housing consumption. By choosing a community, the consumer also chooses the amenity package associated with that community. By specifying a distribution function for the idiosyncratic location preference, we can define a function that determines the fraction of people choosing each community:[23]

(1)                    $$N_c^h = \Phi(r_c, r_s, A) = \alpha_0 r_s^{\alpha_1} r_c^{\alpha_2} A^{\alpha_3},$$

---

22. One might expect that with progressivity there could be a way for high-income homeowners to transfer the tax benefits to low-income households through renting. The tax treatment of housing is essentially symmetric across owners and renters in that mortgage interest and property taxes are deductible for homeowners and landlords, so that this tax advantage is available to both high- and low-income households if they are renters. With respect to ownership, deductibility increases in attractiveness with increasing income (ignoring the recent "phase-out" provisions in the tax code), but it is difficult for high-income households to transfer this advantage to low-income households because it involves losing the benefit of nontaxed imputed rents.

23. Equation (1) is best thought of as an approximation incorporating the implicit indirect utility functions and distribution function for idiosyncratic preferences. Note that we do not

where $N_c^h$ is the number of high-income people choosing a city residence, $r_c$ is the rent in the city, $r_s$ is the rent in the suburb, $A$ is the amenity in the suburb relative to the city, and $\alpha_i$ are the parameters of the function. Given the functional form, $\alpha_1$, $\alpha_2$, and $\alpha_3$ are the elasticities of the number of people choosing the city with respect to changes in suburban rent, city rent, and relative amenities. A similar equation holds for low-income individuals:

$$(2) \qquad N_c^l = \phi(r_c, r_s, A) = \beta_0 r_s^{\beta_1} r_c^{\beta_2} A^{\beta_3},$$

where $N_c^l$ is the number of low-income people choosing a city residence. The number of high- and low-income individuals choosing suburban communities is:

$$(3) \qquad N_s^h = N^h - N_c^h$$

and

$$(4) \qquad N_s^l = N^l - N_c^l.$$

In addition to choosing communities, individuals also choose their consumption of residential land. For simplicity, this model assumes that land consumption is proportional to housing consumption and ignores the trade-off between capital and land in housing. (This assumption is discussed further below.) Abstracting from income effects, the demand for housing depends on the after-tax price of housing, so that for high-income individuals demand is given by:

$$(5) \qquad g_c^h = g^h(r_c, \tau) = \gamma_0(\tau r_c)^{\gamma_1}$$
$$(6) \qquad g_s^h = g^h(r_s, \tau) = \gamma_0(\tau r_s)^{\gamma_1},$$

where $g_i^h$ is the demand for housing in the city and the suburb, $\tau$ is one minus the tax-related subsidy to housing for the wealthy, and $\gamma_i$ are the parameters of the demand function.

Amenities do not enter the housing demand functions; people get the full value of a community's amenities by choosing that community, regardless of the quantity of housing they purchase. The demand functions of low-income individuals differ from those of high-income residents because they are

---

include $r$ in the community-choice function because the houshold receives the same rate of subsidy regardless of community chosen. This assumption is, however, a simplification because $r$ could in theory affect community choice because the absolute value of the subsidy differs across communities depending on rents.

assumed to have sufficiently low incomes to make itemization on tax returns, and hence deductibility, irrelevant. Demand functions for low-income residents are:

(7) $$g_c^l = g^l(r_c) = \delta_0(r_c)^{\delta_1}$$

(8) $$g_s^l = g^l(r_s) = \delta_0(r_s)^{\delta_1},$$

where $g_i^l$ is the demand for housing in the city and the suburb, and $\delta_i$ are the parameters of the demand function.

Note that $\gamma_1$ and $\delta_1$ are the price elasticities of demand for high-income and low-income individuals respectively.

*Land, Amenities, and Developer Behavior*

Total land in the city community is assumed to be fixed, so that:

(9) $$\overline{L}_c = N_c^h g_c^h + N_c^l g_c^l,$$

where $\overline{L}_c$ is the fixed amount of land in the city. Land in the suburb, on the other hand, is determined endogenously and is given by:

(10) $$L_s = N_s^h g_s^h + N_s^l g_s^l.$$

The relative attractiveness of the suburban community and the city community depends on the communities' amenities. Amenities, in turn, are assumed to depend on the number of each type of consumer opting for a suburban residence:

(11) $$A = A(N_s^h, N_s^l) = \theta_0 + \theta_1 N_s^h + \theta_2 N_s^l.$$

For the purposes of this paper, amenities are best thought of as produced public goods such as parks, recreation, education, and public safety.[24] If $\theta_1$ is positive, more high-income people choosing suburban locations increases the relative attractiveness of those locations. If $\theta_2$ is less than $\theta_1$ but greater than zero, an additional low-income resident increases the attractiveness of the suburb, but by less than would a higher-income person. If $\theta_2 < 0$, an additional low-income person choosing a suburban residence will lower the relative attractiveness of the suburban community.

24. Note that these amenities are distinguished from the idiosyncratic preference for city or suburb, which is best thought of as a preference for open space, perhaps for public spaces as in cities or for predominantly private spaces as in suburbs.

The developer plays an important role in this framework in that it is assumed to have a monopoly over suburban land. The developer seeks to choose its price for suburban land to maximize its profits. The developer maximizes profits conditional on the costs of supplying land and on individuals' choosing their communities and land consumption optimally in response to the developer's choice of $r_s$ and the endogenously determined values for $r_c$ and $A$. The developer's profits, $\Pi$, are

$$(12) \qquad \Pi = r_s (N_s^h g_s^h + N_s^1 g_s^1).$$

The developer's unit land cost (its only cost) is assumed to be flat or to increase with $L_s$:

$$(13) \qquad C = C(L_s) = \rho_0 L_s^{\rho_1}.$$

As developers increase $r_s$, both the number of people choosing suburban locations and the amount of housing they consume decrease. The tradeoff is more complicated than simply the total price elasticity of suburban land (including the effects on amount of land to consume and the effects on community choice) because the suburban community's attractiveness depends on the number of rich and poor choosing to live there. Thus if low-income individuals reduce the amenities of the community, an increase in low-income individuals reduces the number of people that would willingly choose a suburban location for any given rent. In this context, we can compare the incentives to pursue exclusionary zoning policies: Is it more profitable for the developer to sell suburban housing to the largest market, including both high- and low-income individuals, or is it more profitable to exclude low-income residents? How is the developer's decision about whether or not to exclude low-income residents affected by the tax treatment of housing? And finally, does the developer's decision have significant effects on the equilibrium locations of the rich and poor as well as on the relative prices of each community?

## Caveats and Extensions

Before turning to simulation of the model, a number of simplifications in the model warrant further comment. First, the assumption that residential land demand is proportional to housing demand is not realistic. In general, as land prices increase, households substitute capital for land in the production of housing services. The model here ignores this potential margin for substitution.

Generalizing the model to include this margin would not affect the qualitative implications of the model as long as capital has a diminishing marginal product in the production of housing services. The key is that land is a fixed factor in the city, and while one can expand housing services in the city by substituting capital for land, at some point the productivity of capital in housing production will fall enough to make additional housing production in the city prohibitively expensive relative to the suburban alternative. Thus while the substitution of capital for land can loosen the constraint imposed by having a fixed amount of land in the city, it cannot eliminate its ultimate impact.

Another simplification of the model is the assumption of a single monopoly developer setting suburban land prices to maximize its profits. Once again, this is not realistic, as there are typically many developers active in a metropolitan area's suburban housing market. The key question is: What would be the consequence of having additional developers that essentially reduce the ability of individual developers to set prices above marginal costs? In the limit, perfectly competitive developers would drive profits to zero, with or without zoning, so that comparing the relative profitability of the two regimes would not be informative. Even in this case, the tax treatment of housing may have implications for the aggregate value of land under constrained and unconstrained regimes, but our framework would have to be recast somewhat to explicitly examine the aggregate land values with and without zoning under a zero-profit constraint.

If we reinterpret the developer as a property-value-maximizing local government, however, the idea of competing communities, each supplying different local bundles of attributes, is consistent with the commonly held Tiebout view of local jurisdictions. Since these communities are providing a differentiated product, it is likely they would retain some pricing power, and in theory we should be able to evaluate how the tax treatment of housing affects zoning choices in the context of many suburban communities, each with some power to affect land prices. While it is our conjecture that the tax treatment of housing would have similar implications in that context, verification of that conjecture is left to future research.

Another area in which the framework could be extended is the developer's choice set. In our model, the developer is limited to either selling to both high- and low-income households or to high-income households alone.[25] In a richer framework, the developer (or community) may optimally set rules that allow some fraction of the total low-income households seeking housing in their

25. Comments by Alex Anas provided the idea of expanding the developer's choice set.

market to gain access rather than simply accepting or excluding all low-income households. Along these lines, the model might be recast in terms of a land-value-maximizing community that chooses minimum lot sizes, rather than zoning that fully constrains low-income households. In this context, we could reevaluate how changes in housing taxation affect the choice of minimum lot size, which is a common type of suburban zoning. Again, this topic is left for future research.

## Model Simulation: Are There Tax Incentives for Exclusionary Zoning?

In models similar to the one described above, but without a developer setting suburban rents, Voith and Gyourko analyze the effects of housing tax subsidies on equilibrium location choices, land consumption, and rental rates.[26] They found that, in the presence of land-market constraints such as zoning, tax-related housing subsidies result in increased sorting of high- and low-income households, greater land consumption by high-income households, and in the case of endogenous amenities, ambiguous effects on rents in the city. The models analyzed by Voith and Gyourko are more general in that they do not assume a specific functional form. However, in those models, suburban rents are assumed to be an arbitrary function only of amenity levels. Essentially, rents are assumed to increase with amenities, but not so much that they offset the location incentives of the amenities—that is, amenities are not fully capitalized. In the framework of the current paper, suburban rents are determined by an optimizing developer and therefore necessitate no ad hoc assumptions about the relationship between amenities and suburban rents.

Conditional on a given level of suburban rents, the basic findings of the Voith-Gyourko model would obtain in this framework as well. In the framework presented in the model above, comparative statics analysis is more complex because the optimizing developer's choice of suburban rents depends on the price elasticity of demand for suburban housing, the elasticity of location choice with respect to the developer's choice of suburban rents, and the endogenously determined city rent levels and amenity levels, as well as the developer's cost function.

Comparative statics, however, plays a less important role for the question addressed in this paper: its goal is to compare alternative equilibria for economies with and without zoning constraints to see not only how the tax

26. Voith and Gyourko (1998).

treatment of housing affects the developer's choice of suburban rent but also whether it is more profitable for a developer to adopt exclusionary strategies. And, if housing subsidies result in exclusionary strategies that are profit-maximizing, what are the effects on location choice and housing consumption?

### Simulation Strategy

To examine the role of the tax treatment of housing on the decision to zone, the first step is to examine the model with a baseline set of parameters under two regimes: (1) unconstrained, in which both low- and high-income individuals can choose either city or suburban locations; and (2) constrained, in which low-income individuals are prevented from choosing a residence in the suburban community.[27] Choosing values for many of the parameters of the model is essentially arbitrary, since there is little empirical evidence on the effects of rents on choice between city or suburban communities, nor is there evidence on the effects of amenities on location choice.[28] Indeed, the model does not precisely define amenities; amenities simply reflect differences in relative attractiveness in the systematic component of utility across communities.[29] This work therefore cannot bring empirical evidence to bear on the magnitude of the relative effects of high- and low-income people on the attractiveness of city and suburban communities. Thus this study examines a range of parameters for the location-choice function and the amenity-production function.

With respect to the four equations for price elasticity of demand for housing, this work centers on an elasticity of demand of $-1$. As will be evident in the simulations, housing price elasticity plays an important role in how the housing tax code affects the incentive to adopt exclusionary zoning. This work examines a range of elasticities from $-.7$ to $-1.3$. The last parameters to be selected are in the residential-land-supply function. Here we examine a range from perfectly elastic supply to steeply upward-sloping. Note that although

27. We do not specify the mechanism for exclusion here, but minimum-lot-size zoning would be entirely consistent with this framework.

28. A potentially interesting exercise in this regard would be to examine how alternative specifications of the distribution of idiosyncratic preferences affect the equilibrium outcomes. In this paper, we simply assert a functional form and parameter values for the location-choice function rather than parameterize a utility function and a probability-distribution function over idiosyncratic preferences.

29. If amenities were more precisely defined, one could use existing studies of the value of neighborhood attributes to infer monetary values for these amenities and perhaps realistically calibrate the location-choice function.

we must choose values for the multiplicative parameters (or the additive parameters in the case of the amenity-production function), this work does not consider a range for these parameters. These are essentially scale parameters, but scale in this model (such as rent per square foot or square mile, or number of people in the community) is essentially arbitrary, and so this work does not focus on these parameters.[30]

## Reference Simulation

The reference simulation is characterized by a price elasticity of housing demand of $-1$ ($\gamma_0 = \delta_0 = -1$); modestly upward-sloping supply of housing ($\rho_1 = 1.2$); identical community-choice parameters for rich and poor, with symmetrical responses to city and suburban rents ($\alpha_1 = \beta_1 = .5$, $\alpha_2 = \beta_2 = -.5$); moderate location response to amenities ($\alpha_3 = \beta_3 = -.5$); the adverse effect of low-income residents on community amenities ($\theta_2 = -.5$); and the noneffect of high-income residents on amenities ($\theta_1 = 0$).

As one would expect, an increase in housing subsidies for high-income individuals results in increasing rents in both the city and the suburbs because demand for housing shifts upward. The upper panel of figure 1 shows the path of suburban rents as subsidies increase. In both the constrained and unconstrained case, suburban rents rise, but the suburban rent level is much higher in the unconstrained case. The constrained case has lower rents because, in the absence of demand from low-income people, it is more profitable to attract additional residents to the suburbs by lowering rent. Recall that because the price elasticity of residential demand is $-1$, changing the rent will not affect revenue for any given resident, but it will have an effect on the total number of residents through the location function.

City rents increase in both the constrained and unconstrained simulation as well (lower panel). Note that city rents are initially higher in the constrained case but rents rise faster in the unconstrained case, because the number of

---

30. These parameters can, however, affect the magnitude of movements along the demand curve in a given community in response to a change in rents relative to the magnitude of the effect of a change in rents on land consumption resulting from shifting across communities. That is, when rents change, people in a community adjust their land consumption. Changing rents also may induce moving from one community to another, in which case there will be discrete changes in land consumption, as the rents in the new community could be considerably different from rents in the original community. These scale parameters can affect the relative importance of the shifts along the margin within a community when compared to the shifts in consumption associated with changing communities.

**Figure 1. Rents, Suburban and City**

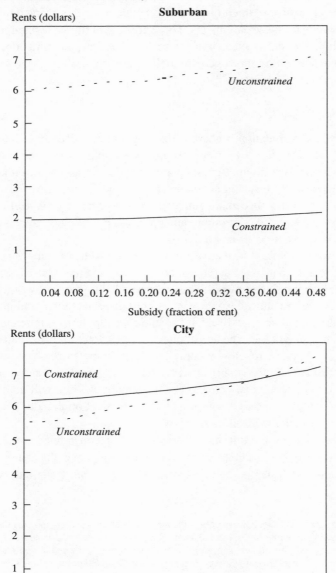

**Figure 2. High-Income City Residents**

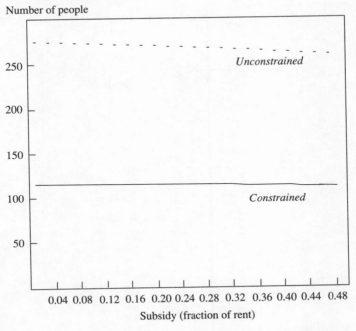

high-income people choosing city residences is much higher in the unconstrained case. Consistent with the comparative statics derived in Voith and Gyourko, the number of high- and low-income individuals choosing city locations declines as subsidies increase under both regimes, but the number of high-income people choosing city residences is much higher for all levels of subsidy in the unconstrained case (figure 2).[31] The decline in the number of people choosing city residences as subsidies increase results from the fact that the supply of land can expand in the suburban community in response to the increased demand for housing for the rich. The number of high-income people choosing city residences is much lower in the constrained case for two reasons: (1) suburban rents are much lower relative to city rents; and (2) suburban amenities are higher.

31. Voith and Gyourko (1998). Note that the reduction in the number of low-income people choosing the city is the same as the reduction for the high-income residents, even though the low-income residents do not receive the subsidy. This result obtains because the community-choice function depends on rents and amenities only and not on subsidies.

**Figure 3. Amenities**

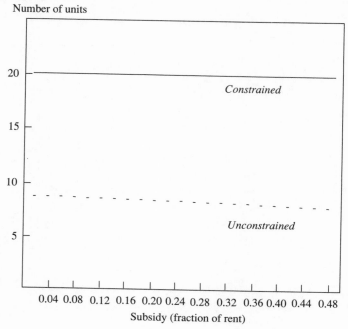

Number of units

Subsidy (fraction of rent)

Figure 3 shows relative city-suburban amenities. In the unconstrained case, suburban amenities are lower and decline with increases in subsidy. This occurs for two reasons: (1) subsidy increases provide an incentive for both high- and low-income individuals to choose suburban locations; and (2) since low-income residents adversely affect amenities, amenities decline with subsidies in the unconstrained case. In the constrained case, amenities are constant because the location choices of high-income individuals are assumed to have no effect on amenities.[32]

Land consumption by high-income consumers depends on the after-subsidy price of housing, while land consumption by low-income consumers depends only on the market price. The upper panel of figure 4 shows land consumption in the city by high-income people increasing moderately with housing subsidies in both the unconstrained and constrained cases. In contrast to city land consumption, suburban land consumption differs sharply between the uncon-

32. This view is consistent with that of Pack (1998), who argues that low-income residents impose higher costs on communities than do high-income residents.

**Figure 4. High-Income Land Consumption, City and Suburban**

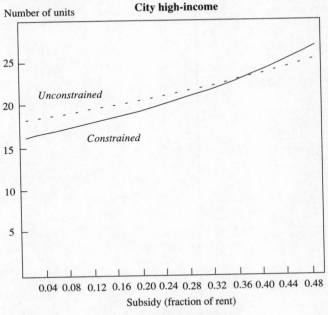

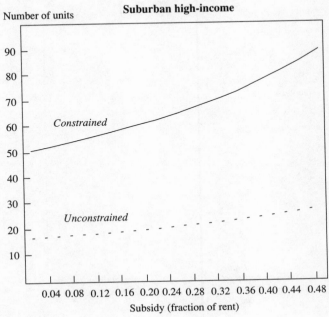

**Figure 5. Low-Income Land Consumption, City and Suburban**

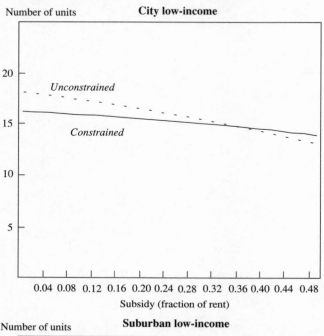

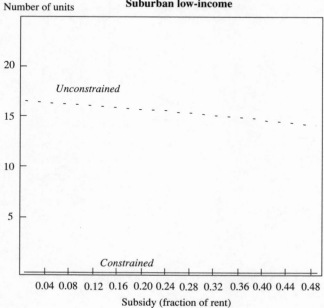

strained and constrained regimes (lower panel). In the unconstrained case, suburban land consumption by high-income residents increases somewhat faster than in the city, reflecting the more elastic supply of suburban land. In the constrained case, however, land consumption by high-income residents is high at low subsidy levels and increases dramatically as subsidies increase. This occurs because suburban rents are very low and rise only modestly with subsidies, so the after-subsidy cost of suburban land is extremely low when subsidies are high.

As the subsidy for high-income residents rises, low-income individuals are generally confronted with higher rents but receive no subsidy, so their housing consumption falls. The upper panel of figure 5 shows the falling land consumption in the city, which is similar in both the unconstrained and constrained cases. The lower panel of figure 5 shows suburban land consumption by low-income residents, which falls modestly as rents rise with subsidies in the unconstrained case. Of course, suburban land consumption is zero for low-income people in the constrained case.

Developer profits, which depend on suburban rents and the aggregate suburban land consumed by high- and low-income individuals, increase with subsidies. The monopolist developer captures part of the value of the subsidy. (The magnitude of the developer's portion depends on the elasticity of supply and demand, as well as on the amenity-production function.) The key questions for this paper are: Which regime would maximize the developer's profits—the unconstrained or constrained model? Assuming that the developer chooses the regime that maximizes profits, how is that choice affected by the rate of subsidy? What are the consequences for development patterns?

Figure 6 shows profits for the developer under the two regimes as housing subsidies increase. Given this parameterization, the developer reaps higher profits from the unconstrained regime if subsidies are less than 17 percent of housing costs, but if subsidies increase beyond that, the constrained regime is more profitable. Thus from the developer's point of view, when housing subsidies for high-income people increase, it prefers to exclude low-income residents. The forces making the constrained regime more profitable are threefold. First, as subsidies increase, developers make more revenue from each high-income resident as their land consumption increases with the subsidy. Second, constraining low-income residents in the city results in a much higher ratio of city-to-suburban rent, so more high-income people choose suburban locations than in the unconstrained cases. Third, the concentration of high-income residents in the suburb results in a higher amenity level in the suburb than that prevailing in the unconstrained case.

**Figure 6. Developer's Profits, Unconstrained and Constrained**

Profits (dollars)

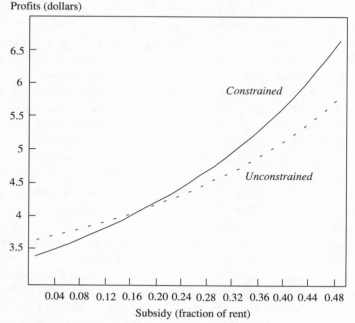

Subsidy (fraction of rent)

Under the reference parameterization, the incentives to choose constrained communities inherent in the tax treatment of housing have dramatic consequences for the patterns of metropolitan development. For discussion purposes, this study refers to the effects of housing subsidies within a regime as the "marginal effects" and the effects associated with shifting regimes when the constrained regime becomes more profitable as "equilibrium effects." In many cases, the equilibrium responses are much greater than the marginal responses.

To show the effects of shifting from unconstrained to constrained equilibria, this study first considers the path of rents, given that the developer is choosing the profit-maximizing regime for each rate of subsidy. Figure 7 shows the path of city and suburban rents as subsidies increase. City rents rise relatively smoothly, but suburban rents fall to one-third of their unconstrained level and rise only slightly as subsidies increase. While at first blush this result may appear surprising, it is consistent with the modestly upward-sloping supply of land in the suburb.[33] As city rents increase relative to suburban rents,

---

33. One might ask what the role of capitalization is in this model. Because the developer is a monopolist, subsidies are capitalized into rents in both the constrained and unconstrained case, and hence rents increase with subsidies. Rents can fall, however, when an increase in sub-

**Figure 7. Rents under Profit-Maximizing Regime**

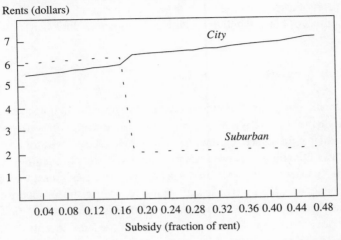

Subsidy (fraction of rent)

the number of high-income residents living in the city declines dramatically with a shift from unconstrained to constrained. The marginal response of high-income residents to an increase in subsidies is for fewer people to choose city residences, but the decline with subsidy increase within a regime is far less important than the decline resulting from a shift in regimes. The shift of high-income residents to the suburb is further accentuated by the positive amenity effect associated with excluding low-income people. High-income residents' housing consumption in the suburb rises dramatically when the developer shifts to a constrained regime. In addition, the rate of increase of housing consumption associated with subsidy increases rises as well. On the other hand, as suburban housing consumption of low-income residents falls to zero and city rents rise, city housing consumption falls.

The reference simulation indicates that the tax treatment of housing has both marginal effects and equilibrium effects on the patterns of metropolitan development. While marginal effects are, by definition, incremental changes and do not imply dramatic changes in the basic patterns of metropolitan development, the equilibrium effects imply potentially dramatic impacts in patterns of development. The reference simulation suggests that the tax treatment of housing provides financial incentives for exclusionary policies that result in fundamental shifts in the structure of land prices, location choice, and com-

sidies causes a shift from an unconstrained regime to a constrained regime, because the entire equilibrium structure of prices changes.

munity characteristics. The next section investigates alternative parameterizations of the model to get a fuller understanding of the conditions under which the tax treatment of housing yields incentives to pursue exclusionary policies.


## Sensitivity Analysis

While the reference simulation indicated that an increase in housing subsidies for high-income individuals can provide incentives for shifts from unconstrained to constrained regimes, these incentives do not exist for all parameterizations of the model. These incentives are likely to exist for empirically plausible parameterizations. To more closely examine these issues, we simulate the model with alternative assumptions regarding the production of amenities and their parameters in the location-choice function, the elasticity of supply, the price elasticity of demand, and finally the effects of rents on location choice. The key focus of our discussion in all cases will be the relationship between subsidies and the difference in profitability of the unconstrained and constrained regimes. In particular, if the difference between unconstrained profits and constrained profits falls as subsidies increase, we view the tax treatment of housing as providing an incentive for exclusionary policies.


### Amenities

Although amenities can play an important role in affecting whether the tax treatment of housing provides an incentive to exclude low-income residents, it is not necessary for low-income residents to have adverse impacts on community amenities to obtain this result. This can be seen by simplifying the reference simulation such that amenities play no role in the location-choice function (and hence no role in any of the variables of interest). Setting $\alpha_3 = \beta_3 = 0$ in the location-choice functions for high- and low-income individuals still results in increasing relative profitability of the constrained regime as subsidies increase. Amenities do, however, play a potentially important role in the relationship between subsidies and the desirability of excluding low-income residents. As shown below, there are combinations of parameters—in particular, either perfectly elastic supply or inelastic demand for housing—that yield a negative relationship between subsidies and the relative profitability of the constrained regime, but this relationship can be reversed if there are sufficiently negative effects of low-income residents on community amenities.

**Figure 8. Price Elasticity of Supply and Relative Profitability**

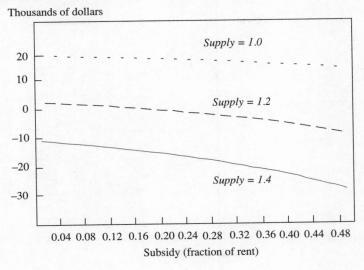

Thousands of dollars

*Subsidy (fraction of rent)*

## Developer Costs

The nature of the developer's costs in supplying residential land can affect the relationship between subsidies and the desirability of the constrained regime. In general, the more that the unit costs increase with quantity supplied, the greater the likelihood that the increased subsidies will favor excluding low-income residents. Figure 8 shows simulations identical to the reference simulation except that the developer's unit costs vary from flat to relatively strongly upward-sloping.[34] Flat costs correspond to the curve marked supply = 1.0 while the other two curves correspond to the reference case, supply = 1.2, and a less-elastic-supply case, supply = 1.4. In each case, increases in subsidies make the constrained option more attractive, but the more upward-sloping the costs, the more subsidies favor the constrained case. It is important to note, however, that for perfectly elastic supply, supply = 1.0, it is easy to generate the reverse relationship. In particular, if there are no amenity effects, perfectly elastic supply results in subsidies favoring the unconstrained case, given the remaining parameter values of the reference simulation.

---

34. Full descriptions of the simulation results are available on request.

**Figure 9. Price Elasticity of Demand and Relative Profitablity**

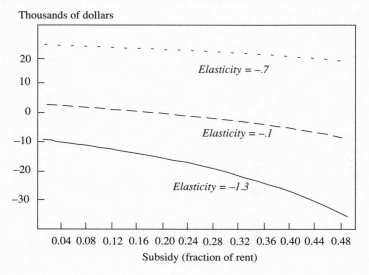

Thousands of dollars

Subsidy (fraction of rent)

## *Price Elasticity of Demand for Land*

Another key parameter affecting the relationship between housing subsidies and the relative profitability of excluding low-income residents is the price elasticity of demand. Figure 9 shows simulations using the same parameters as the reference simulation, but with the demand-elasticity parameter, $\delta_1$, taking on the values of $-.7$, $-1$, and $-1.3$. These simulations show that, given the parameters of the reference simulation, the more elastic residential-land demand is, the more subsidies will favor the constrained regime. Although this is not shown in figure 9, if residential land is inelastic, it is much easier to reverse the relationship between subsidies and the attractiveness of the constrained regime. For example, if supply is perfectly elastic but demand is inelastic, increased subsidies favor the unconstrained regime. Similarly, if low-income residents do not adversely affect the amenities of suburban communities, increased subsidies again favor the unconstrained regime.

## Conclusion

It is well known that tax-related subsidies increase the consumption of housing and, indirectly, of residential land, which results in less dense development patterns. Voith and Gyourko have argued that in the presence of exclusionary zoning these subsidies induce additional geographic sorting by income.[35] This paper has shown that, under plausible parameters, the tax treatment of housing may also provide an incentive to adopt exclusionary zoning policies to maximize the return to suburban developers. The consequences of this incentive are potentially far-reaching. Rather than the incremental shifts in housing demand and location choice suggested in the analysis conducted by Gyourko and Voith, this work suggests that there may be large shifts in rents, location choice, and community characteristics associated with unconstrained and zoning-constrained equilibria. Because the tax code may provide incentives for communities to adopt policies that exclude low-income residents, these policies may cause significant shifts in the overall pattern of development, even when there is no change in preferences.

Further research is required to determine whether the current equilibrium pattern of very dispersed, income-segregated development is simply a reflection of unique American preferences or is in fact a result of policy-related incentives that affect not only individuals' choices on the margin but also communities' choices of institutional rules that shape the equilibrium outcomes. To accomplish this objective, additional research is needed to make the basic modeling framework more realistic, including allowance for the substitution of capital for land in the production of housing services, allowance for competitive developers or competitive suburban communities, and a broadening of the developer's choice set. The findings of this analysis do, however, suggest that the tax treatment of housing could have significant impacts on both the rate of decentralization and the degree of geographic sorting by income in metropolitan areas.

35. Voith and Gyourko (1998).

# Comments

**Jan K. Brueckner**: The purpose of Voith's paper is to explore the effect of the housing tax subsidy on patterns of metropolitan development. Two elements of this exercise are considered in the following comment. The first is Voith's discussion of the effects of the tax subsidy on urban spatial sizes, which is presented mainly in the introduction to the paper. The second is his analysis of the subsidy's effect on the process of income sorting.

The first of these issues, namely the effect of the tax subsidy on urban expansion, relates to the current controversy over "urban sprawl." Critics of urban sprawl claim that cities take up too much space, and Voith's discussion suggests that housing tax benefits may contribute to this outcome. Although the tax code's tendency to stimulate housing consumption has been understood for a long time, the discussion in Voith's introduction serves a useful purpose by drawing a link between this effect and urban land use. The conclusion is that if the preferential tax treatment of owner-occupiers were eliminated (by taxing imputed rental income), then housing consumption would fall, and in the long run, cities in the United States would become more compact.

The part of urban expansion that is due to the housing tax subsidy cannot be ascribed to a market failure such as unpriced road congestion or the failure to value open space around cities. Rather, it is due to a conscious policy decision designed to support home ownership. Thus, while elimination of the tax subsidy might cause cities to shrink, it would involve reversal of a long-standing government policy favoring home ownership. In the end, removal of the tax subsidy would have the same impact as other antisprawl policies such as development taxes or urban-growth boundaries. All such policies raise housing costs, and this cost escalation leads to denser and more compact cities by encouraging consumers to live in smaller dwellings. As with the other policies, attacking sprawl via a reduction in the housing tax subsidy would thus limit a key element in the affluent American life-style: consumption of large

266

amounts of living space at affordable prices. Recognizing this effect, most consumers would probably prefer to leave the current tax subsidy in place, tolerating its consequences for urban structure.

A technical issue arises in deciding how much urban expansion is due to the housing tax subsidy. The important observation is that, if the tax subsidy were eliminated, government revenue would rise. With outlays held constant, other federal taxes could then be reduced, which would raise the disposable incomes of consumers. Since both higher housing costs and higher disposable incomes would result from a balanced-budget removal of the subsidy, an analysis that focuses only on the price effect will overstate the reduction in housing consumption. Instead, the correct magnitude for the reduction corresponds to the pure substitution effect of the subsidy, with its income effect netted out.

To provide a reliable analysis of the impact of such a policy change on urban spatial sizes, the exercise could be carried out using a standard monocentric-city model. In doing so, it should be noted that the exercise is analytically similar to substituting a head tax in place of a property tax, a switch that is analyzed in several existing papers.

The second issue considered by Voith is the effect of the tax subsidy on income sorting. In previous work, which serves as a foundation for the more complex model in the present paper, Gyourko and Voith investigate this issue in a model with two locations, central city and suburbs, and two income groups, with the high-income group benefiting from the subsidy.[1] Households have idiosyncratic locational preferences, so that members of both groups reside in both locations. The price of land (which represents housing) is fixed at the agricultural opportunity cost in the suburbs, where supply is perfectly elastic, but the central-city price is endogenous. If all households are mobile, then an increase in the subsidy causes the populations of both groups to shift toward the suburbs. The higher land demand caused by the subsidy raises the central-city land price, making the suburbs look more attractive by comparison.

If fiscal-zoning restrictions prevent the low-income group from moving to the suburbs, then the release of demand pressure in the central city does not occur as easily when the subsidy rises, so that the central land price increases by more than in the full-mobility case. In response, the movement of high-income households to the suburbs is more substantial. Therefore, in conjunction with zoning, the tax subsidy accentuates suburbanization of the high-income population.

1. Voith and Gyourko (1998).

Although this model is sensible, it seems too specialized to justify any strong conclusions about the effect of the tax subsidy on income sorting. Indeed, a different, more standard approach may give exactly the opposite answer—namely, that the tax subsidy *reduces* the tendency for different income groups to sort spatially. To see this, consider a standard spatial model, with housing consumption and rent given by $q$ and $r$, nonhousing consumption given by $c$, distance and commuting cost per mile given by $x$ and $t$, income given by $y$, and preferences given by $v(c, q)$. Letting $\tau$ denote the high-income consumer's share of housing costs (the government pays $1 - \tau$), the budget constraint is $c + \tau r q = y - t x$ for a household living at $x$. Substituting for $c$ in the utility function, achievement of a spatially uniform utility level $u$ requires that $\max_{\{q\}} v(y - tx - \tau rq, q) = u$. This equation defines the bid-rent function of the high-income consumer, and differentiating yields the following slope:

(1) $$\frac{\partial r}{\partial x} = -\frac{t}{\tau q}.$$

This equation tells how rent must vary with $x$ in order for high-income households to be locationally indifferent.

The spatial sorting envisioned by most urban economists has the rich living in the suburbs and the poor living in the central city. For this to happen, the bid-rent curve of the high-income group should be flatter than that of the low-income group, which ensures that the rich offer higher bids for suburban locations. In other words, the slope expression in equation 1 (above) should be smaller in absolute value than the corresponding expression for the low-income group. This slope comparison should hold where the bid-rent curves intersect.

What happens to this sorting pattern as $\tau$ decreases, indicating a greater tax subsidy? To see what may occur, suppose initially that housing consumption were to stay fixed as $\tau$ decreases (more realistic cases are considered below). Then inspection of equation 1 shows that the bid-rent slope for the rich increases in absolute value as $\tau$ falls. The reason is that when rich households pay a lower share of housing costs, the presubsidy rent, $r$, must decline more rapidly with distance to offset the higher commuting costs associated with a larger $x$. Since the bid-rent curve of the high-income group thus grows steeper, the difference between its slope and that of the bid-rent curve of the low-income group diminishes. But with the bid-rent slopes becoming more equal, the tendency for spatial separation of the two income groups weakens. If the slope of the high-income group's curve increases enough, the curves might look indistinguishable, so the tendency for income sorting would disappear altogether.

This conclusion still emerges when $q$ realistically adjusts in response to a decline in $\tau$. To analyze this case, it is helpful to derive the $\tau$-induced change in the bid-rent slope with the assumption that the height of the bid-rent curve stays constant. This is done by differentiating the denominator expression $\tau q$ in equation 1 with $r$ held fixed. It is easily seen that, if housing demand is price-inelastic, then

$$(2) \qquad \frac{\partial(\tau q)}{\partial \tau}\bigg|_{r=constant} > 0,$$

indicating that the denominator of $\partial r/\partial x$ again becomes smaller as $\tau$ decreases (as the subsidy rises). Since the empirical evidence indicates that housing demand is indeed price-inelastic, the previous conclusion again holds: an increase in the housing tax subsidy steepens the bid-rent curve of the high-income group, weakening rather than strengthening the tendency for income sorting.

Voith's discussion is not inconsistent with this view, given his recognition that the zoning restrictions contained in his model are crucial in generating greater suburbanization of high-income consumers in response to a higher tax subsidy. But given that such restrictions are not a universal feature of suburban communities, it is probably best not to rely on their presence to reach general conclusions about the effect of the tax subsidy and income sorting.

**Douglas Holtz-Eakin**: Voith's paper draws attention to the fact that seemingly uniform federal tax policies may have a differential impact across regions. More specifically, Voith argues that the interaction of income-specific local amenities and income-based tax subsidies to housing may augment decentralization and exclusionary zoning. Viewed in this light, the paper makes three contributions. First, it argues against the notion that decentralization in the United States stems entirely from a preference for increased land per household. Not surprisingly, prices matter. Second, and as its more substantive point, it seeks to show that tax subsidies lead to incentives for income-based exclusionary zoning and result in equilibria characterized by income segregation. Third, and as its most provocative point, it uses a numerical simulation model to demonstrate that these effects can be quite large.

The notions in the paper offer a fresh perspective on U.S. urban decline and provide a new framework within which to analyze the impact of housing policies. What really gets one's attention, however, is the large effect of the subsidy on rents, land use, amenities, and income integration of the two regions. Should we believe this? I think caution is in order. That is, one could easily agree with the basic notions presented in the paper without wholesale adherence to the empirical magnitudes of the simulation model.

Why? First, the simulation results stem directly from assumptions regarding the key elasticities, especially those for the demand and supply of land. Of course, this is a general property of simulation models. In this instance, unfortunately, there is simply a larger gap than usual between the simulations and the depth of our empirical knowledge. While the literature may have made considerable progress in estimating the price elasticity of demand for housing, we are far from having firm estimates of the derived demands for the land and capital necessary to produce this housing. The simulation model takes the shortcut of equating land and housing, and relies heavily on elastic demand for the former (see figures 8 and 9 and the surrounding discussion). With respect to supply elasticities, the situation is even less settled. To be fair, the author presents some sensitivity analysis regarding these elasticities, but under the circumstances I think caution is in order. Changing the parameter values may not affect the qualitative results, but it may considerably alter the size of the impact.

Second, the simulation model is a reduced form, making it difficult to determine the source of the large shifts in prices and locations. For example, we cannot evaluate the simulations compared to any empirical evidence on location choice, as there is no specific choice problem in the model. Similarly, the exact nature of the equilibrium distribution of households will depend upon the distribution of tastes for center-city versus suburban locations. In practice, we have little idea about the shape of this distribution; in the simulations, its role is obscured by the reduced-form nature of the model.

As a third example, consider the functional form for the determination of locational amenities. Amenities are assumed to decline strictly with the number of low-income people. That is, in the model, low-skilled people prefer not to live with other low-income people. One could easily imagine amenities (for example, diversity) that relied on a mixture of types or called for a matching of types. In the context of the model, the assumed functional form provides strong incentives to exclude poor people and a clear impetus to segregation by income.

My strongest caution stems from the fact that the notion of exclusion used in the paper is empirically implausible. In effect, the developer sets up a checkpoint at the city border. After inspection of individuals' Form 1040, low-income individuals are forced to do a U-turn. I think this crucial from two perspectives. First, the mechanism is *costless*. Second, it is devoid of any notion of household choice. Consider each in turn.

In reality, most mechanisms are indirect and costly. To take the most popular example, suppose that the developer or the community imposes a minimum lot size. Because lot size is positively correlated with income, it is a way to exclude low-income, low-amenity households. However, lot size is imperfectly correlated with income (especially in the presence of idiosyncratic tastes for locations—see above), so a minimum lot size will distort the demand decisions of some high-income individuals and lead low-income individuals to voluntarily select living in the city. For these reasons, the mechanism will be costly in terms of both individual welfare and monopoly profits. A developer will have to trade off the benefits of raising amenities with the costs of distorting demand. No such tradeoff exists in the simulations. Not surprisingly, when the monopolist is given two instruments (price and exclusion) to control demand, and one is costless, there will be circumstances in which both will be used to dramatic effect.

The absence of household choice, however, is even more troubling. That is, the simulations do not represent situations in which the low-income households *choose* to live in the city and the high-income households *choose* to live in the suburbs. Accordingly, it is not strictly appropriate to compare the simulations to empirical facts—they are not the results of comparable experiments.

At the same time, it makes the simulations unreliable as a guide to policy evaluation. Without an explicitly choice-based framework, it is difficult to attach any normative significance to policy changes. Certainly, the simulation model does not represent a contribution to the infrastructure needed to calculate the distributional impact or welfare costs of alternative policies.

We tend to think of federal policies as uniform. At times we recognize that policies' impacts will differ spatially because the characteristics of the population differ. The drama in this paper is that there are spatial differences in populations *because of* the federal policies, and these differences are large in magnitude.

This is exciting and insightful research. But a bit of restraint is in order in evaluating the paper. The results rest on a foundation of parametric and functional form assumptions that are not equally appealing. This is par for the course in simulation studies. In this instance, however, the drama of the empirical magnitudes demands a closer inspection of the underpinnings. Thus while Voith shows that a uniform subsidy to high-income individuals creates incentives for spatial segregation of low- and high-income individuals, much work remains to determine whether this is the most important source of decentralization or the least important or falls somewhere in between. And we require considerably more investment in the microfoundations of household choice in order to use the framework to evaluate policies.

# References

Alonso, William. 1964. *Location and Land Use*. Harvard University Press.

Blackley, Dixie M., and James R. Follain. 1983. "Inflation, Tax Advantages to Home-ownership and the Locational Choices of Households." *Regional Science and Urban Economics* 13 (November): 505–16.

Bogart, William T. 1993. "'What Big Teeth You Have!' Identifying the Motivations for Exclusionary Zoning." *Urban Studies* 30 (December): 1669–81.

Brueckner, Jan. 1999. "Urban Sprawl: Diagnosis and Remedies." *Critical Issues Papers*. University of Illinois, Institute of Government and Public Affairs.

DiPasquale, Denise, and William C. Wheaton. 1996. *Urban Economics and Real Estate Markets*. Prentice-Hall.

Epple, Dennis, Thomas Romer, and Radu Filimon. 1988. "Community Development with Endogenous Land Use Controls." *Journal of Public Economics* 35 (March): 133–62.

Feldstein, Martin. 1982. "Inflation, Tax Rules and the Accumulation of Residential and Non-Residential Capital." *Scandinavian Journal of Economics* 84(2): 293–311.

Gyourko, Joseph, and Richard Voith. 1999. "The Price Elasticity of the Demand for Residential Land." University of Pennsylvania, Zell/Lurie Real Estate Center at Wharton.

Hendershott, Patric H. 1982. "Government Policies and the Allocation of Capital between Residential and Industrial Uses." Working Paper 1036. Cambridge, Mass.: National Bureau of Economic Research (December).

Madden, Janice F. 2000. "Examining the Distribution of Income and Poverty within Suburbs of Large Metropolitan Areas." University of Pennsylvania.

Mieszkowski, Peter, and Edwin S. Mills. 1993. "The Causes of Metropolitan Suburbanization." *Journal of Economic Perspectives* 7 (Summer): 135–47.

Mills, Edwin S. 1967. "An Aggregative Model of Resource Allocation in a Metropolitan Economy." *American Economic Review* 57 (May): 197–210.

———. 1987. "Dividing Up the Investment Pie: Have We Overinvested in Housing?" Federal Reserve Bank of Philadelphia *Business Review* (March-April).

Mills, Edwin S., and Luan Sende Lubuele. 1997. "Inner Cities." *Journal of Economic Literature* 35 (June): 727–56.

Muth, Richard F. 1964. "The Derived Demand Curve for a Productive Factor and the Industry Supply Curve." *Oxford Economic Papers* 16 (July): 221–34.

———. 1969. *Cities and Housing: The Spatial Pattern of Urban Residential Land Use*. University of Chicago Press.

Pack, Janet Rothenberg. 1998. "Poverty and Urban Public Expenditures." *Urban Studies* 35 (November):1995–2019.

Pogodzinski, J. M., and Tim R. Sass. 1994. "The Theory and Estimation of Endogenous Zoning." *Regional Science and Urban Economics* 24 (October): 601–30.

Poterba, James M. 1984. "Tax Subsidies to Owner-Occupied Housing: An Asset-Market Approach." *Quarterly Journal of Economics* 99 (November): 729–52.

———. 1991. "House Price Dynamics: The Role of Tax Policy and Demography." *Brookings Papers on Economic Activity* 2: 143–203.

Voith, Richard. 1999. "Does the Tax Treatment of Housing Affect the Pattern of Metropolitan Development?" Federal Reserve Bank of Philadelphia *Business Review,* (March/April).

Voith, Richard, and Joseph Gyourko. 1998. "The Tax Treatment of Housing: Its Effects on Bounded and Unbounded Communities." Working Paper 98–23. Federal Reserve Bank of Philadelphia (December).